REFERENCE WORKS FOR THEOLOGICAL RESEARCH

An Annotated Selective Bibliographical Guide, Second Edition

Robert J. Kepple

UNIVERSITY
PRESS OF
AMERICA

Copyright © 1981 by

University Press of America, Inc.

P.O. Box 19101, Washington, D.C. 20036

All rights reserved

Printed in the United States of America

ISBN: 0-8191-1680-7 (Perfect)

ISBN: 0-8191-1679-3 (Cloth)

Reference Books - Theology

Library of Congress Catalog Card Number: 81-40350

Acknowledgements

I would like to thank Tom Gilbert and Tim Erdel who made various suggestions for this revised edition. Particular thanks should go to Jim Pakala for his careful and thoughtful reading of this work and for his helpful and lengthy written suggestions.

I must also acknowledge the invaluable help of Kathy Kershner in the formatting and proofreading of this work. In addition, Helen Gzanowicz also assisted in the proofreading.

TABLE OF CONTENTS

General Introduction xiii

PART I: THE GENERAL & GENERAL
         RELIGIOUS/THEOLOGICAL LISTS   1

Introduction   1

Chapter 1: BIBLIOGRAPHICAL GUIDES   3
    General Coverage   3
    Religious/Theological--More Current . .   5
    Religious/Theological--Continuing . . .   6

Chapter 2: GENERAL ENCYCLOPEDIAS,
           HANDBOOKS & DIRECTORIES   7
    Encyclopedias   7
    General Coverage--English Language . . .   7
    General Coverage--Foreign Language . . .   8
    Social Sciences   10
    Fact/Statistical Handbooks & Directories   10
    World   11
    United States   12

Chapter 3: RELIGIOUS/THEOLOGICAL
           ENCYCLOPEDIAS   13
    All Religions   13
    Christianity--Protestant Viewpoint . . .   13
    Christianity--Catholic Viewpoint   15
    Christianity--Denominational   17
    Jewish   19

Chapter 4: RELIGIOUS/THEOLOGICAL
           HANDBOOKS AND DIRECTORIES   21
    International and Foreign   21
    American   22

Chapter 5: DIRECTORIES OF UNIVERSITIES,
         COLLEGES, & LIBRARIES 27
    Universities and Colleges--General . . . 27
    Christian Colleges, Bible Colleges,
       Seminaries 27
    Library Directories 29
    Foreign Libraries 29
    American Libraries 30

Chapter 6: BIOGRAPHICAL SOURCES 33
    International--Indexes 33
    International--Sources 34
    American--General 35
    American--Religious 36
    American--Scholars 37
    British 38

Chapter 7: BIBLIOGRAPHIES OF BIBLIOGRAPHIES . 39
    Guides 39
    General 40
    Religious/Theological 41

Chapter 8: RELIGIOUS/THEOLOGICAL
         BIBLIOGRAPHIES 43
    Religions 43
    Library Catalogs 44
    Lists of Selected Works--General 46
    Lists of Selected Works--for Pastors . . 48
    19th Century 50
    Special Topics 51
    Continuing 53

Chapter 9: U.S.A. BIBLIOGRAPHY 55
    Library of Congress &
       National Union Catalogs 55
    Pre-56 Sets 56
    Post-56 Sets 57
    Subject Catalogs 57
    Trade Listings--In-Print 58
    Reprint 60
    Microform 61
    Retrospective 62

Chapter 10: FOREIGN NATIONAL AND
           TRADE BIBLIOGRAPHY 63
    Great Britain--National Library 63
    Great Britain--Current Trade 65
    Great Britain--Retrospective 65
    Germany 66
    France 67

Chapter 11: DISSERTATIONS AND THESES 69
    Bibliographical Guides 69
    Biblios & Indexes--American Dissertations 70
    Biblios & Indexes--American Theses . . . 71
    Biblios & Indexes--Foreign Dissertations 72
    Biblios & Indexes--Religious
                          Dissertations . . . 73

Chapter 12: MULTI-AUTHOR WORKS 75
    General Coverage 75
    Religious/Theological Coverage 76

Chapter 13: BOOK REVIEW INDEXES 79
    General Coverage 79
    Religious/Theological 80
    Other Sources of Book Review Citations . 81

Chapter 14: MANUSCRIPT MATERIALS &
            GOVERNMENT PUBLICATIONS 83
    Archival Materials 83
    Government Publications 84

Chapter 15: PERIODICAL INDEXES:
            GENERAL COVERAGE 87
    Guides 87
    General--American 88
    General--Foreign 90
    Humanities 91
    Social Sciences 92

Chapter 16: PERIODICAL INDEXES:
            RELIGIOUS/THEOLOGICAL COVERAGE . 93
    Guides 93
    More Important 93
    Most Current 96
    Other 96
    Major Denominational 98

Chapter 17: SERIAL PUBLICATION TOOLS 99
          Union Lists--National 99
          Union Lists--Regional Theological . . . 100
          Directories of Current Titles 101
          Books in Series--Bibliographies/Indexes 103

Chapter 18: WRITING AND PUBLISHING TOOLS . . . 105
          Dictionaries 105
          Synonyms and Antonyms 106
          Grammar and Usage 106
          Style/Form 107
          Abbreviations 108
          Other 109

PART II: THE SUBJECT AREA LISTS 111

Introduction 111

Chapter 19: BIBLICAL STUDIES:
            BIBLIOGRAPHICAL GUIDES 113

          General--OT & NT 113
          General--Old Testament 114
          General--New Testament 115
          Commentaries Only--OT & NT 115

Chapter 20: BIBLICAL STUDIES, GENERAL:
            BIBLIOGRAPHIES/INDEXES 119
          Criticism and Interpretation 119
          Versions 121
          Special Topics 123

Chapter 21: BIBLICAL STUDIES, O.T.:
            BIBLIOGRAPHIES/INDEXES 125
          O. T. Proper 125
          Related Areas 127

Chapter 22: BIBLICAL STUDIES, N.T.:
            BIBLIOGRAPHIES/INDEXES 129
          N. T. Proper 129
          Related Areas 132
          The Dead Sea Scrolls 133

Chapter 23: BIBLICAL STUDIES:
        ENCYCLOPEDIAS 135
    General Coverage--Multi-Volume 135
    General Coverage--One Volume 138
    "Bible times" 140
    Archeology 141
    New Testament 142
    Special Topics 143

Chapter 24: BIBLICAL STUDIES: THEOLOGICAL
        DICTIONARIES & WORDBOOKS 145
    OT & NT 145
    Old Testament 146
    New Testament 147

Chapter 25: BIBLICAL STUDIES: OTHER TOOLS . . 149
    Concordances & Topical Bibles 149
    Atlases 151
    Miscellaneous 153

Chapter 26: CHURCH HISTORY: GENERAL COVERAGE . 155
    General History--Bibliographies,
                  Guides, Indexes . . . 155
    Church History--Bibliographies,
                  Guides, Indexes . . . 156
    Church History--Encyclopedias 157
    Church History--Major Works 159
    Church History--Atlases 159

Chapter 27: ANCIENT CHURCH HISTORY
        & PATRISTICS 161
    Bibliographical Guides/Handbooks 161
    Bibliographies/Indexes 162
    Encyclopedias 163
    Patristic Writings--Bibliographies . . . 165
    Patristic Writings--Lexicons and
                  Concordances . . . 166
    Other 167

Chapter 28: MEDIEVAL CHURCH HISTORY 169
    Bibliographies/Indexes 169
    Major Works 171
    Special Topics 171

Chapter 29: THE REFORMATION 173
    General--Bibliographical Guides 173
    General--Bibliographies/Indexes 174
    General--Other Works 175
    In Germany and Switzerland 176
    In Great Britain 177
    Calvin/Calvinism--Main Sequence 179
    Calvin/Calvinism--Other Bibliographies . 180
    Luther 181
    Zwingli 182
    The Radical Reformation 183
    Special Topics 184

Chapter 30: POST-REFORMATION CHURCH HISTORY . 185
    General 185
    The Ecumenical Movement 186
    Denominational Bibliographies 188
    Special Topics 190

Chapter 31: AMERICAN CHURCH HISTORY 191
    General American History 191
    Bibliographical Guides/Bibliographies . 191
    Major Works 192
    Atlases 193
    Special Topics 194

Chapter 32: SYSTEMATIC THEOLOGY 197
    Current State 197
    Bibliographies 197
    Encyclopedias--Protestant 198
    Encyclopedias--Catholic 199
    The Creeds 200
    Special Topics 200

Chapter 33: CHRISTIAN ETHICS 203
    Bibliographies 203
    Dictionaries and Encyclopedias 204
    Bioethics 205
    Specific Issues 206

Chapter 34: PHILOSOPHY OF RELIGION
          & APOLOGETICS 209
    General Philosophy--Bibliographical
                  Guides 209

    General Philosophy--Bibliographies,
                Indexes 210
    General Philosophy--Encyclopedias . . . 211
    General Philosophy--Other 212
    Philosophy of Religion, Apologetics . . 213

Chapter 35: PRACTICAL THEOLOGY 215
    General Works 215
    Church and Society 217
    Church and State 219

Chapter 36: PASTORAL PSYCHOLOGY AND
                COUNSELING 221
    Psychology--Surveys/Guides 221
    Psychology--Indexes 222
    Psychology--Bibliographies 223
    Psychology--Encyclopedias 224
    Pastoral Pyschology/Counseling 225

Chapter 37: MISSIONS, THE THIRD WORLD CHURCH . 227
    Bibliographies/Indexes 227
    Specialized Bibliographies 228
    Encyclopedias & Directories--General . . 230
    Encyclopedias & Directories--U.S. &
                                    Canada . 232
    Other Tools 233
    Asia 234
    Latin America 235
    Africa 236

Chapter 38: CHRISTIAN EDUCATION 237
    Education 237
    Christian Education--Bibliographies . . 238
    Christian Education--Other Tools 240

Chapter 39: WORSHIP & LITURGY,
            CHURCH MUSIC, AND PREACHING . . 243
    Worship and Liturgy 243
    Church Music 244
    Study of Preaching 245
    Homiletical Aids 248

INDEX: To Authors, Editors, Titles,
        & Alternative Titles 251

xii

GENERAL INTRODUCTION

Purpose and Scope

This work is designed to serve as a major resource both for the student and for the instructor in the study of the reference works useful in theological research. It is intended both as a textbook--where students can find the basic "facts" about theological reference works--and as a future resource--to which students may return to refresh their memory as to the most useful works in a given area.

The first edition of this work, which appeared in 1978, was not annotated and listed about 450 tools. In the intervening three years, a number of significant, new reference works have appeared and the need to expand and annotate this work became apparent to the author and such was urged by other librarians.

In comparison to the first edition, this second edition is considerably restructured, greatly expanded, and now includes descriptive annotations.

It should be stressed that, even at its current size, this bibliography is selective and only a limited number of works are included. For additional reference works, particularly the very specialized, the user is urged to consult the various bibliographical guides and bibliographies for each subject area.

Because of the existence of James McCabe's useful work, A Critical Guide to Catholic Reference Books (2nd ed., 1980) [see #A13], this guide has been highly restrictive in including works about the Roman Catholic church or produced under its auspices. However, Roman Catholic works important to the study of Christianity, e.g. The Catholic Encyclopedia, have been included. Those studying the Roman Catholic church or a topic closely related to it will also need to use McCabe's work.

Structure and Use

The table of contents outlines, in some detail, the topical chapters and sections into which this work is divided.

The first 18 chapters form Part I, the General and General Religious/Theological Lists. These are works that cover knowledge in general or religion and/or theology in general. These are divided into chapters primarily on the basis of the bibliographical or reference function of the work.

The last 21 chapters form Part II, the Subject Area Lists. These are works limited by subject to covering, fully or in part, one of the subfields of theological study. These are divided into sections first by the subfield covered, then by (i) type of tool within the subfield (e.g. chapters 19-25), (ii) by time period within the subfield (e.g. chapters 26-30), or (iii) by topical subfields (e.g. chapters 36-39) as appropriate.

In the annotations, material placed within quotation marks is from the subtitle and/or the preface of the work being annotated.

PART I:
THE GENERAL & GENERAL RELIGIOUS/THEOLOGICAL LISTS

INTRODUCTION

The following chapters cover the general reference tools frequently of use in theological study and reference works which cover theology and/or religion in general. Reference works covering only one of the subfields of theology are listed in Part II.

Note that the listings of general reference works are very selective. Only those heavily used and widely available are listed. If one of the listed works is not available, your library may have others which serve the same purpose.

Chapter 1
BIBLIOGRAPHICAL GUIDES

Bibliographical guides are reference tools designed to refer the user to (1) the reference works available on a particular topic and (2) the "standard" or "best" works on a given topic.

Most include brief annotations describing each work, and many provide brief essays on the literature of the various fields and on the methodology of research in those fields.

**GENERAL COVERAGE

   A1. Sheehy, Eugene P. <u>Guide to Reference Books</u>. 9th ed. Chicago: American Library Association, 1976.

The basic working tool of reference librarians. Gives extensive lists of reference tools arranged by subject and function. Most entries have brief annotations. A first place to go to discover what the basic reference tools are in a particular area. Religion is treated on pp. 252-283. Be sure to use the index.

   A2. Sheehy, Eugene P. <u>Guide to Reference Books, Supplement</u>. Chicago: American Library Association, 1980.

The supplement includes a large number of additional works published from mid-1973 to late 1978, using the same subject divisions as the main work. A new section discusses computer-readable data bases.

   A3. Walford, A. J. <u>Guide to Reference Material: vol. 2, Social and Historical Sciences, Philosophy and Religion</u>. 3rd ed. London: Library Association, 1975.

The British equivalent of Sheehy. While coverage

Bibliographical Guides

complements Sheehy, Walford notes important issues of journals and articles and other minor works which Sheehy omits. See also vol. 1 (Science and Technology) and vol. 3 (Generalia, Language and Literature, the Arts).

A4. American Reference Books Annual. Littleton, CO: Libraries Unlimited, 1970-   . Annual.
Intended to be a comprehensive review of new reference books published in the U.S. for each year. Contains long, critical, signed evaluations of c. 1500 new titles each year.
    Classified arrangement. Cumulative author, title, & subject indexes available for v. 1-5 and for v. 6-10. A good place to check out new reference materials.

A5. Rogers, A. Robert. The Humanities: a Selective Guide to Information Sources. 2nd ed. Littleton, CO: Libraries Unlimited, 1979.
A basic and helpful survey. Chapters 1-2 cover general reference tools. Chapters 3-12 treat Philosophy, Religion, the Visual Arts, the Performing Arts, and Languages & Literature. History is NOT included.
    Chapter 13, "The Computer and the Humanities," covers computer-aided research and those resources now available. In all, lists and annotates 1200 titles. Author/title and subject indexes.

A6. Li, Tze-Chung. Social Science Reference Sources: A Practical Guide. Westport, CT: Greenwood, 1980.
An up-to-date basic guide covering both the social sciences in general and the individual disciplines (including history). Lists and annotates over 800 titles published up through late 1978. Name and title indexes. Includes a chapter on data base bibliographic services.

Bibliographical Guides

**RELIGIOUS/THEOLOGICAL--MORE CURRENT

A11. Bollier, John A. <u>The Literature of Theology: a Guide for Students and Pastors.</u> Philadelphia: Westminster, 1979.
A very helpful introductory guide. Lists and annotates 543 works, almost all in English. Classed arrangement with short introductions to each part. Includes lists of Bible versions and commentary series. Author and title index.

A12. Kennedy, James R., Jr. <u>Library Research Guide to Religion and Theology: Illustrated Search Strategy and Sources.</u> Ann Arbor: Pierian, 1974.
A good "how to" introduction for those writing papers. Treats both research techniques and use of selected reference tools. Geared more to undergraduate work, but also helpful for the graduate student. The appendix lists about 250 theological reference works.

A13. McCabe, James Patrick. <u>A Critical Guide to Catholic Reference Books.</u> 2nd ed. Littleton, CO: Libraries Unlimited, 1980.
An extensive guide listing 1100+ "of the most important reference books in English and foreign languages whose contents or point of view relate in some way to Catholicism."
    Emphasis on published works available to the U.S. researcher. Based on a PhD dissertation at the University of Michigan. Author, title, and subject indexes. The place to go if studying the Catholic Church or a closely related topic.

A14. Sayre, John L., & Hamburger, Roberta. <u>Tools for Theological Research.</u> 5th rev. ed. Enid, OK: Seminary Press, 1978.
Includes several hundred annotated entries. Written for a course in Tools for Theological Studies. Classed arrangement with 2 sections: basic tools and more advanced tools. Author and title index. Some inaccurate entries.

Bibliographical Guides

A15. Schwinge, Gerhard. Bibliographische Nachschlagewerke zur Theologie und ihren Grenzgebieten: Systematisch geordnete Auswahl. München: Verlag Dokumentation, 1975. A German bibliographical guide to reference works in theology and related areas, as well as helpful general reference tools. Classed arrangement with commentary at the beginning of each section. Author and title index. Useful for its German and European perspective.

**RELIGIOUS/THEOLOGICAL--CONTINUING

A21. Renewals: a Bibliographic Newsletter of the B.T.I. Boston: Library Development Program, Boston Theological Institute, 1978-1980. 6 issues per year. Publication suspended in late 1980. Includes helpful information on library use and descriptive and critical reviews and annotations of new reference works. Usually, each issue is devoted to a particular topic.

A22. ADRIS Newsletter: Newsletter of the Association for the Development of Religious Information Systems. Bronx, NY: Dept. of Theology at Fordham University, 1971- . Quarterly. This is an important source for current information on publications and activities in theology.
Now includes sections on: (1) calendar of coming events; (2) news, announcements, organizations, and directories; (3) bibliography, information, research, and reference matters (including brief reviews of new works); (4) information from and about serials & periodicals (including reviews and comments); and (5) bulletin of recent books (with brief reviews).

Chapter 2
GENERAL ENCYCLOPEDIAS, HANDBOOKS & DIRECTORIES

**ENCYCLOPEDIAS

These are works that contain articles on all branches of knowledge or comprehensively treat a particular branch of knowledge, usually arranged A to Z by subject.

Note that some encyclopedias, particularly those limited to one subject area, are titled "dictionary" by the publisher, but they really function as encyclopedias.

**GENERAL COVERAGE--ENGLISH LANGUAGE

B1. <u>Encyclopaedia Britannica</u>. 1st-14th editions. Chicago: Encyclopaedia Britannica, 1763-1973.
Generally considered the leading English-language encyclopedia. For the complete history of the 14 editions and their numerous printings, see Sheehy, p. 99 (#A1 above). The following editions are the more important:
  (a) 9th ed., 25 vols., 1875-1889.
     As with the 11th, an outstanding scholarly edition. Emphasis on long detailed articles. Weak index.
  (b) 11th ed., 29 vols., 1911.
     Contains a larger number of more specific articles. Good index.
  (c) 14th ed., 24 vols., 1929-1973.
     With this edition, the encyclopedia began the policy of continuous revision where each year various articles are updated as needed, or left as-is if still current. Be certain to use the comprehensive index to find all the information on a topic.

General Encyclopedias

> B2. <u>The New Encyclopaedia Britannica</u>. 15th ed. 30 vols. Chicago: Encyclopaedia Britannica, 1974- .

A radical restructuring of the encyclopedia which includes: (a) the Propaedia (outline of knowledge) [1 vol.]; (b) the Micropaedia (ready reference and index) [10 vols.]; and (c) the Macropaedia (knowledge in depth) [19 vols.].

The 102,214 short articles in the Micropaedia summarize a subject and refer the user to relevant articles and parts of articles in the Macropaedia. Although it is a poor substitute for the index of the 14th ed., always use the Micropaedia before the Macropaedia.

The 4,207 "in-depth" articles in the Macropaedia are signed by authorities in the field and include selected bibliographies. A continuous revision policy applies to each year's edition.

> B3. <u>Encyclopedia Americana</u>. 30 vols. New York: Americana Corp., 1903- .

A good general encyclopedia comparable in quality to the Britannica. Continuous revision policy. Mostly short specific articles, some with bibliographies (which may not be up-to-date). The last volume is a detailed index which should always be consulted.

> B4. <u>The New Columbia Encyclopedia</u>. 4th ed. New York: Columbia University Press, 1975.

Considered the best one-volume encyclopedia available. Over 50,000 concise articles, many with brief selective bibliographies. Outstanding accuracy. Excellent source for brief, non-specialized, quick-reference information.

**GENERAL COVERAGE--FOREIGN LANGUAGE

> A number of non-English encyclopedias are generally recognized as even more extensive and authoritative than the Britannica. They are usually strongest on subjects related to their own and neighboring countries.

General Encyclopedias

B11. **Brockhaus Enzyklopädie.** 17. völlig neu bearb. Aufl. des Grossen Brockhaus. Wiesbaden: Brockhaus, 1966- .
Contents: v.1-20, A-Z; v.21, Karten; v.22- , Ergänzungen. Latest edition of a standard German work (16th ed. known as **Der Grosse Brockhaus**).

B12. **Meyers enzyklopädisches Lexikon.** 9. völlig neu bearb. Aufl. mit 100 signierten Sonderbeiträgen. 25 vols. Mannheim: Bibliographisches Institut, 1971-1979.
Similar in scope and quality to the Brockhaus. Extensive and up-to-date bibliographies.

B13. **La Grande encyclopédie.** 21 vols. Paris: Larousse, 1971-1978.
One of several major French encyclopedias. Vol. 21 is a detailed index.

B14. **Enciclopedia Italiana di scienze, lettere ed arti.** 26 vols. Roma: Instit. della Enciclopedia Italiana, 1929-39.
A major encyclopedia unparalleled in English. Some articles have Fascist bias.

B15. **Enciclopedia Italiana di scienze, lettere ed arti: Appendice I-III.** 5 vols. Roma: Instit. della Enciclopedia Italiana, 1938-1961.
The supplements are of the same scope and quality as the main work.

B16. **Enciclopedia universal ilustrada europeo-americana.** 80 vols. in 81. Barcelona: Espasa, 1907-33.
Usually referred to as "Espasa." A major Spanish-language work, with strengths in Spanish and Spanish-American history and biography. Since 1935, a number of supplementary volumes have been published.

General Encyclopedias

**SOCIAL SCIENCES

B21. Encyclopedia of the Social Sciences. 15 vols. New York: Macmillan, 1930-1935.
The first comprehensive work in the area. Signed articles by specialists with bibliographies. Especially strong on biography of those active in the social sciences up to 1930.

B22. International Encyclopedia of the Social Sciences. Edited by David L. Sills. 17 vols. New York: Macmillan, 1968.
Based on and complements the above work. "Topical articles are devoted to concepts, principles, theories, & methods in the disciplines of anthropology, economics, geography, law, political science, psychiatry, psychology, sociology, and statistics."
  Lengthy, comparative, analytical articles -- use the index to locate desired information. Weak on biography. Includes bibliographies.

B23. International Encyclopedia of the Social Sciences, vol. 18: Biographical Supplement. New York: Macmillan, 1979.
Includes 215 additional biographies, emphasizing the "intellectual development and contributions to the social sciences" of those included. Those social scientists included have died since the preparation of the original volumes or are now over 70 years old.
  The bibliographies include materials by and about the biographees. No index, but table of contents of biographees.

**FACT/STATISTICAL HANDBOOKS AND DIRECTORIES

  Fact/statistical handbooks are such reference works as yearbooks, almanacs, manuals, etc., which are generally published at regular intervals and provide a source of quick, up-to-date, brief "facts" on various topics.

General Encyclopedias

Directories may be considered specialized fact/statistical handbooks concerned with listing various items, e.g. denominations, associations, addresses, etc.

Most often, you will probably use these tools for specific pieces of information--a group's official name, membership, address, publications, etc.

** WORLD

B31. <u>World Almanac and Book of Facts</u>. New York: Newspaper Enterprise Association, 1868-   . Annual.
Still the best almanac available. Is "a compendium of facts and useful information," e.g. the dates of Easter, cost-of-living statistics, denominational information, etc. Includes extensive index at the front of each volume.
   If the <u>World Almanac</u> is not available, other almanacs will often fill its place, e.g. <u>Information Please Almanac</u>, <u>Reader's Digest Almanac</u>, etc.

B32. <u>Europa Year Book</u>. 1st-   ed. London: Europa Publications, 1959-   . Annual.
Now 2 vols. Has detailed up-to-date information on each country of the world including: historical survey, statistical survey, government, political parties, religion, press, etc. Contains a section on international organizations, as well as maps.

B33. <u>Statesman's Yearbook: Statistical and Historical Annual of the States of the World</u>. New York: St. Martins, 1864-   . Annual.
Publisher varies. Includes the same type of information as <u>Europa Yearbook</u> but in more compact form. Also includes selective bibliographies of statistical sources and reference books for each country. Detailed index.

11

General Encyclopedias

B34. <u>The World of Learning</u>. 2 vols. London: Europa Publications, 1947- . Annual.
Lists, country by country, the (i) academies; (ii) learned societies; (iii) research institutes; (iv) libraries and archives; (v) museums; (vi) universities and colleges; and (vii) other schools of higher education.
Gives addresses, officers, selective listings of faculty, brief description & statistics, etc., as appropriate. Provides a wealth of information. At the back of vol. 2 is an index of institutions by name.

**UNITED STATES

B41. United States. Bureau of the Census. <u>Statistical Abstract of the United States, 1878-   </u>. Washington, DC: U.S. Government Printing Office, 1879-   . Annual.
The standard source for social, political, and economic statistics about the U.S. Besides the current-year data, it often has statistics for the last 5 to 15 years, sometimes back to 1790.

B42. <u>Encyclopedia of Associations</u>. 3 vols. Detroit: Gale, 1961-   . Annual.
Contents: v.1--National Organizations of the U.S. [the basic listing]; v.2--Geographic and Executive Index; v.3--New Associations & Projects. Vol. 1, the main volume, is arranged by 17 broad subject areas, one of which is "Religious."
The extensive index in vol. 1 indexes each entry by name, by important words in the name, and by specific subject. Includes information on full name, address, officers, purpose, activities, membership, publications, etc.

Chapter 3
RELIGIOUS/THEOLOGICAL ENCYCLOPEDIAS

Encyclopedias covering religion and/or theology in general. Encyclopedias covering one subfield of theology are found in the subject area lists.

**ALL RELIGIONS

C1. Die Religion in Geschichte und Gegenwart: Handwörterbuch für Theologie und Religionswissenschaft. Hrsg. von Kurt Galling. 3d. völlig neubearb. Aufl. 7 vols. Tübingen: Mohr, 1957-65.

Known as "RGG," this is an authoritative work in the field. The 1st ed. (1909-13) and 2nd ed. (1927-32) are also still useful, containing excellent articles by specialists with good bibliographies, as does this edition. Many biographies, including living people. German Protestant viewpoint. Vol. 7, the index, includes biographical notes on the contributors.

C2. Encyclopedia of Religion and Ethics. Edited by James Hastings. 13 vols. New York: Scribners, 1908-28.

The most comprehensive work on religion in the English language, limited only by its obvious age. Wide coverage of all aspects of religion and ethics. Signed articles with good bibliographies covering all religions, as well as people and places associated with them. Excellent indexing.

**CHRISTIANITY--PROTESTANT VIEWPOINT

C11. New Schaff-Herzog Encyclopedia of Religious Knowledge. 13 vols. New York: Funk and Wagnalls, 1908-12.

A revision and translation of the 3rd. ed. (1896)

Rel./Theo. Encyclopedias

of the Herzog-Hauck Realencyklopädie. Preceded by the Schaff-Herzog Encyclopedia (1884-91 in various editions) which is based on the 1st & 2nd editions of the Herzog-Hauck Realencyklopädie.
   Strong on historical, biographical, ecclesiastical, & theological topics -- weakest on Bible. Includes some information on non-Christian religions as well.
   Note that bibliography is found 3 places: (i) a general bibliographical survey in the preface; (ii) a bibliographical appendix at the beginning of each volume; and (iii) appended to the individual articles. Has good index.

C12. Twentieth Century Encyclopedia of Religious Knowledge. Edited by Lefferts A. Loetscher. 2 vols. Grand Rapids: Baker, 1955.
Intended to be a supplement to Schaff-Herzog. Includes both supplementary and new articles. The articles are signed and have bibliographies. Concentrates on church history and biography, including biography of living figures. Has an increased number of entries for practical theology and for ecclesiastical terminology.

C13. Encyclopedia of Christianity. 4 vols. Marshalltown, DE: National Foundation for Christian Education, 1964-1972.
Only four volumes, through "G", ever published. Reformed and evangelical in orientation, the work contains some good articles by well-known evangelical scholars.

C14. Cyclopedia of Biblical, Theological, and Ecclesiastical Literature. Edited by John M'Clintock & James Strong. 10 vols. +2 vol. supplement. New York: Harper, 1867-87.
Obviously not up-to-date, but a good source for the prevailing theological viewpoint of that time. Good bibliographies of 19th century and earlier materials accompany the long articles.

Rel./Theo. Encyclopedias

C15. <u>Realencyklopädie für protestantische Theologie und Kirche</u>. Johann Jakob Herzog, ed. 3. verb. und verm. Aufl., hrsg. von Albert Hauck. 24 vols. Leipzig: Hinrichs, 1896-1913.
A basic and extensive German Protestant encyclopedia. Long signed articles by specialists with bibliographies. Still of value. Vol. 22 is an index, vols. 23-24 form a supplement.

C16. <u>Evangelisches Kirchenlexikon; kirchlich-theologisches Handwörterbuch</u>. Hrsg. von Heinz Brunotte & Otto Weber. 4 vols. Göttingen: Vandenhoeck & Ruprecht, 1955-61.
German Protestant viewpoint, with c. 800 contributors. The signed articles include bibliographies, and both emphasize recent literature. Vol. 4 is an important subject index and also includes a name index, the "Biographischer Anhang," which has brief biographical information on 15,000 persons.

C17. <u>Theologische Realenzyklopädie</u>. Hrsg. von Gerhard Krause und Gerhard Müller. Berlin: de Gruyter, 1977-   .
A new Protestant encyclopedia. Completed through Band 6 (-Boehmen) as of December 1980. Much more theological than historical, with long discussions of selected theological issues by specialists. The forthcoming cumulative index will facilitate use (each volume is also separately indexed).
The first volume published, the "Abkürzungsverzeichnis," is a useful listing of abbreviations used by many in theology, not just in the TRE.

**CHRISTIANITY--CATHOLIC VIEWPOINT

C21. <u>Catholic Encyclopedia</u>. 16 vols. New York: Appleton, 1907-1914.
Subtitle: "An International Work of Reference on the Constitution, Doctrine, Discipline, and History of the Catholic Church."
The predecessor of the <u>New Catholic Encyclo-</u>

Rel./Theo. Encyclopedias

pedia, this set complements it on history and biography, especially of the medieval period. Reflects the older, more traditional theology of the Catholic Church.

C22. New Catholic Encyclopedia. 15 vols. New York: McGraw-Hill, 1967.
C23. New Catholic Encyclopedia, vol. 16: Supplement, 1967-74. New York: McGraw-Hill, 1974.
C24. New Catholic Encyclopedia, vol. 17: Supplement, Change in the Church. New York: McGraw-Hill, 1978.

Not just a revision of the above work, but an entirely new production. International in scope, emphasis on American and English-speaking areas.

Contains about 17,000 signed articles, most with bibliographies, by more than 4800 contributors. Vol. 15 is a well done index of c. 600 pages, and also lists the abbreviations and contributors. Be sure to use the index to locate specific topics. Vols. 1-15 cover up to the close of Vatican II. The supplements update the earlier articles and cover new topics.

C25. Encyclopédie des sciences ecclésiastiques redigée par les savants Catholiques le plus eminents de France et de l'étranger. Paris: Letouzey, 1907-   .

The most extensive theological encyclopedia. Represents the best scholarship of French Catholicism. Consists of five major parts, most of which are listed below in the appropriate subject lists. The parts are:
    (1) Dictionnaire d'archéologie chrétienne et de liturgie.
    (2) Dictionnaire d'histoire et de géographie ecclésiastiques.
    (3) Dictionnaire de théologie catholique.
    (4) Dictionnaire de la Bible.
    (5) Dictionnaire de droit canonique.

Rel./Theo. Encyclopedias

C26. <u>Lexikon für Theologie und Kirche</u>. 2. völlig neu bearb. Aufl. hrsg. von Josef Höfer und Karl Rahner. Begrundet von Michael Buchberger. 10 vols. & Register. Freiburg: Herder, 1957-67.
One of the best Catholic encyclopedias. Primarily short signed articles with selective bibliographies, but has some extensive essays. The index volume has an extensive specific-subject index, a classified subject index, a geographical index, and a list of the contributors indicating the entries contributed.

C27. <u>Lexikon für Theologie und Kirche: Ergänzungband, Teil 1-3: Das Zweite Vatikanische Konzil</u>. 3 vols. Freiburg: Herder, 1966-1968.
The supplements include the texts of the Vatican II documents (in Latin and German) along with extensive commentary, a bibliography, & an index.

**CHRISTIANITY--DENOMINATIONAL

C31. <u>Encyclopedia of Southern Baptists</u>. 3 vols. Nashville: Broadman, 1958-1971.
Vol. 3 is the 1971 supplement with a separate A-Z sequence. Treats the history, practices, and worship of the Southern Baptists. Includes articles on organizations, institutions, colleges, newspapers, theology, important people, etc. Signed articles with bibliographies.

C32. Bodensieck, Julius. <u>The Encyclopedia of the Lutheran Church</u>. Edited for the Lutheran World Federation. 3 vols. Minneapolis: Augsburg, 1965.
Broad coverage of the Lutheran church, international and ecumenical in scope. Covers Lutheran doctrine, history, practice, beliefs, persons, etc. Contains c. 3000 articles contributed by 723 Lutherans from 34 countries. No index, few (and weak) bibliographies.

Rel./Theo. Encyclopedias

C33. Lueker, Erwin L. <u>Lutheran Cyclopedia</u>. rev. ed. St. Louis: Concordia, 1975.
Substantially revised and expanded from the 1st ed. of 1954. Strongest on Lutheranism, but does include material on other denominations. Has brief articles on history, practice, teaching, significant individuals, etc., of the Lutheran church. Includes bibliographies.

C34. Hege, Christian, & Neff, Christian. <u>Mennonitisches Lexikon</u>. 4 vols. Frankfort a. Main: the Authors, 1913-1967.
Issued in parts over 55 years! Has signed articles with bibliographies. International perspective with European emphasis.

C35. <u>The Mennonite Encyclopedia: a Comprehensive Reference Work on the Anabaptist-Mennonite Movement</u>. 4 vols. Hillsboro, KS: Mennonite Publishing House, 1955-1959.
Covers the history, theology, practices, ethics, biography, etc., of the Mennonites from their beginning to the present. Signed articles with bibliographies. Builds upon, but does not duplicate, the <u>Mennonitisches Lexikon</u> (see C34).

C36. Harmon, Nolan B. <u>Encyclopedia of World Methodism</u>. History of the United Methodist Church. 2 vols. Nashville: United Methodist Publishing House, 1974.
Sponsored by the World Methodist Council and the Commission of Archives and contains articles on Methodist history, doctrine, biography, sites, etc. Emphasis on the coverage of the United Methodist Church and American Methodism. Signed articles with bibliographies, general index.

C37. Nevin, Alfred. <u>Encyclopaedia of the Presbyterian Church in the United States of America</u>. Philadelphia: Presbyterian Publishing, 1884.
Includes articles on significant individuals,

Rel./Theo. Encyclopedias

presbyteries, congregations, history & growth of Presbyterianism in the U.S., and other institutions & topics. Good coverage of the 19th century and earlier.

**JEWISH

Only two major English-language Jewish encyclopedias are included here. Students of the Christian religion will find them useful for backgrounds and Jewish perspectives.

C41. <u>Encyclopaedia Judaica</u>. 16 vols. Jerusalem: Encyclopaedia Judaica, 1971-1972.
The major new Jewish encyclopedia, often cited as THE authority on Jewish topics. A comprehensive view of world Jewry and its history. The 25,000+ signed articles, most with bibliographies, include many biographies, including living figures.
   Use the extensive (c. 200,000 entries) index (vol. 1) for best results. This index uses letter-by-letter, not word-by-word, alphabetizing.

C42. <u>Jewish Encyclopedia</u>. Ed. by Isadore Singer. 12 vols. New York: Funk & Wagnalls, 1901-6.
Subtitle: "A Descriptive Record of the History, Religion, Literature, and Customs of the Jewish People from the Earliest Times to the Present Day." The older standard work, now dated. Still useful for its bibliographies of older material and historical and biographical information.

Rel./Theo. Handbooks

Chapter 4
RELIGIOUS/THEOLOGICAL HANDBOOKS AND DIRECTORIES

Use these tools for information about religious organizations and denominations such as addresses, membership, names of officers, and other statistical information. Some of these tools also contain historical and/or theological information about the sects and denominations.

**INTERNATIONAL AND FOREIGN

D1. <u>World Christian Handbook, 1968</u>. Edited by H. Wakelin Coxil & Kenneth Grubb. London: World Dominion Press, 1968.
Parts 1 & 2 are survey articles and world church statistics. Part 3 is a directory of: Protestant & Anglican churches, missions & Christian organizations, ecumenical & international Christian organizations, and lists of African independent churches in separate sections. Good index.

D2. Gründler, J. <u>Lexikon der christlichen Kirche und Sekten, unter Berücksichtigung der Missionsgesellschaften und zwischenkirchlichen Organisationen</u>. 2 vols. Freiburg: Herder, 1961.
Includes c. 2600 entries in alphabetical order. For most organizations gives name, address, historical background, type of church or sect, and religious connections. Includes bibliography.

D3. Mol, Hans, ed. <u>Western Religion: a Country by Country Sociological Enquiry</u>. The Hague: Mouton, 1972.
Contains essays about 28 countries (arranged A-Z) by prominent sociologists of religion. Each describes and analyzes the religious situation in that country, and includes a bibliography and statistical tables. Includes indexes of names and

Rel./Theo. Handbooks

subjects. Useful for the data included and for its sociological perspective. Excludes South American countries and Rumania.

D4. Annuaire protestant ... la France protestante et les Églises de langue française. Paris: Centrale du livre protestant, 1862- . Annual.
Subtitle and publisher varies. Gives directory & institutional information on each entry for French protestant churches and other French-speaking churches.

**AMERICAN

D11. Melton, J. Gordon. The Encyclopedia of American Religions. 2 vols. Wilmington, NC: Consortium, 1978.
"Explores the broad sweep of American religions and describes 1200 churches" (preface). Classed arrangement, use the extensive table of contents and the detailed name, title, & subject indexes in each volume to find specific groups. Gives considerable detail and covers many minor groups, e.g. "snake handlers" and "flying saucer groups."

D12. Melton, J. Gordon, & Geisendorfer, James V. A Directory of Religious Bodies in the United States. New York: Garland, 1977.
Compiled from the files of the Institute for the Study of American Religion. Includes 1200+ entries for all religious bodies in the U.S.
    Gives basic information about each -- name, address, major publication, etc. Also includes an interesting systematic classification of these religious bodies into 17 "philosophical" groups. Particularly helpful for its data on non-Christian (Hindu, Jewish, Sufi, Buddhist, Muslim, Sikh, etc.) groups.

D13. Mayer, Frederick E. The Religious Bodies of America. 4th ed., rev. by Arthur C. Piepkorn. St. Louis: Concordia Publishing, 1961.

Rel./Theo. Handbooks

Classified arrangement by major church groups. Gives a description of most American religious groups including doctrines, practices, & history. Also includes a bibliography for each group, and a name/subject index.

D14. Mead, Frank S. <u>Handbook of Denominations in the United States.</u> new 7th ed. Nashville: Abingdon, 1980.

Intended to give a brief, impartial account of each body -- its history, doctrine, present status, etc. Also gives an evaluation of the group's doctrinal beliefs. Includes a glossary of terms, a list of addresses of denominational headquarters, a 14-page bibliography of material about each denomination, and a name & subject index.

D15. Piepkorn, Arthur Carl. <u>Profiles in Belief: The Religious Bodies of the United States and Canada.</u> 7 vols. New York: Harper & Row, 1977- .

Four volumes published thus far. Classed arrangement. Strong on historical backgrounds of each group and in describing the origin, significance, and meaning of the many sub-branches of each group. Includes indexes and bibliographical notes.

Contents: v.1--Roman Catholic, Old Catholic, Eastern Orthodox; v.2--Protestant; v.3--Holiness and Pentecostal; v.4--Evangelical, Fundamentalist, and other Christian churches; v.5--Metaphysical bodies; v.6--Judaism; v.7--Oriental, Humanist, and Unclassified.

D16. U.S. Bureau of the Census. <u>Religious Bodies, 1936.</u> 3 vols. Washington, DC: Government Printing Office, 1941.

Subtitle: "Selected Statistics for the United States by Denominations and Geographic Divisions." This and 3 previous reports (1906, 1916, 1926) provide a wealth of historical statistical information. Vol. 1 is summary and statistics; vols. 2 & 3 cover the various denominations. No further reports were done after 1936.

Rel./Theo. Handbooks

D17. National Council of Churches of Christ. Bureau of Research and Survey. <u>Churches and Church Membership in the United States</u>. New York: the Council, 1956-58.
"An Enumeration and Analysis by Counties, States, and Regions." A series of volumes giving detailed statistics, not only by denomination, but by state, county, & city, and by social-economic characteristics.

D18. Geisendorfer, James, ed. <u>Directory of Religious Organizations in the United States</u>. 2nd ed. Wilmington, NC: Consortium, 1980.
Compiled by the editorial staff of McGrath Publishing Co. Gives the name, address, brief description, membership, officers, facilities, publications, etc., of 1800+ organizations active in the field of religion.
    Entries are arranged alphabetically by the name of the organization. A detailed subject index & cross-reference system give access by key words in each group's name and by its function. The 1st ed., 1977, included 1569 organizations and is arranged topically.

D19. <u>Religion in America, 1979-80</u>. Princeton: Princeton Religion Research Center, 1979.
Prepared by a non-denominational group using the Gallup research facilities. Provides current statistics and interpretative comment. This is one title of an ongoing series of current statistical analyses of religion in the U.S.

D20. <u>Yearbook of American and Canadian Churches</u>. Nashville: Abingdon, 1916-   . Annual.
Exact title varies. The standard directory, sponsored by the National Council of Churches. Does not include cults and small groups. Gives extensive information on each group, including: various sub-bodies within the denomination, addresses, brief description of its organizational set-up, names and addresses of officers, membership statistics, etc.

Rel./Theo. Handbooks

Indexed by name of organization and denomination. Along with the directory this work also contains a statistical and historical section on Christianity in the U.S. and Canada.

D21. Catholic Almanac. 65th-   ed. Huntington, IN: Our Sunday Visitor, 1969-   . Annual. Previously titled the National Catholic Almanac. Gives information primarily for the U.S., but covers the entire RC Church worldwide. Includes: special reports; the history, hierarchy, and government of the RC Church; biographical data on officials, saints, & popes; and summaries of the beliefs, practices, & activities of the RC Church. Use the extensive index at the front.

NOTE: Most denominations also publish directories of their churches, officers, etc. If you are working with a particular denomination, use their directory.

College & Library Directories

Chapter 5
DIRECTORIES OF UNIVERSITIES, COLLEGES, & LIBRARIES

**UNIVERSITIES AND COLLEGES--GENERAL

There are numerous directories of universities and colleges. Listed below are just two of the better known guides. If they are not available, most libraries will have some other directory of this type.

E1. Peterson's Annual Guide to Graduate Study. Ed. by Karen G. Hegener. 6 vols. Princeton: Peterson Guides, 1966-   . Annual.
New ed. each year. Arranged by major subject areas, then by names of the schools. Gives brief information on each graduate program.

E2. Lovejoy, Clarence. Lovejoy's College Guide. 14th ed. New York: Simon & Schuster, 1979.
A directory, with brief information, of undergraduate schools. Arranged by state, subarranged by name of the school. Indexed by school and by "career curricula and special programs."

**CHRISTIAN COLLEGES, BIBLE COLLEGES, SEMINARIES

E11. "Church-Related and Accredited Colleges and Universities in the United States." Section in each volume of Yearbook of American and Canadian Churches (see #D20 above).
Includes all colleges in some way related to those groups listed in the Yearbook. Does not include Bible colleges.

E12. "Guide to Higher Education." Christianity Today 20 (Nov. 7, 1975):147-153.
A selected list of Christian liberal arts colleges and Bible colleges, including brief statistical

College & Library Directories

information. The Christian colleges were selected for their commitment to some type of Christian perspective in their education program. Somewhat dated but useful.

E13. Doors '81: Guide to Educational and Employment Opportunities for Christian Students. Philadelphia: Eternity Magazine, 1980.
To be published annually? Includes lists, with addresses & brief information, of seminary and graduate schools; mission organizations; broadcasting, broadcasting schools, record companies; publishers; and Christian agencies.
Also has articles on Christian education and employment as well as numerous seminary ads.

E14. American Association of Bible Colleges. Directory. Wheaton, IL [box 543; 60187]: AABC, 1948- . Annual.
Lists all members and candidates for membership. Gives name, address, church affiliation, brief statistical information, and names of officials. The AABC is the major accrediting body for Bible colleges.

E15. Council on the Study of Religion. Directory of Departments and Programs of Religion in North America. 1978 ed. Waterloo: the Council, 1980.
Lists all 4-year colleges and universities with undergraduate or graduate programs in religion, as well as graduate seminaries. A useful guide.
All known schools and their addresses are listed in Appendices A, B, and C, but only those which paid a fee have entries in the full directory -- which gives a department profile, institutional facilities, listings of faculty, etc. Index of the faculty in the participating schools.

E16. Council on the Study of Religion. Graduate Studies in Religion: a Guide to the Programs of the Council on Graduate Studies in

College & Library Directories

Religion. Waterloo: the Council, 1979.
A much briefer guide, listing only the graduate programs of the 30 schools which are members of the council. Gives program description, financial and academic requirements, and listing of the faculty. No index.

E17. Association of Theological Schools in the United States & Canada. *Directory*. Vandalia, OH: the Association, 1975- . Annual.
Previous editions under old name, American Association of Theological Schools. Published as an issue of the Association's *Bulletin*. ATS is the major accrediting body for graduate seminaries in the U.S. and Canada.

Lists accredited & associate members. Gives address and brief statistical information about each school. Appendices list schools by (i) denominational affiliation and nation, and (ii) by geographical location.

**LIBRARY DIRECTORIES

Library directories provide helpful information about the libraries included such as location, hours, personnel, address, size, collection strengths, and lending policies. Most are arranged or indexed by location, subject, and/or institutional name.

**FOREIGN LIBRARIES

E21. Ruoss, George M. *A World Directory of Theological Libraries*. Metuchen, NJ: Scarecrow Press, 1968.
Gives basic information on 1779 theological libraries (Catholic, Jewish, Orthodox, and Protestant) in the world. Arranged by country, then by city. Effective date of contents: December 1966. Has A-Z index of institutions and religious groups. No subject index.

College & Library Directories

E22. Lewanski, Richard C. <u>Subject Collections in European Libraries</u>. 2nd ed. New York: Bowker, 1978.
Lists around 10,000 special subject collections, primarily in NW Europe. Arranged by subject using the dewey classification: then, within each subject, alphabetically by country. Subject index. Gives for each collection its size, location, and special conditions of access.

E23. Robert, Stephen Andrew, et al. <u>Research Libraries and Collections in the United Kingdom: a Selective Inventory and Guide</u>. Hamden, CT: Linnet Books, 1978.
Contains 4 major sections, each arranged alphabetically: (1) national, special, & public libraries; (2) university libraries; (3) polytechnical libraries; and (4) Scottish central institutions.
   For each, it gives the library name, address, collection strength(s), use and access policies, etc. Has 3 indexes: by subject, by name of collection, and by geographical location.

AMERICAN LIBRARIES

E31. <u>American Library Directory</u>. 32nd ed. New York: Bowker, 1923-   . Annual.
Frequency, subtitle, and compiler varies. Lists 30,000+ U.S. and 300+ Canadian academic, public, special, and government libraries. Arranged by state/province, then by city, then alphabetically by name. Also includes 400+ networks, consortia, and cooperative efforts.
   The information given includes: full name, address, telephone, personnel names, special collections owned, statistics on size and service. Has name index. Very helpful for locating most libraries in a given geographical area.

E32. Ash, Lee. <u>Subject Collections: a Guide to Special Book Collections and Subject Emphases</u>. 5th ed. New York: Bowker, 1978.
"As Reported by University, College, Public, and

College & Library Directories

Special Libraries and Museums in the United States and Canada."

Entries are arranged under numerous specific subject headings which are in alphabetical order. Under each subject, libraries with strengths in that subject are listed, along with brief address and holdings information.

NOTE: In addition to the directories listed above, many state, city, & regional library groups issue directories of libraries within their scope. Check with your reference librarian to find out what is available for your area.

Biographical Sources

Chapter 6
BIOGRAPHICAL SOURCES

There are numerous publications designed to provide biographical information on individuals of note -- a small sample of some of the more important & useful for your purposes are listed below.

Remember that most encyclopedias do include biographies of significant individuals. In addition, biographical encyclopedias for church history figures are given in the church history section, rather than here.

Many denominations also issue a biographical dictionary, a ministerial directory, "fasti," etc., of ministers and leading figures of the denomination, past and/or present. These types of works are NOT included in this list.

**INTERNATIONAL--INDEXES

F1. Hyamson, Albert M. <u>A Dictionary of Universal Biography of All Ages and of All People</u>. 2nd ed.. New York: Dutton, 1951.
An index to 23 major biographical sources, e.g. the <u>Dictionary of National Biography</u>. Includes individuals who died before the late 1940's, but stronger on 19th century and earlier. Lists c. 120,000 individuals alphabetically and directs the user to the appropriate biographical tool.

F2. Arnim, Max. <u>Internationale Personalbibliographie, 1800 - 1943</u>. 2 Aufl. 2 vols. Stuttgart: Hiersemann, 1952.
Primarily a list of bibliographies of materials by & about individuals, but includes some basic biographical information (e.g. occupation/profession, dates) & often leads to other biographical tools. International in scope, but emphasis on Germany.

Biographical Sources

F3. Arnim, Max. <u>Internationale Personalbibliographie Bd. III-IV, 1944-1975</u>. Fortgefuhrt von Franz Hodes. 2. überarbeitete & bis zum Berichtsjahr 1975 fortgefuhrte Aufl. von Bd. III (1944-1959). Mit Nachträgen zur zweiten Aufl. von Bd. I/II (1800-1943) Hrsg. Gerhard Bock. Stuttgart: Hiersemann, 1978-   .
Currently being published by fascicle. Extends coverage of the original set up through 1975, and includes new references for individuals already included in vols. 1 - 2. Vol. 4 of this work will provide an index to all four volumes.

F4. <u>Biography Index: a Cumulative Index to Biographical Material in Books and Magazines</u>. New York: Wilson, 1947-   . Quarterly.
Annual & 3-year cumulations. Indexes all types of biographical material found in English-language periodicals (articles, tributes, obituaries, etc.). Arranged by name of biographee, indexed by occupation or profession.

**INTERNATIONAL--SOURCES

F11. <u>Webster's Biographical Dictionary: a Dictionary of Names of Noteworthy Persons, with Pronunciations and Concise Biographies</u>. Springfield, MA: Merriam, 1967.
Gives brief information about 40,000 persons, living and dead. Helpful in giving a syllabic division and pronunciation for all names included. A number of minor revisions have kept it somewhat up-to-date.

F12. <u>Who's Who in the World</u>. 1st ed.-   . Chicago: Marquis, 1971-   .
Published about every 3 years. Includes 25,000+ living biographees from 150+ countries.

F13. <u>International Who's Who</u>. London: Europa, 1935-   .
Annual. Gives short (100-150 word) biographies of living world notables. Includes an obituary list

Biographical Sources

of those in the previous edition who have died. Particularly good coverage of heads of state, the performing arts, and writers.

F14. <u>New York Times Obituary Index, 1858-1968</u>. New York: New York Times, 1970.
Lists the 353,000+ names which have appeared under the heading "Deaths" in the <u>New York Times Index</u> from 1858-1968. Gives year, day, section, page, & column where the notice is located in the New York Times (available on microfilm at many libraries).

**AMERICAN--GENERAL

F21. <u>Who's Who in America</u>. Chicago: Marquis, 1899-   . Annual.
Subtitle varies. Now published in two volumes. Brief biographical information on living prominent Americans. Includes addresses and lists of published works. Accuracy of information included varies -- it is supplied by the biographee.

F22. <u>Who was Who in America: Historical Volume, 1607-1896</u>. Chicago: Marquis, 1963.
Includes "individuals who have made a contribution to or whose activity was in some manner related to the history of the U.S." Other features: lists of major historical events, vice-presidents and presidents, cabinet officers, supreme court justices, congressional leaders, state governors, etc.

F23. <u>Who was Who in America: a Companion Biographical Reference Work to Who's Who in America</u>. Chicago: Marquis, 1942-   .
Now 6 volumes covering 1897-1976. Includes the biographical entry (with death date) of those who were dropped from <u>Who's Who in America</u> at death. Each volume also includes a cumulative index for itself and the preceding volumes.

F24. <u>Dictionary of American Biography</u>. Published under the Auspices of the American Council of Learned Societies. 20 vols. & Index. New

Biographical Sources

York: Scribner, 1928-37.
The major scholarly American biographical tool. Includes long essays with bibliographies by specialists. Planned to include all noteworthy persons of all periods who lived in the area of the U.S. Indexed by: names of biographees, contributors, birthplaces, schools and colleges attended, occupations, and topical subjects.

F25. Dictionary of American Biography: Supplement 1-   . New York: Scribner, 1944-   .
Now 6 volumes including individuals who died up to 1960. Supplements the above, similar in scope and purpose. Each supplementary volume also includes a cumulative index to the individuals included in all supplements.

**AMERICAN--RELIGIOUS

Works covering 20th century only. See chapter 31, "Church History: United States," for other works covering American religious biography.

F31. Who's Who in Religion. 2nd ed. Chicago: Marquis, 1977.
1st ed., 1975. Now includes about 18,000 living religious leaders in the United States. Coverage is somewhat spotty. Gives brief biographical data on each individual as supplied by the biographee.

F32. Williams, Ethel L. Biographical Directory of Negro Ministers. 3rd ed. Boston: G. K. Hall, 1975.
1st ed., 1965; 2nd ed., 1970. Gives basic biographical data on living black ministers who are active and influential in local or national affairs. Geographical index.

F33. Bowden, Henry Warner. Dictionary of American Religious Biography. Westport, CT: Greenwood, 1977.
Brief articles on 425 individuals "from all denom-

inations who played a significant role in our nation's past." Emphasizes the wide pluralism of American religion. Includes bibliographies of material by and about each individual.

F34. Who's Who in the Clergy: Vol. 1, 1935-36. Edited by J. C. Schwarz. New York: the author, 1936.
Lists c. 7000 clergy alive and prominent in 1936. Gives brief biographical data including birthdate, education, positions and posts, and publications.

   This work, and the volume below, will provide information on the more obscure religious authors of the period who are not included in other biographial sources. Pages 1223-24 list divinity schools and theological seminaries in 1936.

F35. Religious Leaders of America: v. 2, 1941-42. Edited by J. C. Schwarz. New York: the author, 1941.
Later edition of the above work, similar in form and content.

**AMERICAN--SCHOLARS

F41. Directory of American Scholars: a Biographical Directory. Ed. by the Jacques Cattell Press. 7th ed. 4 vols. New York: Bowker, 1978.
Includes around 39,000 scholars "currently active in teaching, research, and writing." The 4 vols. are divided by subject -- vol. 4 includes Philosophy, Religion, and Law.

   Each volume has geographic index. Vol. 4 has a cumulative index of the persons found in all four volumes. Gives brief biographical information, stressing academic background and accomplishments. Includes current addresses.

F42. National Faculty Directory. 1st- ed. Detroit: Gale, 1970-   . Annual.
An alphabetical listing of faculty members at junior colleges, colleges, and universities in the

Biographical Sources

United States as well as at selected schools in Canada. Gives name, address, and department, but no other information.

**BRITISH

F51. Who's Who: an Annual Biographical Dictionary, with which is incorporated "Men and Women of the Time." London: Black, 1849- .
Includes brief biographical sketches of living prominent British persons. Also has a list of the members of the royal family. An obituary section lists those who have died who were in the previous edition.

F52. Who was Who, a Companion to Who's Who. London: Black, 1929- .
Now six vols., covering 1897-1970. Includes the entries for those who were removed from Who's Who at death. Each new supplement includes a cumulative index for itself and the previous volumes.

F53. Dictionary of National Biography. Edited by Leslie Stephen and Sidney Lee. 22 vols. London: Smith, Elder, 1908-09.
A scholarly biographic source for Britons & those of significance to the history of Britain who died before 1900, including numerous clergymen. Long articles by specialists with bibliographies.

F54. Dictionary of National Biography: Index and Epitome. Edited by Sidney Lee. 2 vols. London: Smith, Elder, 1903-13.
Adds new entries to the above. The index contains very brief biographical data on each man and gives the location in the DNB of the full article.

F55. Dictionary of National Biography: 2nd Supplements. Oxford: Univ. Press, 1912- .
Now 7 volumes, covering 1901 and 1960. Same scope and purpose as the main work. Each new volume includes a cumulative index to the individuals in itself and in the previous supplements.

Chapter 7
BIBLIOGRAPHIES OF BIBLIOGRAPHIES

The bibliography of bibliographies is a bibliography limited to listing only bibliographies. It may be universal or be also limited by subject, date, language, and/or other considerations.

These tools may be used to determine if a bibliography has ever been produced which covers an area of interest. If one is listed, the user must then go to that bibliography to find the listing of works on that topic.

**GUIDES

G1. Collison, Robert L. *Bibliographies, Subject and National: a Guide to Their Contents, Arrangement, and Use*. 3rd ed. London: Lockwood, 1968.
A good basic guide to major bibliographies in a given field or country. Lists 400-500 works with annotations. Includes entries for major works containing bibliographies (e.g. encyclopedias).
   Part 1 lists subject bibliographies by major subjects; Part 2 lists universal and national bibliographies. Includes an interesting introduction about bibliographies and their compilation.

G2. Gray, Richard A. *Serial Bibliographies in the Humanities and the Social Sciences*. Ann Arbor: Pierian, 1969.
Note subject limits. Arranged in classified order via dewey decimal numbers. Lists a large number of ongoing bibliographies, many of them published as sections in various journals. Fairly helpful, but is now somewhat dated.
   The amount of information given for each item varies greatly. Includes indexes by title; by author, sponsor, publisher; and by subject.

Biblio. of Biblio.

**GENERAL

G11. Besterman, Theodore. A World Bibliography of Bibliographies and Bibliographical Catalogues, Calendars, Abstracts, Digests, Indexes and the Like. 4th ed. 5 vols. Lausanne: Societas Bibliographica, 1965-66.
The major listing by the all-time great bibliographer. Includes c. 117,000 SEPARATELY PUBLISHED bibliographies. This edition covers through 1963.
 Arranged by specific subject headings in alphabetical order (c. 16,000 headings and subheadings). Gives the number of items in each bibliography. An author index is in vol. 5.
 Some sections of this work have also been reprinted separately.

G12. Toomey, Alice F. A World Bibliography of Bibliographies, 1964-1974. 2 vols. Totowa, NJ: Rowman & Littlefield, 1977.
Subtitle: "A List of Works Represented by Library of Congress Printed Catalog Cards: a Decennial Supplement to Theodore Besterman, A World Bibliography of Bibliographies."
 The subtitle describes its purpose and extent which is much more limited than Besterman. Consists of reproductions of c. 18,000 LC printed cards arranged under c. 6000 specific subject headings. Note the headings of "Dissertations, Academic," and "Festschriften." Somewhat disappointing considering its predecessor, but helpful.

G13. Bibliographic Index: a Cumulative Bibliography of Bibliographies, 1937-   . New York: Wilson, 1938-   . 3x a year.
Annual cumulations. Intends to list any published bibliography (whether separate or part of a larger work) with 50+ entries. Surveys about 2200 periodicals as well as books and other materials.
 Arranged by specific subject headings. Fairly comprehensive, strongest in the Western European languages.

**RELIGIOUS/THEOLOGICAL

G21. Barrow, John G. <u>A Bibliography of Bibliographies in Religion</u>. Ann Arbor: Edwards, 1955.

Lists c. 4000 separately published bibliographies; see pp. iii-iv for types of works not included. Covers up to c. 1952, fairly complete to 1950. Dated but not superseded.

Classified arrangement, (but no section for Systematic Theology) -- use the detailed table of contents for specific subjects. Title and author index. Includes fairly good critical annotations and some information on the location of copies.

G22. Smith, Wilbur M. <u>A List of Bibliographies of Theological and Biblical Literature Published in Great Britain and America, 1595-1931: with Critical, Biographical, and Bibliographical Notes</u>. Coatesville, PA: the author, 1931.

Note limits of coverage: "theology" in strict "systematic theology" sense; does not include church history or practical theology. Lists only separately published materials.

Includes brief annotations and biographical information on the author of each bibliography. Well done, but hard to use since entries are arranged by date. Author index.

G23. Shunami, Shlomo. <u>Bibliography of Jewish Bibliographies</u>. 2nd enl. ed. with corrections. Jerusalem: Magnes, 1969.

Introductory matter in English & Hebrew. Includes 4700+ entries for bibliographies on Jewish literature, ancient Israel, the Bible & books about it.

Chapter 8
RELIGIOUS/THEOLOGICAL BIBLIOGRAPHIES

Two primary uses for these bibliographies are (1) a subject approach to theological literature, and (2) verification and location of the more obscure, esoteric, or rare works in the field of religion.

Note that (1) bibliographies covering only one subfield of religious or theological studies are NOT included here (they are in the subject area lists), and (2) none of the bibliographies listed here are comprehensive; each employs some set of criteria to limit its contents.

**RELIGIONS

Only three of the better and more recent of the bibliographies covering religion in general are listed below.

H1. Adams, Charles J., ed. <u>A Reader's Guide to the Great Religions</u>. 2nd ed. New York: Free Press, 1977.
1st ed., 1965. A collection of authoritative bibliographical essays on the world's major religions as well as ancient and primitive religions by 13 outstanding scholars.
Each essay is a brief, thorough, and well-written introduction to the basic and important works for study of the respective religion. Includes author and subject indexes.

H2. Mitros, Joseph F. <u>Religions: a Select, Classified Bibliography</u>. Louvain: Nauwelaerts, 1973.
Classed arrangement with brief introductory paragraphs to each of the major areas and brief annotations to some works. Gives a select bibliography, favoring recent English-language titles,

Theological Bibliographies

of important works for the study of each religion. About 1/2 of this book covers Christianity, the other 1/2 non-Christian religions. Author index, detailed table of contents, NO subject index. More extensive than Adams.

H3. Karpinski, Leszak M. The Religious Life of Man: Guide to Basic Literature. Metuchen, NJ: Scarecrow, 1978.

A well-written survey primarily for undergraduates and the public, but also helpful for advanced students. Classified arrangement with index of authors, titles, and subjects. Entries have brief annotations. Includes, for each major subsection in the bibliography, a list of major periodicals.

**LIBRARY CATALOGS

H11. Union Theological Seminary, N.Y. Library. Alphabetical Arrangement of the Main Entries from the Shelf List of the Union Theological Seminary in New York City. 10 vols. Boston: G. K. Hall, 1960.

A listing of the 191,000+ titles held in 1961 by one of the largest seminary libraries in the world. Only one listing per title, usually the author (= main entry), arranged in alphabetical order. Very helpful for verifying older and obscure theological titles.

H12. Union Theological Seminary, N.Y. Library. The Shelf List of the Union Theological Seminary in New York City in Classification Order. 10 vols. Boston: G. K. Hall, 1960.

Includes the same books as the above set, but now arranged by call number. This allows the listing to be used as a classified subject listing. You must determine the Union Seminary call number where the subject you are interested in will be found -- see next entry.

H13. Pettee, Julia. <u>Classification of the Library of Union Theological Seminary</u>. rev. & enl. ed. New York: the Seminary, 1967.
A listing of the classification system used at Union Theological Seminary which will enable you to effectively use the above set.
   Use the index of this work to find the call number(s) of the topic of interest. Then, use that call number to find the correct location in the above set listing books on that topic.

H14. Hebrew Union College - Jewish Institute of Religion. Library. <u>Dictionary Catalog of the Klau Library, Cincinnati</u>. 32 vols. Boston: G. K. Hall, 1964.
Includes author, title, and subject entries (in one alphabetical listing) for c. 200,000 volumes of Judaica and related materials. Vols. 1-27 are of Roman alphabet materials, vols. 28-32 of Hebrew-language materials.

H15. <u>The Library of Congress Shelflist: Religion, BL-BX</u>. microfiche ed. Ann Arbor: University Microfilms, 1979.
These 156 microfiche are part of a larger project which filmed the entire LC shelflist. Reproduces, in call number order, the catalog cards for 332,000+ titles classified by the Library of Congress under "religion." Using the LC classification guides, you can determine the call numbers for specific subjects and use this as a subject listing.

H16. <u>CORECAT: Cooperative Religion Catalog, 1/1/1979-   </u>. Princeton, NJ: Committee for Theological Library Development, 1979-   . Semiannual.
A union catalog which lists all works cataloged by the theological libraries at Andover-Harvard, Princeton Seminary, Union Seminary, and Yale Divinity School since 1978.
   Each new set of microfiche cumulates and

Theological Bibliographies

completely supersedes the previous. Includes entries for authors, titles, series, subjects, etc., in one alphabet. Published on microfiche.

H17. Graduate Theological Union, Berkeley. Library. <u>Union Catalog of the Graduate Theological Union Library</u>. 15 vols. Berkeley, CA: the Library, 1972.
An author-entry only catalog covering up to 1972. Includes the holdings of the San Francisco/Berkeley area Graduate Theological Union libraries. Helpful as an extensive general theological bibliography up to 1972.

**LISTS OF SELECTED WORKS--GENERAL

H21. Trotti, John, ed. <u>Aids to a Theological Library</u>. Missoula, MT: Scholars Press for the American Theological Library Association, 1977.
Written as a guide for theological libraries, intends to stress the bibliographical, reference and book-buying resources that a theological library should have. Classed arrangement, but NO table of contents or index. Earlier editions included a listing of scholarly periodicals in religion.

H22. <u>Guide to Catholic Literature: v. 1-8, 1888-1967</u>. Edited by Walter Romig. Detroit: Romig, 1940-1968.
Includes entries by author, title, and specific subject, but the FULL entry is found only under the author's name. Includes books by and about Catholics in all languages. In total, contains about 1/4 million entries with notes.
  In 1968, merged with the <u>Catholic Periodical Index</u> to form the <u>Catholic Periodical and Literature Index</u>.

H23. <u>A Theological Book List</u>. Compiled by Raymond P. Morris. London: the Fund, 1960.
"Produced by the Theological Education Fund of the

46

Theological Bibliographies

International Missionary Council for Theological Seminaries and Colleges in Africa, Asia, Latin America and the Southwest Pacific."
  Includes 5472 works, primarily in English, considered to be basic for developing theological libraries in the Third World. Detailed classed arrangement, author index, brief annotations.

H24. *A Theological Book List, [1963]*. London: the Fund, 1963.

H25. *A Theological Book List, 1968*. London: the Fund, 1968.

H26. *A Theological Book List, 1971*. London: the Fund, 1971.

The above three works supplement the original work (H23). Compilers and subtitles vary from volume to volume. Each includes separate sections for works in English, French, German, Spanish, and Portuguese.

H27. Katholieke universiteit te Leuven. Faculteit der godgeleerdheid. *Bibliographia academica*. Samengesteld door G. Dreesen. Louvain: the University, 1972.
Lists a selection of theological books by the faculty of a Dutch theological institute.

H28. Heintz, Jean-Georges. *Bibliographie des sciences théologiques*. Paris: Presses universitaires de France, 1972.
A selective bibliography of theological works from a French perspective. Prepared in consultation with the Protestant theological faculty at the University of Strasbourg.
  Classified arrangement, NO annotations. Of interest for its French and European perspective on "basic" works in each area of theology.

H29. Merchant, Harish D., ed. *Encounter with Books: a Guide to Christian Reading*. Downers Grove, IL: InterVarsity Press, 1970.
A selective bibliography of books in all subject areas designed to "acquaint Christians with the

Theological Bibliographies

range of published literature and help them build sound reading habits." (preface) Classed arrangement with annotations. Author index.
 Helpful for its listings of books with Christian perspectives on all areas of life. Written by authors of the "historic evangelical Protestant tradition."

H30. Batson, Beatrice. A Guide to Religious Literature. Chicago: Moody, 1968.
An introduction to the "classics" of Christian literature from the Middle Ages and later, including the influence of Christian thought on outstanding literary works. Concentrates on the 17th to 19th centuries.
 Each chapter surveys the historical and cultural developments of a period, briefly mentions its literary masterpieces, and then analyzes several important religious literary works of the period. Includes bibliography and index.

**LISTS OF SELECTED WORKS--FOR PASTORS

 A large number of these lists have been produced. Listed here are a few of the more recent and more widely circulated lists.

H41. Barber, Cyril. The Minister's Library. Grand Rapids: Baker, 1974.
A classed bibliography with brief annotations intended for pastors. Selections and annotations have a decidedly evangelical and dispensational orientation.
 Child's evaluation that " ... his advice is very misleading. Barber seems mainly concerned with the orthodoxy of the author and he has little judgment of quality" is unfortunately correct.
 Includes some information for the pastor on how to organize his library. Includes author, title, and subject indexes.

Theological Bibliographies

H42. Barber, Cyril. *The Minister's Library: Periodic Supplement #1-3.* Grand Rapids: Baker, 1976-80.
Updates the above work with recently published materials.

H43. Sayre, John, ed. *Basic Books for a Minister's Library.* Enid, OK: Seminary Press, 1979.
Compiled by members of a course on the minister's library, its purpose is "providing only a limited number of the first most recommended books in each field, all of which (as of the date of publication) are in print."
Classified subject arrangement, brief annotations, no index. Excludes reference tools and commentaries (Sayre lists those elsewhere).

H44. Todd, Robert W. "A Suggested Bibliography for Ministers." *Trinity Journal* 4 (Spring 1975): 119-167.
A selected bibliography based on recommendations by the faculty at Trinity Evangelical Divinity School. Classified arrangement with brief annotations. Scholarly, evangelical viewpoint.

H45. Union Theological Seminary, Va. *Essential Books for a Pastor's Library.* 5th ed. Richmond, VA: Union Theological Seminary, 1976.
Intended (i) to list subject areas which should be represented in a pastor's library and (ii) to suggest, in each category, one or more important books. Classified arrangement with brief annotations. No indexes.

H46. Southwestern Baptist Theological Seminary. *Essential Books for Christian Ministry: Basic Readings for Pastors, Church Staff Leaders, and Laymen.* Fort Worth, TX: the Seminary, 1972.
Lists c. 1000 titles, selected by the seminary faculty, in order to "assist students, alumni, and Christian lay workers in selecting the most

Theological Bibliographies

helpful books for their libraries." (preface)
Classified arrangement with brief annotations but no indexes. Includes 18 pages on church music and 15 pages on religious education.

**19TH CENTURY

The nineteenth century was a fruitful period for extensive bibliographies of theological works. Only a few of the more important and English-language oriented works are listed.

H51. Cave, Alfred. <u>An Introduction to Theology: Its Principles, Its Branches, Its Results, and Its Literature</u>. 2nd ed. Edinburgh: T & T Clark, 1896.
1st ed., 1886. An introduction to the study of theology which includes large bibliographies of recommended books for each section. Includes English, German, and French works. Author and subject indexes. Strongest on biblical studies.

H52. Darling, James. <u>Cyclopedia Bibliographica</u>. 2 vols. London: Darling, 1854-59.
Subtitle: "A Library Manual of Theological and General Literature, and Guide to Books for Authors, Preachers, Students, and Literary Men: Analytical, Bibliographical, and Biographical.
Vol. 1 is a list of authors (with biographical information) and their writings.
Vol. 2 is a classified bibliography of material on the Bible, the major portion of which is a listing, in Bible-passage order, of materials on particular passages (including sermons).
A projected 3rd volume; "General Subjects in Theology," was never published.

H53. Hagenbach, Karl R. <u>Theological Encyclopedia and Methodology: on the Basis of Hagenbach</u>. Trans. & enl. by George R. Crooks & John F. Hurst. New York: Phillips & Hunt, 1884.
A comprehensive work on theology which also includes many extensive bibliographies that list

c. 5000 books. Includes index. Based on the original German work, enlarged by the addition of English and American titles.

H54. Hurst, John F. Literature of Theology: a Classified Bibliography of Theology and General Religious Literature. New York: Hunt & & Eaton, 1896.
Based on his 1882 work: Bibliotheca Theologica. An extensive classified bibliography of "the best and most desirable books in theology and general religious literature published in Great Britain, the United States, and the Dominion of Canada." Detailed classified arrangement, see 9-page table of contents. Includes author & subject index.

H55. Malcom, Howard. Theological Index: References to the Principle Works in Every Department of Religious Literature. Boston: Gould & Lincoln, 1868.
Includes c. 70,000 titles under 2000 specific subject headings. Unfortunately, the entries are given in a very abridged form (author's last name, short title, and [sometimes] date) which makes identification difficult.

NOTE: On the theological bibliography of the EIGHTEENTH CENTURY, see: Krentz, Edgar. "Theological Bibliography in the Eighteenth Century." In Essays on Theological Librarianship, pp. 47-66. Edited by Peter de Klerk & Earle Hilgert. Philadelphia: American Theological Library Association, 1980.

**SPECIAL TOPICS

H61. Berkowitz, Morris I., & Johnson, J. Edmund. Social Scientific Studies of Religion: a Bibliography. Pittsburgh: University of Pittsburgh Press, 1967.
A classified bibliography of 6000+ items. Emphasis on recent English-language works that relate religion to social science variables. Author index.

Theological Bibliographies

H62. Crysdale, Stewart, and Montminy, Jean P. La religion au Canada: bibliographie annotée des travaux en sciences humaines des religions, 1945-1970. Avec la collaboration de Henrique Urbano et Les Wheatcroft. Quebec: Presses de l'Univ. Laval, 1974.
English title: Religion in Canada: Annotated Inventory of Scientific Studies of Religion, 1945-1970. An annotated bibliography of social scientific studies of religion in Canada.

H63. Erbacher, Hermann. Personal-Bibliographien aus Theologie und Religionswissenschaft mit ihren Grenzgebieten: eine Bibliographie. Neustadt: Degener, 1976.
An index to where bibliographies of works by and/or about 1843 persons of significance in the study of religion and theology can be found. Arranged by names of the individuals included. Lists nearly 2500 items found in books, periodical articles, etc.

H64. Williams, Ethel L. The Howard University Bibliography of African and Afro-American Religious Studies: with Locations in American Libraries. Wilmington, DE: Scholarly Resources, 1977.
An updated version of the author's bibliography, Afro-American Religious Studies (Scarecrow, 1972). Lists over 13,000 items from 230+ libraries and archives (gives location information). Includes all types of primary and secondary materials with brief descriptions of some items. Use the detailed table of contents to find the material classed under 5 major headings with numerous subdivisions. Author index.

H65. Borchardt, C. F. A., and Vorster, W. S. South African Theological Bibliography: Suid-Afrikaanse Teologiese Bibliographie. Pretoria: University of South Africa, 1980.
A bibliography of 6,008 items which aims "to index all Festschrifts and periodical literature pub-

lished in South Africa covering the theological field." Also includes relevant dissertations submitted at South African universities. Classified arrangement with a detailed table of contents and an author index.

H66. Die Inslag van die Calvinisme in Suid-Afrika: 'n Bibliografie van Suid-Afrikaanse tydskrifartikels. 4 vols. Potchefstroom, S. Africa: Potchefstroomse Universiteit, 1980.
Lists c. 12,500 articles having something to do with Calvinism taken from c. 60 Afrikaans-language periodicals. Classified subject arrangement with cumulative author and subject indexes.
   Contents: v.1--Histories en principieel, v.2 --Godsdienstig en teologies, v.3--Wetenskaplik en opvoedkundig, v.4--Maatskaplik en staatkundig.

H67. "Bibliography [on Christianity and Literature]." In Christianity and Literature, 1970?- . Quarterly.
Each issue of the journal includes abstracts of books, periodical articles, etc., in a classed arrangement. Through mid-1980 there were a total of 6199 abstracts. Annual author & subject index.

**CONTINUING

H71. Religious Reading, 1973- . Wilmington, NC: Consortium, 1975- . Annual.
A classified subject listing of new religion books for the year that the Library of Congress and/or the British National Bibliography recorded. The descriptive annotations (which most entries include) are supplied by the publisher. Title index. Useful for browsing to "see what was published" but not complete or accurate.

H72. Theology Digest. St. Louis: St. Louis University, 1953- . Quarterly.
Contains both "condensations of recent significant articles selected from over 400 of the world's theological journals" (translated into English if

Theological Bibliographies

in a foreign language) and a "book survey." The book survey lists, with descriptive annotations, a large number of new theological books.

H73. Theologische Literaturzeitung: Monatsschrift für das gesamte Gebiet der Theologie und Religionswissenschaft. Leipzig: Hinrichs, 1876- . Monthly.
A periodical which includes bibliographical essays on important topics and numerous reviews and short descriptions of numerous new books. Cumulative annual indexes.

H74. Bibliographisches Beiblatt der Theologischen Literaturzeitung: Die theologische Literatur des Jahres 1921-1942. Leipzig: Hinrichs, 1922-43.
An annual cumulation of Theologische Literaturzeitung, issued in the years indicated. Classified subject arrangement, title index.

H75. Theologische Rundschau. Tübingen: Mohr, 1897- . Quarterly.
Includes long bibliographical essays on the literature of various important theological topics. Also includes additional brief book reviews. Contains many valuable bibliographies and critical reviews of research by authorities in each field.

H76. Theologischer Jahresbericht, 1881-1913. 33 vols. Leipzig: Heinsius, 1882-1916.
Published annually in period indicated. Publisher varies. Arranged by a detailed classification system with author index. Each section of these listings has a bibliography of relevant materials, followed by a bibliographical essay discussing and evaluating each item.

U.S.A. Bibliography

Chapter 9
U.S.A. BIBLIOGRAPHY

National and trade bibliographies are listings of the books published in a given country compiled by official (i.e. "national") agencies or by commercial (i.e. "trade") firms. Ideally, they provide a comprehensive listing of the works published in that country.

The U.S. has no official national library and no official national bibliography. However, the Library of Congress and its extensive National Union Catalog come closest to filling those roles.

Remember however, that the holdings of the Library of Congress, as well as the other members of the National Union Catalog group, include extensive amounts of non-U.S. published materials. Thus the National Union Catalog functions both as a "selective universal" bibliography as well as a "national" bibliography.

**LIBRARY OF CONGRESS & NATIONAL UNION CATALOGS

    The sets of volumes listed here are interrelated and are based on 2 sets of catalog cards produced by and located at the Library of Congress [LC]:
    (1) the LC printed catalog cards which LC sells to other libraries, and
    (2) the catalog cards of the National Union Catalog [NUC] which represents the books in 700+ U.S. libraries (including LC) and indicate which of those libraries holds each title.

    Except for the Subject Catalog volumes (at the end of the list below), all the LC/NUC volumes are arranged by the "main entry"

55

U.S.A. Bibliography

(usually author) and NO title or subject access is possible. Few cross-references are provided.

The LC/NUC catalogs are most useful for (1) verification of bibliographical information when you have an incomplete or incorrect citation; (2) compiling a bibliography of works BY (not ABOUT) an individual, and (3) locating libraries where copies of a wanted book are located so that it may be requested on interlibrary loan.

**PRE-56 SETS

J1. National Union Catalog, Pre-1956 Imprints: a Cumulative Author List Representing Library of Congress Printed Cards and Titles Reported by Other American Libraries. 685 vols. London: Mansell, 1968-1980.
Known as "Mansell" or "Pre-56." A bibliography of all books published before 1956 reported to the National Union Catalog. Very extensive (over 10 million books are included) and useful, essential for in-depth bibliographical research.

Under voluminous authors a logical classified arrangement (usually by original title, subarranged by language) is used. An outline of the arrangement used is given at the beginning of the entries for such authors.

Vols. 53-56 include all works entered under "Bible." See #AB11 below for further information on these volumes.

Each entry also lists libraries reported as holding each title. The quality and accuracy of the entries varies considerably depending on the contributing library. Some duplicate or conflicting entries for the same works will be found.

This work supersedes all of the earlier LC & NUC catalogs up to and including the 1953-1957 NUC cumulative (the 1956 & 1957 titles in the NUC were added to the 1958-1962 cumulation of the NUC).

U.S.A. Bibliography

J2. <u>National Union Catalog, Pre-56 Imprints: Supplement</u>. London: Mansell, 1980-   .
A supplement listing titles and added locations reported to the National Union Catalog since the beginning of the Pre-56 project. To be about 70 volumes.

**POST-56 SETS

J11. <u>National Union Catalog: 1958-1962</u>. 54 vols. New York: Rowman & Littlefield, 1963.
J12. <u>National Union Catalog: 1963-1967</u>. 67 vols. Ann Arbor: Edwards, 1969.
J13. <u>National Union Catalog: 1968-1972</u>. 119 vols. Ann Arbor: Edwards, 1973.
J14. <u>National Union Catalog: 1973-1977</u>. 135 vols. Totowa, NJ: Rowman & Littlefield, 1978.

Subtitle: "A Cumulative Author List Representing Library of Congress Printed Cards and Titles Reported by Other American Libraries." The above works are 5-year cumulations of the monthly NUC. Author-entry only, alphabetically arranged.

J15. <u>National Union Catalog: a Cumulative Author List</u>. Washington, DC: Library of Congress, Cataloging Distribution Service Division, 1959-   . Monthly.

Quarterly & annual cumulations. The information found in the above cumulations first appears in this monthly NUC listing. U.S. published books are usually listed 6 to 18 months after publication. Author-entry only.

**SUBJECT CATALOGS

J21. U.S. Library of Congress. <u>Books: Subjects, 1950-1954</u>. 20 vols. Ann Arbor, MI: Edwards, 1955.
J22. U.S. Library of Congress. <u>Books: Subjects, 1955-1959</u>. 22 vols. Paterson, NJ: Pageant, 1960.
J23. U.S. Library of Congress. <u>Books: Subjects,</u>

U.S.A. Bibliography

    1960-1964. 25 vols. Ann Arbor, MI: Edwards, 1965.
J24. U.S. Library of Congress. Books: Subjects, 1965-1969. 42 vols. Ann Arbor, MI: Edwards, 1970.
J25. U.S. Library of Congress. Books: Subjects, 1970-1974. 100 vols. Totowa, NJ: Rowman & Littlefield, 1975.
J26. U.S. Library of Congress. Subject Catalog. Washington, DC: Library of Congress, 1950- . Quarterly.

"A Cumulative List of Works Represented by Library of Congress Printed Cards." Annual cumulations. The above sets list the books cataloged by the Library of Congress, & are arranged by the Library of Congress subject heading(s) which are assigned to each book.

    Offers a helpful subject approach to recently published books, but limited to those actually cataloged by LC.

NOTE: Some of the above sets have been reprinted by a number of commercial publishers, some in single-sequence cumulations. Often available in printed copy or on microfiche. Your library may have those instead of the above.

    In addition, some publishers have issued title and/or other indexes to the LC/NUC catalogs in various formats. Use them if they are available to you.

**TRADE LISTINGS--IN-PRINT

  Up-to-date listings of materials which are currently or will be shortly available for purchase.

J31. Books in Print. New York: Bowker, 1948- . Annual.

Lists currently available books from 8000 U.S. publishers and foreign publishers with an American distributor. NOTE: some types of publications

U.S.A. Bibliography

are excluded and some publishers are not represented (esp. small and reprint publishers).
Two separate A-Z sections: Authors & Titles. A section at the end of the Title volumes lists publisher addresses. Use carefully, the alphabetizing of the publisher-supplied bibliographical entries results in some strange sequences.

J32. Subject Guide to Books in Print. New York: Bowker, 1957-   . Annual.
Similar in scope and form to the above, but lists books by subject, A-Z under Library of Congress subject headings.

J33. Forthcoming Books; now including New Books in Print. New York: Bowker, 1966-   . Bimonthly.
Includes two types of books: (i) those too new to be listed in the latest Books in Print and (ii) new books due to appear in the next five months (according to the publisher). Separate author and title lists. For forthcoming books, gives author, title, publisher, and projected date & price. A separate "Subject Guide" is also available.

J34. Publishers' Trade List Annual. New York: Bowker, 1873-   . Annual.
A uniformly sized & bound compilation of publisher catalogs, arranged alphabetically by publisher. Completeness, indexing, and accuracy of information varies since actual printing copy is supplied by the publishers -- who pay to be included. Thus, not all publishers are found herein.
The yellow pages at the beginning of volume 1 include (i) an alphabetical index of included publishers and (ii) brief catalogs, printed by Bowker, for the publishers not supplying catalogs for the main section.

J35. American Book Publishing Record. New York: Bowker, 1960-   . Monthly.
Annual & 5-year cumulations. Also know as "BPR." A list of books actually published, arranged by

U.S.A. Bibliography

dewey classification number. Author and title index. Useful (i) for retrospective bibliography back to 1960, (ii) as a source of LC cataloging copy, and (iii) for current awareness of books newly published in the U.S.

J36. Religious Books and Serials in Print, 1978/79-   . New York: Bowker, 1978-   . Annual.
Includes 50,000+ entries in the author and title indexes, from 1700+ publishers, over 100 of which are not in BIP. Gives BIP type of information on each book. Also includes a "Sacred Works Index" (including 71 headings for versions of the Bible & 13 other headings).
   For religious books, this work is more complete than Books in Print & offers better subject access. The subject indexing of serials is also more extensive than that found in Ulrich's (#U22).

**REPRINT

J41. Guide to Reprints. Kent, CT: Guide to Reprints, Inc., 1967-   . Annual.
Now a 2 volume author and title listing, much like Books in Print. Includes reprints of both books and periodicals from 300+ reprint publishers, some of which are not in Books in Print. A separate Subject Guide to Reprints is also available.

J42. Books on Demand: 93,000 Out-of-Print Books Available as Reprints. 3 vols. Ann Arbor: University Microfilms, 1980.
A new edition now appears annually. Subtitle of earlier editions varies. One volume each for Author Guide, Title Guide, & Subject Guide.
   Lists books of which UM will provide a "demand" reprint on a "30-day" delivery basis. Listed books are available in paper, hardback & microfilm. An expensive way to get a book -- check first that it is not available from other sources.

U.S.A. Bibliography

**MICROFORM

J51. Guide to Microforms in Print, Author/Title: Incorporating International Microforms In Print. Westport, CT: Microform Review, 1977-   . Annual.
Author and title entries arranged in one A-Z sequence. Includes bibliographical information on each title and special coding which describes the type of microform that is available. Includes University Microform materials, but is NOT a complete listing of them. Lists books, periodicals, newspapers, and other types of materials on microform. A "Subject Guide" companion volume is also available.

J52. National Register of Microform Masters, 1965-1975. 6 vols. Washington, DC: Library of Congress, 1976.
"The Register reports master microfilms of foreign and domestic books, pamphlets, serials, and foreign doctoral dissertations." Includes a brief bibliographical entry, LC card # (when available), location of the master, and the form & character of the microform. Supplements are issued yearly.

J53. American Theological Library Association. Board of Microtext. [List of Microfilms Available]. Princeton, NJ: the Board. Irregular.
The ATLA Board of Microtext has and is filming a large number of theological materials. Lists of materials available from the board are issued at irregular intervals, and lists of new materials are published in the ATLA Newsletter.

J54. Microform Publishers Trade List Annual. Westport, CT: Microform Review, 1979-   .
An extensive collection of the catalogs of microform publishers from throughout the world. Issued on microfiche, with printed index to the catalogs and instructions for use. Necessary for any extensive microform buying.

U.S.A. Bibliography

**RETROSPECTIVE

J61. Cumulative Book Index: a World List of Books in the English Language, 1928/32- . New York: Wilson, 1933- . Monthly.
Quarterly, annual, and multi-year cumulations. An extensive and accurate worldwide listing of English-language books. Has author, title, and subject entries in one alphabetical list. The author entry for each book is the most complete.

J62. American Book Publishing Record Cumulative, 1876-1949: an American National Bibliography. 14 vols. Ann Arbor: Bowker, 1980.
Intends to list "every book published and/or distributed in the United States during that 74-year span." Includes 600,000+ entries arranged by subject via the dewey decimal system. Author, title, & subject indexes. Extensive and helpful.

J63. American Book Publishing Record Cumulative, 1950-1977: an American National Bibliography. 15 vols. Ann Arbor: Bowker, 1978.
Similar to the above. A massive bibliography of 920,000+ titles arranged by dewey decimal number. Separate author, title, and subject indexes.

J64. Evans, Charles. The American Bibliography. 14 vols. Chicago: the Author, 1903-59.
"Chronological Dictionary of all Books, Pamphlets and Periodical Publications Printed in the United States of America from the Genesis of Printing in 1639 down to and including the year 1820."
Subtitle describes the scope of this work. Works are arranged in chronological order. Each volume has author, subject & printer/publisher indexes. Vol. 14 is a cumulative author index. Gives full bibliographical information & locations of copies in American libraries.

Chapter 10
FOREIGN NATIONAL AND TRADE BIBLIOGRAPHY

See the introductory note to Chapter 9.

GREAT BRITAIN--NATIONAL LIBRARY

L1. British Museum. Department of Printed Books. <u>General Catalogue of Printed Books</u>. Photolithographic ed. to 1955. 263 vols. London: Trustees of the British Museum, 1959-66.

One of the most comprehensive listings of English-language books, this work includes over 4 million entries for virtually all the printed books in the Library of the British Museum. Also strong on French materials and other foreign-language materials. Periodicals are listed in 3 separate volumes under the word "Periodicals."

Entries are primarily by author, with some title entries. Entries under an author also include cross-references to works about the author. Under an author, a logical classified arrangement of titles and editions is used.

Under the names of sacred books (primarily the Bible), are listed both texts of that book & books about that sacred book (e.g. commentaries). There are 3 volumes for the Bible with an index.

L2. British Museum. Department of Printed Books. <u>General Catalogue of Printed Books: Ten Year Supplement, 1956-1965</u>. 50 vols. London: Trustees of the British Museum, 1968.

L3. British Museum. Department of Printed Books. <u>General Catalogue of Printed Books: Five Year Supplement, 1966-1970</u>. 26 vols. London: Trustees of the British Museum, 1971-72.

Supplements to the above. Periodicals are now listed under title, not "Periodicals."

Foreign Bibliography

L4. British Library. __General Catalogue of Printed Books: Five-Year Supplement, 1971-1975.__ 13 vols. London: Britism Museum Publications, 1978-1979.
Includes 400,000 works under 600,000 entries. Printed in a new 3-column format. Will be the last supplement published -- superseded by the cumulative volumes of the __British National Bibliography__ (see #L12).

NOTE: A cumulation of all the above sets is in the process of being published by C. Bingley and by Saur under the title: __The British Library General Catalogue of Printed Books to 1975.__ To be c. 360 volumes.

L5. Peddie, Robert A. __Subject Index of Books Published Before 1880.__ 4 vols. London: Grafton, 1933-48.
Each volume forms a "series." Each series is an alphabetical subject index of about 1/4 of the 50,000 pre-1881 books included. Most of the books listed are found in the British Library.
   Many specific subject headings are used, but no personal names are included. Primarily English-language and British-publisher in scope, but does include foreign-publisher and foreign-language titles.

L6. British Museum. Department of Printed Books. __Subject Index of the Modern Works Added to the Library, 1881-1900.__ 3 vols. London: the Museum, 1902-03.

L7. British Museum. Department of Printed Books. __Subject Index of the Modern Works Added to the Library: Supplements, 1901/05-1956/60.__ London: the Museum, 1906-1974. Quinquennial.
Exact title varies. An ongoing alphabetical subject catalog, listing over 900,000 books. Often uses very general subject headings with numerous subdivisions. Personal names are not included -- that is covered in the main author catalog.

Foreign Bibliography

No overall index or table of contents, and subject headings also vary from volume to volume. Thus, it is often difficult to use effectively. Since 1950, the subject access of the British National Bibliography (#L12) is superior & easier to use.

**GREAT BRITAIN--CURRENT TRADE

L11. British Books in Print: the Reference Catalogue of Current Literature. London: Whitaker, 1965-   . Annual.
An annual listing of books currently in print and on sale in the United Kingdom. A single alphabetical listing of author, title, and subject entries. Includes listing of publishers and addresses.

L12. The British National Bibliography. London: Council of the British National Bibliography, 1950-   . Weekly.
Monthly, annual, & 5-year cumulations. An excellent listing of any work published in Great Britain or by any publisher having an office there. Arranged by detailed dewey-decimal-like classification system, with author, title, and extensive subject indexing. Excellent source for post-1949 bibliography of English-language titles.

**GREAT BRITAIN--RETROSPECTIVE

L21. Pollard, Alfred W., and Redgrave, G. R. A Short-Title Catalogue of Books Printed in England, Scotland, and Ireland, and of English Books Printed Abroad, 1475-1640. London: Bibliographical Society, 1926.
Known as the "STC." Arranged alphabetically by author. Includes a bibliographical description of each book and lists locations of copies (all locations of rarer titles). The subtitle describes the scope of the books included.

Foreign Bibliography

L22. Pollard, Alfred W., and Redgrave, G. R. Short-Title Catalogue of Books ... 1475-1640. 2nd ed., rev. & enl., begun by W. A. Jackson and F. S. Ferguson, completed by Katharine F. Pantzer. 2 vols. London: Bibliographical Society, 1976- .
Only vol. 2 published thus far. Revised and corrected edition of the above work.

L23. Wing, Donald G. Short-Title Catalogue of Books Printed in England, Scotland, Ireland, Wales, and British America, and of English Books Printed in Other Countries, 1641-1700. 3 vols. New York: Index Society, 1945-51.
Continues the STC for the time period indicated. Similar contents to the STC, giving locations in 200+ libraries. Be sure to read the description of its scope, entry form, and entry-selection policies in the introduction.

L24. Wing, Donald G. Short-Title Catalogue of Books . . . 1641-1700. 2nd ed. New York: Modern Language Association, 1972.
Vol. 1 published thus far. Revised edition of the above, expanding and correcting previous entries. Now includes locations information for c. 300 libraries.

NOTE: For 1950-   , the annual and cumulative volumes of the British National Bibliography (see above) may also serve as a retrospective bibliography.

**GERMANY

L31. Verzeichnis lieferbarer Bücher, 1971/72-   . Frankfurt am Main: Verlag der Buchhändler-Vereinigung, 1971-   . Annual.
A German "Books in Print" of currently available titles. Now has 3 volumes, forming a single alphabet of authors, titles, & subject key-words. Also lists addresses of German publishers. A companion "Subject Guide" is also available.

L32. Gesamtverzeichnis des deutschsprachigen Schrifttums (GV): 1911-1965. Hrsg. von Reinhard Oberschelp; bearb. unter der Leitung von Willi Gorzny, mit einem Geleitwort von Wilhelm Totok. Müchen: Verlag Dokumentation, 1976- .
To be 150 vols. A cumulation and single listing of the main entries from some 15 German-language bibliographical tools. Entries are from the Deutsches Bücherverzeichnis, Deutsche Bibliographie, Deutsche Nationalbibliographie and various dissertation lists. Does not entirely supersede these works, esp. their subject access.

L33. Gesamtverzeichnis des deutschsprachigen Schrifttums (GV): 1700-1910. Bearb. unter d. Leitung von Peter Geils und Willi Gorzny; bibliograph. und red. Beratung, Hans Popst & Rainer Schöller. München: Saur, 1979- .
Probably will be c. 100 vols. Similar to the above, but for the earlier period indicated.

**FRANCE

L41. Paris. Bibliothèque Nationale. Catalogue général des livres imprimés: Auteurs. Paris: Impr. Nationale, 1897- .
An alphabetical author list -- does not include periodicals, government or corporate authors, or entries for anonymous or classical works. Under voluminous authors, a detailed title index shows volumes, title changes, editions, etc.
Includes most of the collection up through 1959, although the earlier volumes had earlier cut-off dates. Some post-1959 supplements have been published and others are being prepared.

L42. Les Livres de l'année--Biblio, 1971- . Paris: Cercle de la Librairie, 1972- . Annual.
An annual listing of all French-language books published in that year. Includes author, title, and subject entries in a single alphabet.

Foreign Bibliography

L43. <u>Les Livres disponibles</u>. Paris: Cercle de la Librairie, 1977- .
Also titled <u>French Books in Print</u>. Issued now in three parts: author, title, classified subject. Lists French-language books, regardless of place of publication. Includes a listing of publishers and distributors with addresses.

NOTE: For additional national and trade bibliographies for these and other countries, see the applicable section in Sheehy (#A1).

Chapter 11
DISSERTATIONS AND THESES

Unpublished dissertations and theses are often valuable sources for research in any field. Fortunately, a number of tools are available which list dissertations and theses, index them by author and subject, and/or give abstracts.

In general, doctoral dissertations receive much better coverage than masters theses. However, this list does include some bibliographies of masters theses as well.

**BIBLIOGRAPHICAL GUIDES

M1. Chauveinc, Marc. *Guide on the Availability of Theses*. Groningen: University Library, 1978.
Gives information on obtaining copies of theses from 60 institutions in 60 countries. Includes information on interlibrary loan, in-library use, availablity of copies, etc. The information was gathered by questionnaire and the quality of the information varies.

M2. Reynolds, Michael M. *Guide to Theses and Dissertations: an Annotated International Bibliography of Bibliographies*. Detroit: Gale, 1975.
A "retrospective international listing of [separately published] bibliographies of theses and dissertations produced through 1973." Arranged by subject with special sections for universal and national bibliographies of theses.
  See esp. pages 499-514 which cover "Religion and Theology." Includes indexes of institutions, names, titles, and specific subjects. Has brief annotations.

Dissertations & Theses

M3. Black, Dorothy M. <u>Guide to Lists of Master's Theses</u>. Chicago: American Library Association, 1965.
Includes four sections: (i) sources of such lists; (ii) a few general lists of masters theses; (iii) lists by specific subjects covered; and (iv) lists of theses prepared at individual institutions. Gives descriptive annotations.

**BIBLIOS & INDEXES--AMERICAN DISSERTATIONS

M11. <u>Comprehensive Dissertation Index, 1861-1972</u>. 37 vols. Ann Arbor: University Microfilms, 1973.
Known as "CDI." Includes virtually all doctoral dissertations done in the U.S. up to 1973. Includes, but is not limited to, the entries in <u>Dissertation Abstracts</u> (see #M15 below).
　　Vols. 33-37 are a listing of the dissertations arranged by author. Vols. 1-32 are divided into 6 major subject sections including history (v.28) and philosophy and religion (v.32). Subject indexing is done by listing the dissertation under each of the important words that occur in its full title.
　　Thus, to use effectively you must think of the major words and their synonyms which dissertations of interest probably had in their title. Not perfect, but still very good subject access.

M12. <u>Comprehensive Dissertation Index: Five-Year Supplement, 1973-1977</u>. 19 vols. Ann Arbor: University Microfilms, 1979.
A supplement to the above. Same format, but also includes indexing by "key phrases" (i.e. multiple-word keys) as well as by key words.

M13. <u>Comprehensive Dissertation Index, [Annual Supplement], 1973-   </u>. Ann Arbor: University Microfilms, 1974-   . Annual.
Published yearly to update the above two works. Similar content and format.

Dissertations & Theses

M14. American Doctoral Dissertations, 1955/56- .
Compiled for the Association of Research Libraries. Ann Arbor: University Microfilms, 1957- . Annual.
Earlier volumes (through 1962/63) had varying titles. Lists dissertations (without abstract) by subject area, then by school, then alphabetically by author and title. Includes author index.
  Valuable for its relatively quick publication and for its breakdown of new dissertations by subject area and by granting institution.

M15. Dissertation Abstracts International. Ann Arbor: University Microfilms, 1938- . Monthly.
Often referred to as "DAI." Title varies, v.1-11: Microfilm Abstracts; v.12-29: Dissertation Abstracts. Now divided into three subseries: A = Humanities & Social Sciences; B = Sciences & Engineering; and C = European Abstracts.
  Dissertations are listed by broad subject areas with monthly key-word and author indexes that are cumulated annually. Primarily valuable because it includes abstracts of each dissertation, generally written by the author.
  To find dissertations, it is easier to use Comprehensive Dissertations Index (see above) and then read the abstracts here (CDI includes the DAI abstract location). Most of the dissertations listed can be ordered from University Microfilms.

**BIBLIOS & INDEXES--AMERICAN THESES

M21. Masters Abstracts: A Catalog of Selected Masters Theses on Microfilm. Ann Arbor: University Microfilms, 1962- . Quarterly.
Subtitle and format vary slightly. Format is the same as in Dissertation Abstracts. Indexes and abstracts selected masters theses from selected schools. Includes relatively few of the masters theses done annually. Most issues have cumulative author indexing for that year's preceding issues.

Dissertations & Theses

M22. Cumulative Subject and Author Index to Volumes I-XV of Masters Abstracts. Ann Arbor: University Microfilms, 1978.
A complete author and subject index to the 10,500 theses listed in Masters Abstracts up through 1977. Gives complete bibliographical and ordering information, but not the abstract.

**BIBLIOS & INDEXES--FOREIGN DISSERTATIONS

M31. Retrospective Index to Theses of Great Britain and Ireland, 1716-1950. Vol. 1: Social Sciences and Humanities. Santa Barbara, CA: Clio Press, 1975.
A listing of masters and doctoral level theses. Includes two parts: (i) by specific subject (not just by key word); and (ii) by author. Both parts give full bibliographical information including author, title, year, degree, and school -- no abstracts. Includes some availability information.

M32. Index to Theses Accepted for Higher Degrees in the Universities of Great Britain and Ireland, 1950/51-   . London: ASLIB, 1953-   . Annual.
Title varies. Theses and dissertations are listed in a classified subject arrangement; then alphabetically by institution within each subject. Subject and author indexes are provided. Includes information on availability.

M33. Dissertation Abstracts International C: European Abstracts. Ann Arbor: University Microfilms, 1976-   . Quarterly.
"Abstracts of Dissertations Submitted for Doctoral & Post-Doctoral Degrees at European Institutions." Foreign-language dissertations include an English translation of the title and an English abstract. Selective in the schools that are included--seems to stress English-language dissertations.
   Many of the dissertations are available from U.M. Author & key-word subject indexes. Includes a survey of "European Higher Education Practices."

Dissertations & Theses

**BIBLIOS & INDEXES--RELIGIOUS DISSERTATIONS

M41. Sonne, Niels H. A Bibliography of Post-Graduate Master's Theses in Religion. Chicago: American Theological Library Association, 1951.
Lists c. 2700 ThM and STM theses divided into 37 subject areas. Author index. Dated but the only tool of this type. Does not include Catholic or Jewish seminary theses.

M42. Council on Graduate Studies in Religion. Doctoral Dissertations in the Field of Religion, 1940-1952. New York: Columbia University Press for the Council, 1954.
"Their Titles, Location, Field, and Short Precis of Contents." Published as a supplement to the Review of Religion, v.18. Only lists dissertations from universities or seminaries offering a PhD in religion and done under the "religion" or "theology" department.
Lists 425 items with brief abstracts arranged alphabetically by author. Of primary value where CDI or DAI are not available. Includes an "index" listing entry numbers under 14 subject headings.

M43. Council on Graduate Studies in Religion. Dissertation Title Index. Iowa City, IA: the Council, 1952-1977. Annual.
Continues the above. Annual listing of the titles of new dissertations in the area of religion. Continued by the following item.

M44. Religious Studies Review. Waterloo, Ontario, Canada: Council on the Study of Religion, 1975-   . Quarterly.
Regularly includes a list of "Recent Dissertations in Religion" & less frequently a list of "Dissertations in Progress." Dissertations are primarily from schools in the Council, but items from other schools are included if supplied. Arranged under broad subject headings. Gives author, title, degree, school, & date; but includes no abstract.

Chapter 12
MULTI-AUTHOR WORKS

A number of books are published each year which consist of essays by different authors. These works are known as multi-author works (MAW).

The most common of these in academic circles is the festschrift, "a volume of writings by different authors presented as a tribute or memorial esp. to a scholar." Other types of MAWs include volumes of papers from conferences and volumes of essays on the same topic.

A number of special reference tools exist which index (usually by subject and author) the individual essays within these MAWs. Those of general interest & those relating to religious/theological studies are included in this list.

**GENERAL COVERAGE

N1. American Library Association. <u>The "A.L.A." Index: an Index to General Literature.</u> 2nd ed. Boston: Houghton Mifflin, 1901.
The standard general-coverage MAW index, covering up to 1900. Includes only English-language titles. A supplement, published in 1914, indexes some additional works from 1901-1910, but these are largely incorporated in the work listed below.

N2. <u>Essay and General Literature Index, 1900- .</u> New York: Wilson, 1934- . Semiannual.
Annual & 5-year cumulations. Continues the coverage of the above work. Detailed indexing of MAWs by author, subject, & some titles. Covers English-language materials, primarily in the humanities. Indexes, in total, over 10,000 MAWs.

Multi-Author Works

**RELIGIOUS/THEOLOGICAL COVERAGE

N11. Religion Index Two: Festschriften, 1960-1969. Edited by Betty O'Brien and Elmer O'Brien. Chicago: American Theological Library Association, 1980.
An author and subject index to the individual essays in 783 religious/theological festschriften for the time period indicated. Same format and style as #N13 below. Includes 13,000+ author/editor entries and 33,000+ subject entries.

N12. Religion Index Two: Multi-Author Works, 1970-1975. Chicago: American Theological Library Association, [forthcoming in 1982].
Designed to fill the gap between the O'Brien index and the beginning of Religion Index Two.

N13. Religion Index Two: Multi-Author Works, 1976-___. Chicago: American Theological Library Association, 1978-___. Annual.
Two major sections: (i) a name index for the editors (of the whole MAW) & authors (of the individual essays) ; and (ii) a subject index that analyzes both the whole MAW and the individual essay by subject.
   The entry under editor in the first section has the full bibliographical information about the MAW and lists its contents. Uses the same subject headings, format, and typeface as Religion Index One (see #T12 below).

N14. Berlin, Charles. Index to Festschriften in Jewish Studies. Cambridge: Harvard College Library, 1971.
Includes two listings: (i) by author and (ii) by specific subject. The "List of Festschriften Indexed" gives full bibliographical entries for the 243 volumes of festschriften dealing with Jewish studies that are included.

N15. Erbacher, Hermann. <u>Bibliographie der Fest- und Gedenkschriften für Persönlichkeiten aus evangelischer Theologie und Kirche</u>. Neustadt: Verlag Degener, 1971-   .
Two volumes thus far: vol. 1 covers 1881-1969; vol. 2 covers 1969-1975.

Each volume has two sections. The first is a listing of the festschriften included (arranged by the name of the honoree), with indexing by key title words and by series or journal (if any) of which the festschrift is a part.

The second is a classified subject listing of the individual articles, prefaced by a detailed outline of the subject classification scheme. Also has author, personal name, geographical name, subject, and biblical reference indexes.

Book Review Indexes

Chapter 13
BOOK REVIEW INDEXES

A number of reference works which direct the user to reviews of a particular book are available. Most are arranged by author of the book reviewed, and several also provide subject access.

Both the book's subject and its publication date are important when looking for a review. Choose a book review index with subject coverage the same as or broader than the subject of the book. Since most book reviews appear 1/2 to 3 years after a book is published, look for reviews in journals published during that time period.

When using the book review indexes, remember that there is an additional time lag between when the journal issue appears and when the index which covers the journal issue appears.

**GENERAL COVERAGE

P1. Book Review Digest. New York: Wilson, 1905- . Monthly.
Annual and multi-year cumulations. Indexes and briefly summarizes the reviews in c. 75 English & American, general-coverage (c. 4 religious in nature) periodicals. Reviews are arranged by author of the book reviewed. Includes subject and author indexes. Very selective and generally not too helpful in theological studies.

P2. Book Review Index. Detroit: Gale, 1965- . Bimonthly.
Annual cumulations. Indexes all reviews in (currently) c. 300 periodicals, c. 10 of which are religious in nature. Reviews are listed by author of the book reviewed; reviewer is not named in the index. Title index in 1976 and later issues.

Book Review Indexes

P3. <u>Current Book Review Citations</u>. New York: Wilson, 1976- . Monthly.
Annual cumulations. "An author and title cumulation of reviews indexed in other Wilson indexes." Covers over 1200 periodicals, including a number of religious, psychological & historical journals.
Two major parts: (i) a listing of the books reviewed & the locations of the reviews, arranged by the author of the book reviewed; and (ii) a title index. Valuable for its wide coverage and fairly rapid appearance.

**RELIGIOUS/THEOLOGICAL

P11. <u>Book Reviews of the Month: an Index to Reviews Appearing in Selected Theological Journals</u>. Fort Worth, TX: Fleming Library, Southwestern Baptist Theological Seminary, 1965- . Monthly.
Lists the reviews that have recently appeared in 100+ theological journals. Entries for the works reviewed are arranged using a detailed subject classification, with an outline/table of contents & author index included in each issue.
Cumulative author indexes are available for most years. Not published from June 1965 to May 1968. Valuable for its rather wide and current listing of reviews of theological books.

P12. Mills, Watson E. <u>An Index of Reviews of New Testament Books Between 1900-1950</u>. Danville: VA: Association of Baptist Professors of Religion, 1977.
Indexes the numerous reviews in 52 major journals of books on the New Testament published between 1900 and 1950. Arranged by author of the book reviewed. A helpful supplement to the listing of book reviews in <u>New Testament Abstracts</u>.

Book Review Indexes

**OTHER SOURCES OF BOOK REVIEW CITATIONS

Many periodical indexes include sections listing book reviews, or include indexing of book reviews within the main index. A few of the major religious/theological periodical indexes which include book review indexing are listed below. See the main annotation for full information on each.

T11. Index to Religious Periodical Literature, 1949-1976.
T12. Religion Index One, 1977-   .

Book reviews are listed in a separate section at the back of each issue and cumulation.

T13. Catholic Periodical Index, 1930-1966.
T14. Catholic Periodical and Literature Index, 1967-   .

Book reviews are found under the heading "book reviews" in the bimonthly issues but in a separate section at the back of the cumulated volumes.

T34. Christian Periodical Index, 1956-   .

Book reviews are found in a separate section at the back of each issue.

NOTE: Many of the specialized periodical indexes listed in Part II, THE SUBJECT AREA LISTS, also index relevant book reviews.

Mss. & Government Pub.

Chapter 14
MANUSCRIPT MATERIALS & GOVERNMENT PUBLICATIONS

**ARCHIVAL MATERIALS

Often, the primary materials for historical research will be the papers, original records, etc., of the individual or institution under study. The tools below help the researcher locate available materials and learn the conditions for using those materials.

R1. National Union Catalog of Manuscript Collections, 1959/61-   . Washington, DC: Library of Congress, 1962-   . Annual.

The major guide & index to mss. collections in the U.S. Gives a detailed description (contributed by the holding institution) of 30,000+ collections in over 900 repositories in the U.S.

Information given includes number of items, scope and extent, access restrictions, location, microfilm copy availability, etc. Includes annual index (cumulated every 5 years) of those collections by topical subject, personal, family, corporate, and geographical names.

R2. U. S. National Historical Publications Commission. A Guide to Archives and Manuscripts in the United States. Philip M. Hamer, ed. New Haven, CT: Yale Univ. Press, 1961.

Arranged by state, then by city, with good index. Gives a brief description of the collections found in each archive, indicating scope, size, and individual names of prominence in the collection. Includes bibliographical references to published guides to the various collections.

Mss. & Government Pub.

R3. U. S. National Historical Publications and Records Commission. <u>Directory of Archives and Manuscript Repositories</u>. Washington, DC: the Commission, 1978.
Updates but does not supersede Hamer (above). Includes information on 2700+ archives and mss. repositories. Arranged geographically, extensive name and subject indexes. Includes information on hours, use provisions, & holdings; descriptions of special collections; and bibliographical citations to other material where the collections are described more fully.

**GOVERNMENT PUBLICATIONS

A government publication is any document published at government expense. Each year, the government publishes millions of pages of material, including a great deal of basic statistical information. For those working in religion and theology, particularly the sociological aspects, government documents may be a valuable source of information.

The methods of classification, the means of identification, and the reference tools for using government documents are quite specialized. Below are listed only two works which will provide an introduction to these documents and their use.

R11. Newsome, Walter L. <u>New Guide to Popular Government Publications for Libraries and Home Reference</u>. Littleton, CO: Libraries Unlimited, 1978.
An up-to-date guide to 2500+ government publications "that are of current or long-term popular interest." Entries are arranged by subject. Helpful in listing some of the better popular-level material, but does not serve as an introduction to the whole range of public documents as does the next work.

Mss. & Government Pub.

R12.   Morehead, Joe. <u>Introduction to United States Public Documents</u>.   2nd ed.   Littleton, CO: Libraries Unlimited, 1978.
A good introduction to the use and bibliographical control of government publications. Four chapters discuss the production, distribution, and control of government documents. Seven additional chapters are a guide to the access and use of these publications.

General Periodical Indexes

Chapter 15
PERIODICAL INDEXES: GENERAL COVERAGE

Both indexes proper and abstracting tools are included in this list.

The main function of periodical indexes is to provide SUBJECT access to the individual articles published in magazines and journals. Many indexes also include access by the author of the article, and a few by title as well.

Some indexes, particularly the more specialized subject ones, also index book reviews, books, dissertations, and/or articles in multi-author works.

Abstracting tools, besides providing the subject (and usually author) access of the periodical index, also provide a short descriptive and/or critical summary of each item included.

Periodical indexes are arranged in a number of different ways. The most common is a single alphabetical listing of author and specific subject entries. Some are arranged in two sections: one for subjects and another for authors. Others have a classified arrangement with author and/or specific subject indexes. Be sure you understand the arrangement of each index which you use.

**GUIDES

S1. Marconi, Joseph V. <u>Indexed Periodicals: a Guide to 170 Years of Coverage in 33 Indexing Services</u>. Ann Arbor: Pierian, 1976.
A guide which tells the user where, in the 33 periodical indexes covered, over 11,000 periodicals have been indexed. Covers up to about 1973. Indexes included are the more popular ones, e.g. most of those published by Wilson.

General Periodical Indexes

Religious periodical indexes analyzed are: Index to Religious Periodical Literature, Index to Jewish Periodicals, Catholic Periodical Index, and Catholic Periodical and Literature Index. Helpful for finding out where a particular periodical you are interested in has been indexed in the past.

**GENERAL--AMERICAN

S11. Poole's Index to Periodical Literature, 1802-1881. rev. ed. 2 vols. Boston: Houghton, 1891.
S12. Poole's Index to Periodical Literature: Supplements, 1882-1906. 5 vols. Boston: Houghton, 1887-1908.
Provides only subject, NOT author, access. A general-coverage index, but much theological material is included. Indexes c. 590,000 articles found in c. 300 periodicals in the 19th century.

The bibliographical citation gives only the volume number and the first page of the article. Despite the problems, the major source of indexing of 19th-century English-language periodicals.

S13. Wall, C. Edward. Cumulative Author Index for Poole's Index to Periodical Literature, 1802-1906. Ann Arbor: Pierian, 1971.
A "quick and dirty" computer-compiled author index to Poole's Index. Author names are cited as they appear in the original index -- no attempt has been made to make all the entries for the same person exactly the same.

Under each author's name, the user is given a volume, page, and column in Poole's Index where an article by that author is listed. Better than no author access, but still difficult to use.

S14. Nineteenth Century Readers' Guide to Periodical Literature, 1890-1899; with Supplementary Indexing 1900-1922. 2 vols. New York: Wilson, 1944.
Originally intended to cover all of the 19th century, but only this volume was ever published.

General Periodical Indexes

Same format and layout as Readers' Guide (see below). "Supplementary" in that it supplements the coverage of the first 22 years of Readers' Guide by indexing some additional titles.

S15. The Readers' Guide to Periodical Literature, 1900-   . New York: Wilson, 1905-   . Semi-monthly.

Annual and multi-year cumulations. A general index to popular periodical titles. Includes author and subject entries in a single alphabet. Stays very current in its coverage and is easy to use. Particularly useful for its indexing of news magazines. Available at most public libraries.

S16. International Index: a Guide to Periodical Literature in the Social Sciences and Humanities. 18 vols. New York: Wilson, 1907-1965.

A good general-coverage periodical index but of more scholarly magazines. Includes religion, philosophy, and psychology. Good indexing; easy to use. Superseded by the following title.

S17. Social Sciences and Humanities Index. 7 vols. New York: Wilson, 1966-1974.

Continues #S16 above, but restricted to the humanities and social sciences. Indexes 200+ scholarly periodicals. Similar in layout, format, and ease-of-use to Readers' Guide. Continued by Humanities Index (#S41) and Social Sciences Index (#S51).

S18. Public Affairs Information Service. Bulletin. New York: the Service, 1915-   . Weekly.

10-week and annual cumulations. Known as "PAIS." Selectively indexes about 1000 English-language journals, government publications, books, pamphlets, and reports for material about political and social conditions.

General Periodical Indexes

S19. New York Times Index. New York: the Times, 1913- . Weekly.
Quarterly & annual cumulations. A carefully done subject index to the news stories in the New York Times. A brief abstract of the article is also included. Very helpful in locating brief summaries of past news stories and for finding the location of the full text in the New York Times.

**GENERAL--FOREIGN

S31. Subject Index to Periodicals, 1915-1961. 44 vols. London: Library Association, 1919-1962.
Primarily British, covering the humanities, technology, and education. Later volumes index 300+ British titles. Primary section is arranged by subject. Author index.

S32. France. Centre National de la Recherche Scientifique. Bulletin signalétique. Paris: the Centre, 1948- .
Actually an entire series of periodical indexing tools that includes abstracts of the articles (in French). International, attempts to be exhaustive. Each part has a classified arrangement, with specific subject and author indexes. Early coverage, up to about 1960, is somewhat sketchy. For religion & theology, see #T16 below.

S33. Internationale Bibliographie der Zeitschriftenliteratur aus allen Gebieten des Wissens, 1963/64- . Osnabrück: Dietrich, 1965- . Semiannual.
Known as "IBZ." Arranged by specific subject entry, with author indexing. Uses German subject headings, with references to them from the French and English equivalents. Worldwide coverage of a large number of periodicals, transactions, yearbooks, etc. Continues the following two works.

General Periodical Indexes

S34. Bibliographie der deutschen Zeitschriftenliteratur, mit Einschluss von Sammelwerken, 1896-1964. 128 vols. Leipzig: Dietrich, 1897-1964.
An index of German-language periodicals, transactions, yearbooks, etc. Subject arrangement with author index. Original coverage of 275 periodicals grew to c. 4500 titles before it merged with #S35 to form #S33.

S35. Bibliographie der fremdsprachigen Zeitschriftenliteratur; 1911-1915, 1925/26-1962/64. 73 vols. Leipzig: Dietrich, 1911-1964.
Complement to the above work for non-German-language periodicals, etc. The first series (1911--1915) has subject access only; the later series also includes an author index. Good coverage of American, English, French, and Italian periodicals. At the end, indexed about 1400 titles.

**HUMANITIES

S41. Humanities Index. New York: Wilson, 1974- . Quarterly.
Continues, in part, Social Sciences and Humanities Index (#S17). Includes history. Typical Wilson format, with a single alphabet of author & subject entries. Includes separate book review section. Indexed 260 humanities journals in first volume.

S42. British Humanities Index, 1962- . London: Library Association, 1963- . Quarterly.
Annual cumulations. Intends to cover "all material relating to the arts and humanities." In 2 parts, subject & author, each with full entries. Indexes around 380 British journals. Continues, in part, Subject Index to Periodicals (#S31).

S43. Arts and Humanities Citation Index. Philadelphia: Institute for Scientific Information, 1978- . 3x a year.
Annual cumulations. Rather than indexing by sub-

General Periodical Indexes

ject, a citation index "indexes" the material by the works which are cited in the footnotes of the article being indexed.
   Thus, using this index, you can discover what (i) articles have cited a given work or article and (ii) what works are cited by a given indexed article. Also provides for modified author and subject access. Includes some religious and theological journals.

**SOCIAL SCIENCES

S51. Social Sciences Index. New York: Wilson, 1974-   . Quarterly.
Annual cumulations. Continues in part the Social Sciences and Humanities Index (#S17 above). Regular Wilson layout with a single alphabet of author and subject entries. Includes separate book review section. Vol. 1 indexed 263 titles.

S52. Social Sciences Citation Index, 1970-   . Philadelphia: Institute for Scientific Information, 1974-   . 3x a year.
Annual & 5-year cumulations. Rather than indexing by subject, a citation index indexes the material by the works which are cited in the footnotes of the article being indexed.
   Thus, using this index, you can discover (i) what articles have cited a given work or article and (ii) what works are cited by a given indexed article. Also provides for modified author and subject access. Covers around 2000 titles.

Rel./Theo. Periodical Indexes

Chapter 16
PERIODICAL INDEXES: RELIGIOUS/THEOLOGICAL COVERAGE

Periodical indexes which cover religion and/or theology in general. Periodical indexes covering one subfield of theological studies are found in the subject area lists.

**GUIDES

T1. Kepple, Robert J. A Study and Evaluation of Religious Periodical Indexing. (ERIC document #ED 150 984). Arlington, VA: ERIC Document Reproduction Service, 1978.
Consists of two parts: Part I is a detailed examination of 26 tools which provide indexing of religious periodical literature. Citation, frequency of publication, and a descriptive narrative on the state and usefulness of each tool is given.
  In Part II, the coverage and completeness of past indexing is examined and the overlap of coverage among current indexes is evaluated.

T2. Regazzi, John, and Hines, Theodore C. A Guide to Indexed Periodicals in Religion. Metuchen, NJ: Scarecrow, 1975.
An alphabetical listing of some 2700+ periodicals indexed in 17 abstracting and indexing services. The title of each periodical is given and the indexing tools which cover it are indicated. Also included is a key-word index to aid in locating the periodical titles. As noted in several reviews, this work includes some inaccurate data.

**MORE IMPORTANT

T11. Index to Religious Periodical Literature, 1949-1976. 12 vols. Chicago: American Theological Library Association, 1953-1977.

Rel./Theo. Periodical Indexes

T12. Religion Index One: Periodicals. Chicago: American Theological Library Association, 1977- .
Now issued semiannually with 2-year cumulations. "RIO" continuing "IRPL," is the major American religious periodical index. Now indexes 200+ journals, mainly in English and from North America although some other titles are included. Covers a wide range of journals from all areas of theology.
Through 1976, this index had 2 A-Z sections: (i) author and subject entries for the articles; and (ii) a listing of book reviews arranged by author of the book reviewed.
Since 1977, has three A-Z sections: (i) subject entries, (ii) author entries with abstracts whenever they are available, & (iii) book reviews.

T13. Catholic Periodical Index. 13 vols. Haverford, PA: Catholic Library Association, 1930-1966.

T14. Catholic Periodical and Literature Index. Haverford, PA: Catholic Library Association, 1967- . Bimonthly.
2-year cumulations. The Catholic Periodical and Literature Index continues both the Catholic Periodical Index and the Guide to Catholic Literature. (see #H22 above). Now indexes 130+ periodicals either by or of-interest-to Catholics. Its periodical coverage deliberately minimizes overlap with the Index to Religious Periodical Literature. Since 1967, it has also included books of interest to or by Catholics.
For books & periodical articles, the author & subject entries are arranged in a single A-Z list. In the bimonthly issues, book reviews are listed under the heading "Book Reviews." In the cumulations, they are gathered in a separate listing at the back of the volume.
Includes indexing of papal, conciliar, diocesan, & other official church documents, whether in original language or in translation. Overall, a useful index covering the literature and periodicals of the Catholic Church.

Rel./Theo. Periodical Indexes

T15. "Elenchus Bibliographicus" in <u>Ephemerides Theologicae Lovanienses</u>. Louvain: Universitas Catholica Lovaniensis, 1924-   . Annual.

"ETL." Currently published as a separately paged section of the journal, this is the most extensive bibliography of theology and canon law published today. While it covers all areas of theology, dogmatic theology is stressed.

Lists monographs, festschriften, conference proceedings, & dissertations, as well as indexing over 500 theological journals. The journals are in many languages, scholarly in nature, and include a large number of Roman Catholic works.

Entries are arranged by a fairly detailed classified subject system -- see the table of contents at the back of the volume. Author index. Very useful for current work but hard to search retrospectively due to its numerous separate numbers. Particularly valuable for its coverage of topics in systematic theology.

T16. <u>Bulletin signalétique 527: Histoire et sciences des religions</u>. Paris: Centre de Documentation du C.N.R.S., 1979-   . Quarterly.

Published since 1947, title varies. Since 1970, a major international work, indexing and abstracting relevant material in over 1500 journals and proceedings (both secular and religious). Book reviews are included, listed under the author of the book. In its earlier numbers, coverage was much less extensive.

BS527 covers all areas of religious studies including history of religion, comparative religion, Christian doctrine, church history, biblical studies, & the study of non-Christian religions.

Organized in 4 parts: (i) a classified listing of articles with abstracts (in French); (ii) a detailed listing of the periodicals abstracted; (iii) a set of detailed subject indexes; and (iv) an author index. Indexes are cumulated annually. Valuable for its current and extensive coverage.

Rel./Theo. Periodical Indexes

**MOST CURRENT

T21. Subject Index to Select Periodical Literature. Dallas: Mosher Library, Dallas Theological Seminary, 1970-1979.

T22. Mosher Periodical Index. Dallas: Mosher Library, Dallas Theological Seminary, 1980- .
Provides very current monthly indexing of the periodical issues just received at the Mosher Library. Currently indexes 250 periodicals, primarily English-language. Articles are listed under specific subject entries, with an author index.

The issues are not cumulated. Most useful for its very current coverage, often 8 to 12 months in advance of the same indexing in Religion Index One.

T23. Zeitschriften Inhaltsdienst Theologie. Indices Theologici. Tübingen: Universitätsbibliothek, 1975- . 9x a year.
Annual indexes. Provides very current coverage of theological journals by reproducing the tables of contents of over 400 journals received at the Tubingen University theological library. Also includes festschriften and collected-essay works.

Arrangement is in 12 sections by major theological subject areas, subarranged by title of the journal. Includes author and biblical reference indexes. A convenient way to quickly scan a large number of recent journals.

**OTHER

T31. Richardson, Ernest C. An Alphabetical Subject Index and Index Encyclopedia to Periodical Articles on Religion, 1890-1899. 2 vols. New York: Scribners, 1907-1911.
Vol. 1 lists 58,000 articles from 600+ journals under specific subject headings. Vol. 2, which lists the same articles alphabetically by author, is titled Periodical Articles on Religion. Includes materials in French, German, Italian, and English.

Each subject heading also gives references to encyclopedia articles on the topic and (for subjects) a brief definition of the term or (for people) brief biographical information.

Gives extensive and well-indexed coverage for the 1890-1899 decade, attempting to list all religious articles published during that period.

T32. *Guide to Social Science and Religion in Periodical Literature.* National Periodical Library, 1970- . Quarterly.

Annual and 3-year cumulations. Formerly titled *Guide to Religious and Semi-Religious Periodicals* (1965-1969) and *Guide to Religious Periodicals* (1964-1965). Indexes c. 100 semi-scholarly and popular English-language periodicals in the fields of the social sciences and religion.

Concentrates on material relating religion to the social sciences and to modern society. Only gives subject entries, and those are few and broad. Most of the periodicals indexed here are indexed elsewhere.

While its less-than-perfect subject headings, subject-only indexing, and time lag detract from its value, it still is occasionally of some use for locating popular-level materials on the relationships between religion and the social sciences and with modern society.

T33. *Index to Jewish Periodicals.* Cleveland: College of Jewish Studies Press, 1963- . Semiannual.

Now indexes 44 English-language American & British Jewish periodicals. Lists author & subject entries in a single A-Z sequence. Book reviews are listed, by author of the book reviewed, within the main sequence. Valuable as a source of popular & scholarly Jewish opinion on a variety of topics.

T34. *Christian Periodical Index.* Buffalo: Christian Librarians' Fellowship, 1956- . Quarterly.

Annual and multi-year cumulations. Indexes c. 60

Rel./Theo. Periodical Indexes

popular and scholarly, primarily evangelical and fundamentalist publications. Includes entries for authors & specific subjects in a single alphabetic sequence. Book reviews are listed in a separate section at the back. Fairly current, provides needed coverage of popular evangelical literature.

T35. Religious and Theological Abstracts. Myerstown, PA: Religious and Theological Abstracts, Inc., 1958-   . Quarterly.
Annual author and Scripture reference indexes. Includes brief (5-15 lines) abstracts in English, arranged in classified subject order.

Now indexes c. 180 journals, primarily Protestant and English-language, although some French, German, & Dutch titles are included. Valuable for its abstracts, but it and Religion Index One index many of the same titles.

**MAJOR DENOMINATIONAL

T41. Southern Baptist Periodical Index. Nashville: Historical Commission, Southern Baptist Convention, 1965-   . Annual.
No cumulations. An author and specific subject index to Southern Baptist periodicals. Particularly helpful for its indexing of the popular and Christian education periodicals of that group.

T42. United Methodist Periodical Index. Nashville: United Methodist Publishing House, 1960-   . Quarterly.
Annual & 5-year cumulations. An author & subject index to c. 60 Methodist periodicals, including a good deal of Christian education material. Vols. 1-5 were titled: Methodist Periodical Index.

Serial Publication Tools

Chapter 17
SERIAL PUBLICATION TOOLS

Periodicals, irregular and annual repeat publications, and monograph series are all included under the term "serial." This list includes several types of reference tools which will help you deal with these types of publications.

**UNION LISTS--NATIONAL

Once you have located a periodical article of interest to you, it is still necessary to locate a copy of that periodical issue. If your library does not have it, a union list will help you find a library that does.

A union list is an alphabetical list of the serials (including periodicals) which are owned by the various libraries that contributed information to the union list. The list also specifies which issues of a serial the library does have, if it does not have them all.

U1. Union List of Serials in Libraries of the United States and Canada. 3rd ed. 5 vols. New York: Wilson, 1965.
Known as "ULS." Includes 156,000 periodical and serial titles which began publication before 1950 and are held by one or more of 956 libraries. Gives history of periodical name changes, numbering irregularities, etc. Libraries holding a given serial are indicated with a listing of the extent of their holdings.

The abbreviations for holding libraries are NOT in complete alphabetical order -- you must scan the entire list. In addition, discovering the form of name under which a periodical is entered may require several attempts.

Serial Publication Tools

U2. New Serial Titles, a Union List of Serials Commencing Publication after December 31, 1949: 1950-1970 Cumulative. 4 vols. Washington, DC: Library of Congress, 1973.

U3. New Serial Titles: 1971-1975 Cumulation. Washington, DC: Library of Congress, 1976.

Updates the above work for serials beginning or ending within the indicated time periods.

U4. New Serial Titles. Washington, DC: Library of Congress, 1953- . Monthly.

Annual cumulations. An ongoing service which provides up-to-date information on new serials and other serial changes.

**UNION LISTS--REGIONAL THEOLOGICAL

Hundreds of various local and regional union lists exist. Your librarian will know those most helpful in your location. Listed below are some of the more important union lists involving theological libraries.

U11. Boston Theological Institute. B.T.I. Union List of Periodicals. Preliminary checking ed. Boston: the Institute, 1974.

The Boston Theological Institute includes Andover Newton, Harvard Divinity School, Boston University School of Theology, Weston School of Theology, Gordon-Conwell, and other theological seminaries.

U12. Chicago Area Theological Library Association. Union List of Serials. Chicago: the Association, 1974.

U13. Chicago Area Theological Library Association. Union List of Serials: Supplement. Chicago: the Association, 1980.

Lists the periodicals held by 23 theological libraries in the Chicago area, including Seabury-Western, The Univ. of Chicago Divinity School, the Jesuit-Kraus-McCormick library, and others. Arranged by title with holdings indicated.

Serial Publication Tools

U14. Matthews, Donald N., ed. <u>Union List of Periodicals of the Southeastern Pennsylvania Theological Library Association</u>. 2nd key ed. Gettysburg, PA: the Association, 1981.
A union list of the periodical holdings of 13 theological seminary libaries in Southeastern Pennsylvania including Westminster Theological Seminary, Lutheran Theological Seminary (Philadelphia), Eastern Baptist Seminary, and others.

Entries are arranged strictly by the title of the periodical, with cross-references linking the entries of periodicals with title changes. Gives full holding information for each library.

U15. Theological Education Association of Mid-America. <u>TEAM-A Serials: a Union List of the Serials Holdings</u>. Louisville, KY: Southern Baptist Theological Seminary, 1972.
TEAM-A includes the Southern Baptist, Asbury, Louisville Presbyterian, St. Meinard, and Lexington seminaries.

U16. Matthews, Donald N., ed. <u>Union List of Periodicals of the Members of the Washington Theological Consortium and Contributing Institutions</u>. 3rd ed., rev. Gettysburg, PA: Lutheran Theological Seminary, 1979.
A union list of periodical holdings of 15 theological libraries including Catholic University of America, Howard University School of Religion, Wesley Theological Seminary, the Washington Theological Union Library.

**DIRECTORIES OF CURRENT TITLES

Several publishers issue listings of currently published serials. These tools give such information as publisher, cost, and circulation; and are arranged by major subject areas. They are useful for finding subscription information, for information on newer serials not yet in union lists, and for a broad subject approach to serials.

Serial Publication Tools

The four lists below are among the more comprehensive. There are other similar tools by other publishers, and you may find that your library has those as well.

U21. Oxbridge Directory of Religious Periodicals. New York: Oxbridge Communications, 1979-   . Annual.
Lists 3077 U.S. and Canadian titles -- magazines, newspapers, directories, educational materials, annual reports, etc. Entries include publisher, address & phone, editor, year established, circulation, etc. Arranged by title with key-word title index.

U22. Ulrich's International Periodicals Directory: a Classified Guide to Current Periodicals, Foreign and Domestic. 1st- ed. New York: Bowker, 1932-   . Biennial.
Titles of earlier editions vary. This and the following two works are complementary in coverage. It, along with the works below, intend to give comprehensive coverage to all serials currently published.
   Arranged in broad subject categories with title and publishing organization indexes. Gives bibliographical and subscription information including price, circulation, and tools in which indexed. Includes only serials published more than once per year on a regular basis.

U23. Irregular Serials & Annuals: An International Directory. 1st- ed. New York: Bowker, 1967-   . Biennial.
"A Classified Guide to Current Foreign and Domestic Serials, excepting Periodicals Issued more Frequently than Once per Year."
   Titles of earlier editions vary. Includes those serials published at irregular intervals, yearly, or less frequently. Thus, it complements the coverage of the above tool. Gives the same type of information in a similar format.

Serial Publication Tools

U24. <u>Ulrich's Quarterly: a Supplement to Ulrich's International Periodicals Directory</u> and <u>Irregular Serials and Annuals</u>. New York: Bowker, 1977-   . Quarterly.
An ongoing publication designed to update the listings in the above two tools by listing serials which have appeared since publication of the latest editions of <u>Ulrich's</u> and <u>Irregular Serials and Annuals</u>. Come here for data on new serials.

NOTE: For American religious serials in particular, see the list of religious serials in <u>Religious Books and Serials in Print</u> (#J36).

**BOOKS IN SERIES--BIBLIOGRAPHIES/INDEXES

Another problem with serials is determining the individual titles and authors of books which are part of a monograph series.

The tools listed below are designed to provide author and title information on volumes in a series when only the series name (and possibly the number assigned to the book in the series) is known. Also helpful for their listing of titles included in each series.

U31. Baer, Eleanora A. <u>Titles in Series: a Handbook for Librarians and Students</u>. 3rd ed. 4 vols. New York: Scarecrow Press, 1978.
Lists series in order by title or responsible body. Under each series, the individual authors and titles of works in the series are listed. Indexed by authors, titles of individual volumes, titles of series, and alternative names and titles for series.

U32. <u>Books in Series</u>. 3rd ed. 3 vols. New York: Bowker, 1980.
"Original, Reprinted, In-Print, and Out-of-Print Books, Published or Distributed in the United States in Popular, Scholarly, and Professional Series."

Serial Publication Tools

   Includes 200,000+ titles (in 21,000+ series) of all books in series published in the U.S. from 1950 to the present. The main section is arranged in alphabetical order by the name of the series, with a listing of all included volumes under each series. Has author, title, and subject-of-series indexes. The "series heading index" serves as a table of contents.

Writing & Publishing Tools

Chapter 18
WRITING AND PUBLISHING TOOLS

In this section are listed some of the basic tools which should be used in writing in the field of theology. The list is highly selective and emphasizes basic tools of which any writer in theology should be aware.

**DICTIONARIES

V1. <u>Webster's Third New International Dictionary of the English Language, Unabridged</u>. Springfield, MA: Merriam, 1961.
Today's standard unabridged dictionary, used as an editorial standard by many publishers. Includes c. 400,000 words; proper nouns are excluded. Note that meanings are given in chronological order, not in order of importance or frequency.
   Basic philosophy is to be "descriptive," i.e. how the language is used, not "prescriptive," i.e. how the language should be used. The 2nd ed. followed the prescriptive model and is still preferred by some users.

V2. <u>Webster's New Collegiate Dictionary</u>. rev. ed. Springfield, MA: G & C Merriam, 1977.
An abridged desk dictionary based on Webster's 3rd (see #V1 above), following the same principles and arrangement for use. Includes c. 152,000 words.
   Appendices include: foreign words & phrases, biographical names, geographical names, colleges & universities, signs & symbols, and a handbook of style. The one to own and to use in writing.

V3. <u>The American Heritage Dictionary of the English Language</u>. Boston: American Heritage Pub. Co., 1969.
In contrast to the two above, this dictionary places its emphasis on offering guidance to good

Writing & Publishing Tools

use. An abridged desk dictionary but larger than most others, this work includes c. 155,000 entries. A legitimate alternative to Webster's.

V4. **The Oxford American Dictionary**. Edited by Eugene Ehrlich. New York: Oxford ,1980.
Intended as "a compact up-to-date guide to American English." Another good desk dictionary which traces its heritage to the **Oxford English Dictionary**. Gives brief definitions; Labels "old," "informal," and "slang" usages as such. Just published, but will probably soon become acceptable as a writing standard.

**SYNONYMS AND ANTONYMS

V11. **Roget's International Thesaurus**. 4th ed. Revised by Robert L. Chapman. New York: Thomas Y. Crowell, 1977.
A major listing of synonyms and antonyms with a long publishing history. Entries are put into categories by concept, grouping similar words together. Use the alphabetical index of individual words to locate the needed section.

V12. **Webster's Collegiate Thesaurus**. Springfield, MA: G & C Merriam, 1976.
"A wholly new book resulting from long study and planning and differing from existent thesauruses in a number of significant respects." Very helpful and easier to use than Roget's.
Entries are arranged in regular A-Z order. Each entry gives synonyms & antonyms, related terms, contrasting terms, and cross-references.

**GRAMMAR AND USAGE

V21. Hodges, J., & Whitten, M. **The Harbrace College Handbook**. 8th ed. New York: Harbrace, 1977.
One of the many useful guides to English grammar, punctuation, etc. All writers should have at least one such work and consult it regularly.

Writing & Publishing Tools

V22. Ebbitt, Wilma R. Writer's Guide and Index to English. 6th ed. Glenview, IL: Scott, Foresman, & Co., 1978.
5th ed. by P. G. Perrin. An established source of information about current written English. Every writer should be acquainted with this book!
   Part 1, the Writer's Guide, discusses such topics as writing, developing ideas, persuading & proving, elements of style, the research paper, etc. Part 2, the Index to English, lists in alphabetical order particular words and phrases which often trouble the writer & indicates correct use.

V23. Strunk, William, Jr., and White, E. B. The Elements of Style. 3rd ed. New York: Macmillan, 1979.
A small paperback which has become a classic on writing style. Covers elementary rules of usage, elementary principles of composition, matters of form, words and expressions commonly misused, and comments on style. Must reading.

**STYLE/FORM

V31. A Manual of Style: for Authors, Editors, and Copywriters. 12th ed., rev. Chicago: University of Chicago Press, 1969.
For theology, this is the style manual most widely used by book and journal publishers. Has a wealth of detailed information on many matters of style & publishing. An indispensable tool for writers.
   While Turabian summarizes parts of this work, it is still necessary for other features, e.g. the chapter on "Foreign Languages in Type" (which includes information on capitalization) and the chapter on "Indexes" and their preparation. Has detailed index.

V32. Turabian, Kate L. A Manual for Writers of Term Papers, Theses, and Dissertations. 4th ed. Chicago: Univ. of Chicago Press, 1973.
Summarizes and adapts the University of Chicago Manual of Style (see #V31 above) for the person

Writing & Publishing Tools

producing a typewritten thesis, dissertation, paper, etc. Stresses information on typewritten style and footnote & bibliography forms. Many schools use this as their standard. Good index.

At times, the information in the text and the examples is unclear and/or contradictory. Reference to the actual Manual of Style will usually resolve such problems.

V33. "Instructions for Contributors." Journal of Biblical Literature 95 (1976): 331-346.
Gives instructions for handling special matters of style in biblical studies papers. Intended to supplement the Univ. of Chicago Press Manual of Style. Also published in 1980 as part of the SBL Member's Handbook. A number of other theological journals now follow these guidelines.

In particular, it gives an extended list of permissible (i) abbreviations for the biblical books, pseudepigraphical books, early patristic works, Dead Sea Scroll texts, Targumic materials, Mishnaic & related literature, other Rabbinic works, & the Nag Hammadi texts; and (ii) "abbreviations of commonly used periodicals, reference works, and serials."

**ABBREVIATIONS

V41. Taylor, John T. An Illustrated Guide to Abbreviations: for Use in Religious Studies. Enid, OK: Seminary Press, 1976.
Includes both an explanation of the use of abbreviations in religious studies and an extensive listing of abbreviations. Topics covered include abbreviations of (i) journals and periodicals, (ii) reference materials, and (iii) classical and early Christian literature.

Each section includes an extensive list of standard abbreviations. A helpful work, particularly on topic (iii). Note that these abbreviations do not always agree with the standard JBL list (see #V33 above).

V42. Schwertner, Siegfried. <u>Internationales Abkürzungsverzeichnis für Theologie und Grenzgebiete: Zeitschriften, Serien, Lexika, Quellenwerke, mit bibliographischen Angaben</u>. New York: de Gruyter, 1974.
An "International Glossary of Abbreviations for Theology and Related Subjects: Periodicals, Series, Encyclopedias, Sources, with Bibliographical Notes. A contribution towards the standardization of title abbreviations, offering suggested standard abbreviations for c. 7,500 titles." Includes two major sections: one arranged alphabetically by the abbreviations and one arranged alphabetically by the names being abbreviated.

**OTHER

V51. van Leunen, Mary-Claire. <u>A Handbook for Scholars</u>. New York: Knopf, 1978.
Billed as "the first complete modern guide to the mechanics of scholarly writing," this is a very useful book. Covers matters of form & style, the problem of when & where to quote and to footnote, and peculiarities of scholarly style. Includes a helpful appendix on the writing of academic resumes. Includes index.

V52. <u>Directory of Publishing Opportunities in Journals and Periodicals</u>. 4th ed. Chicago: Marquis, 1979.
Lists, under 73 "fields of interest," over 3400 specialized and professional periodicals. For each, gives address and manuscript information for submissions. Includes indexes of periodical titles, specific subjects, sponsoring organizations, and editorial staff members.
Good for determining (i) what periodicals might be interested in publishing your article and (ii) in what form to submit an article to a given journal.

PART II: THE SUBJECT AREA LISTS

INTRODUCTION

The following chapters cover (1) the reference tools which are concerned only with a specific subfield of theological studies and (2) basic reference tools from related "secular" disciplines which may be helpful in that subfield.

Note that each of these subject areas will also require the use of reference works of "general" or general "religious/theological" coverage to fill gaps where specialized tools are not available.

These lists are limited in scope and highly selective. The reader is urged to consult the bibliographical guides listed for each subject area in which listings of additional relevant works will be found.

Study in a number of the specialized areas of theology also requires knowledge of the research methods and literature of a related "secular" discipline. While a few of the basic reference works in such fields are listed below at appropriate spots, it is imperative that the reader obtain one of the bibliographical guides available for that field and use it.

Chapter 19
BIBLICAL STUDIES: BIBLIOGRAPHICAL GUIDES

These guides provide a basic survey of the literature of the field and direct you to the "best" works on a particular topic.

GENERAL--OT & NT

AA1. Marrow, Stanley B. <u>Basic Tools of Bibical Exegesis: a Student's Manual</u>. Rome: Biblical Institute Press, 1976.
Most recent guide. Well organized with an excellent selection of 215 scholarly tools, most with descriptive annotations. Includes an author/title index and a list of important biblical studies journals (p. 83).
   Covers the Apocrypha, pseudepigrapha, background studies, texts & versions, dictionaries, grammars, lexicons, and concordances. Does not include commentary listings. An excellent tool, always worth consulting.

AA2. Danker, Frederick W. <u>Multipurpose Tools for Bible Study</u>. 3rd ed. St. Louis: Concordia, 1970.
A basic work which discusses the bibliography, history, and use of the various biblical reference tools by a Lutheran biblical scholar. Covers texts, concordances, grammars, lexicons, dictionaries, versions, and commentaries. Particularly helpful for its examples of how various tools can be effectively used.

AA3. Glanzman, George S., & Fitzmyer, Joseph A. <u>An Introductory Bibliography for the Study of Scripture</u>. Westminster, MD: Newman Press, 1961.
An older list by two Catholic biblical scholars. Includes 342 items with evaluative annotations,

Biblical Studies: Biblio. Guides

arranged in 21 subject areas. Has chapters on periodicals and on series. Author index. Dated, but still helpful for its listing of periodicals.

AA4. Kelly, Balmer H., and Miller, Donald G. Tools for Bible Study. Richmond, VA: John Knox Press, 1956.
Includes 11 bibliographical essays by prominent Protestant biblical scholars. Originally published in the journal Interpretation in 1947-1949. Still helpful for its discussion of the reference tools and the illustrations of their use.

AA5. A Bibliography of Bible Study for Theological Students. 2nd rev. & enlarged ed. Princeton, NJ: Princeton Theological Seminary, 1960.
An annotated and classified list with an emphasis on commentaries. Somewhat dated but still helpful. No annotations or index.

**GENERAL--OLD TESTAMENT

AA11. Childs, Brevard S. Old Testament Books for Pastor and Teacher. Philadelphia: Westminster, 1977.
A good prose discussion of the various O.T. study tools by a leading American O.T. scholar. Directed toward the needs of the pastor and teacher, Childs offers critical evaluation of major tools.
   The largest part of the book (54 pages) discusses commentaries. A bibliography at the back gives full information for the books cited in short form in the text.

AA12. Barker, Kenneth L., and Waltke, Bruce K. Bibliography for Old Testament Exegesis and Exposition. 3rd rev. ed. Dallas: Dallas Theological Seminary, 1975.
More extensive listings than Childs but no annotations. Conservative viewpoint. Includes commentary listings. The 1st ed. also rated the works by "quality" and "theological position."

Biblical Studies: Biblio. Guides

**GENERAL--NEW TESTAMENT

AA21. Scholer, David M. <u>A Basic Bibliographic Guide for New Testament Exegesis</u>. 2nd ed. Grand Rapids: Eerdmans, 1973.
This and France (immediately below) complement one another. Scholer provides better coverage of the central topics of N.T. study. Entries are topically arranged, and include some annotation and discussion. The final section lists 3 to 5 "best" commentaries on each N.T. book. Author index.

AA22. France, R. T. <u>A Bibliographical Guide to New Testament Research</u>. 3rd ed. Sheffield, England: J.S.O.T. Press, 1979.
Like Scholer, also includes listings for O.T., inter-testamental, early church, and other background tools. Concentrates more on background information and reference works -- no commentary listings. Some annotations & discussion, British orientation. Includes a list of 49 periodicals of particular importance in N.T. research.

AA23. Gaffron, H.-G., and Stegemann, H. <u>Systematisches Verzeichnis der wichtigsten Fachliteratur für das Theologiestudium: Vorausdruck für das Einzelfach Neues Testament, gemäss dem Stand im Frühjahr 1966</u>. Bonn: H. Bouvier, 1966.
A selective bibliography for the study of the New Testament which was written to be part of a larger work (never published). Classified arrangement, no annotations, name index. Special characteristics of the books (e.g. "priority for acquisition") are indicated through symbols (see p. 12).

**COMMENTARIES ONLY--OT & NT

Individual commentaries and sets of commentaries will not be enumerated in this guide. Rather, the user is referred to the bibliographies of commentaries given below.

Biblical Studies: Biblio. Guides

AA31. Stegmüller, Friedrich. <u>Repertorium Biblicum Medii Aevi</u>. 7 vols. Madrid: Consejo Superior de Investigaciones Científicas, Instituto Francisco Suárez, 1950-1961.
A thorough treatment of early & medieval biblical commentaries. Vol. 1 covers apocryphal writings and lists prologues to the Bible. Vols. 2-7 list patristic and medieval biblical commentaries, giving the incipit, explicit, editions, manuscripts, and bibliographies.

AA32. Sayre, John L. <u>Recommended Reference Books and Commentaries for a Minister's Library</u>. 3rd ed. Enid, OK: Seminary Press, 1978.
Compiled by members of a class at Phillips Seminary on the minister's library. While some other types of books are listed, the majority of this work (17 pages) is a list of recommended commentaries. No annotations or index.

AA33. Spurgeon, Charles H. <u>Commenting and Commentaries</u>. rev. ed. Grand Rapids: Kregel, 1954.
First published in 1876. An old classic which contains (i) 2 lectures on commentaries and their use, and (ii) an annotated bibliography (over 100 pages) of 1437 commentaries, arranged in canonical order. Particularly valuable as an historical bibliography of pre-1900 commentaries. Conservative theological viewpoint but good critical judgment.

AA34. Goldingay, John. <u>Old Testament Commentary Survey</u>. American ed., with additions & editing by Mark Branson & Robert Hubbard. Madison, WI: Theological Students Fellowship, 1977.
A bibliographic essay listing, evaluating, and discussing O.T. commentaries from a scholarly evangelical viewpoint. The first few pages discuss "general resources," an evaluation of

some commentary sets is next, followed by a book-by-book analysis. The final page lists "Some 'Best Buys'" as a summary. Very helpful and relatively up-to-date.

AA35. Thiselton, Anthony C. <u>New Testament Commentary Survey</u>. Revised by Don Carson. Madison WI: Theological Students Fellowship, 1977.
A bibliographic essay listing, evaluating, and discussing N.T. commentaries from a scholarly evangelical viewpoint. General comments on a number of commentary sets are followed with a book-by-book analysis. The final page lists "Some 'Best Buys'" as a summary. Very helpful and relatively up-to-date.

NOTE: See also items #193-217 (Bible), #242-244 (O.T.), and #279-286 (N.T.) in Bollier, <u>The Literature of Theology</u> (#A11).

Chapter 20
BIBLICAL STUDIES, GENERAL: BIBLIOGRAPHIES/INDEXES

Most of the works listed here include both periodical articles & books. Usually, they give access to the material by subject and author.

CRITICISM AND INTERPRETATION

AB1. *Elenchus Bibliographicus Biblicus.* Rome: Biblical Institute Press, 1920- . Annual. Vols. 1-48 (1920-1967) issued as part of *Biblica*. Known as "EBB." The most extensive bibliography for biblical studies. Published annually, usually 2-3 years after the date of the material included. The latest issue covered 1100+ journals as well as books, dissertations, etc., in the field.

Classified subject arrangement; see the table of contents at the back of each volume. Includes indexes of authors & subjects, Hebrew words, Greek words, & words in other languages. No abstracts.

While the index goes back to 1920, it was not so extensive then and its structure and indexing were poor. Note that from 1960 to 1966 supplements to this bibliography were published in *Verbum Domini*. This is a "must" tool for extensive biblical studies research.

AB2. *Internationale Zeitschriftenschau für Bibelwissenschaft und Grenzgebiete: International Review of Biblical Studies, 1951/52-* . Düsseldorf: Patmos, 1952- . Annual.
"IZBG." Not as extensive as EBB, but does include abstracts (usually in German) of each item indexed and has an arrangement that is easier to use. Covers articles in 400+ periodicals, plus festschriften, reports, and book reviews. Classified subject arrangement, use the table of contents at the back of each volume. Author index.

Biblical Studies: Indexes

AB3. Langevin, Paul-Émile. Bibliographie Biblique; Biblical Bibliography ... 1930-1970. Québec: Presses de l'Univ. Laval, 1972.
Indexes the biblical studies articles in 70 Catholic journals (from 1930 to 1970) as well as 286 Catholic books. Classified subject arrangement with 5 major sections: Introduction, O.T., N.T., Jesus Christ, and Biblical Themes.
The introduction, table of contents (at the BACK of the book), subject headings, and subject heading index are repeated in French, English, German, Italian, and Spanish. Indexed by author.

AB4. Langevin, Paul-Émile. Bibliographie Biblique; Biblical Bibliography II, 1930-1975. Québec: Presses de l'Univ. Laval, 1978.
A companion volume to the above, with the same format. Updates the 70 Catholic journals for 1971-1975, and indexes 50 other major non-Catholic biblical studies journals for 1920-1975.
Indexes 1094 additional monograph works, analyzing 812 of them chapter by chapter. Used together, these two volumes are an important starting point for bibliography compilation.

AB5. École Biblique et Archéologique Francaise, Jerusalem. Bibliothèque. Catalogue de la Bibliothèque de l'École Biblique et Archéologique Francaise. 13 vols. Boston: G. K. Hall, 1975.
"Catalog of the Library of the French Biblical and Archeological School, Jerusalem, Israel."
Contains reproductions of 215,000 catalog cards representing author and subject entries for (i) 50,000+ books; and (ii) the articles in 300 journals in the library. Material on particular Bible passages is listed directly under the name of the biblical book, arranged by chapter & verse.
One of the world's best biblical collections, the library covers the biblical sciences, Palestinology, epigraphy, etc. As the center for study of the Dead Sea Scrolls, the Institute's library holds all significant materials on that topic.

Biblical Studies: Indexes

AB6. L'Année philologique: bibliographie critique et analytique de l'antiquité gréco-latine. Paris: Société d'édition "Les Belles Lettres," 1924- . Annual.
Covers antiquity in general but contains material on the O.T., N.T., early church history, and other related areas. Entries are arranged topically (see table of contents) and often includes brief annotations. Indexed by ancient names, collective titles, geographical locations, and authors.

AB7. Rounds, Dorothy. Articles on Antiquity in Festschriften: the Ancient East, the Old Testament, Greece, Rome, Roman Law, Byzantium; An Index. Cambridge: Harvard Univ. Press, 1962.
In part, a supplement to Metzger (see #AD3 below). Contains, in a single alphabet, an author and subject index to the articles in 1178 festschriften published before 1955. Bibliographical entries for the festschriften themselves are also included in the main listing.

**VERSIONS

AB11. The Bible: Texts and Translations of the Bible and the Apocrypha and Their Books from the National Union Catalog, Pre-1956 Imprints. 5 vols. London: Mansell, 1980.
Separate release of the Bible volumes from Pre-56. The first 4 volumes list 63,000+ books, both texts of the Bible and commentaries which include the text (but Bible-related materials without the text are usually excluded). Arranged by Bible "uniform title" main entry.
 Vol. 5 is an 18,000+ entry index of the first 4 volumes -- by editor, translator, and variant titles. Vol. 5 is NOT part of the Pre-56 set, but most of the same cross-references are found scattered in the other Pre-56 volumes.

Biblical Studies: Indexes

NOTE: Vols. 17-19 of the British Museum Library Catalogue of Printed Books (see #L1 above) are a similar list of Bibles and works containing the biblical text. Arranged in a similar, but not identical manner to the above, with a number of helpful indexes at the end of vol. 19. Includes a number of items not in Pre-56.

AB12. Darlow, T. H., and Moule, H. F. Historical Catalogue of the Printed Editions of Holy Scripture in the Library of the British and Foreign Bible Society. 2 vols. in 4. London: the Bible House, 1903-1911.
Lists all Bibles in that library up to about 1900. Vol. 1 lists 1410 English-language editions, arranged by publication date. It has indexes by (i) translator, revisor, & editor; (ii) printer, publisher, etc.; and (ii) place of publication, printing, etc.
  Vol. 2, published in 3 parts, first lists polyglot editions, then those in all other languages, A to Z. Under each language, the 8438 entries are arranged by date of publication. Indexed by (i) languages & dialects; (ii) translator, revisor, etc.; (iii) printer, publisher, etc.; (iv) place of printing or publication; and (v) general subjects. This index, at the end of vol. 2, also includes indexing of vol. 1 as well.
  The major bibliography of Bible editions up to 1900. Herbert (#AB13) updates vol. 1. Separate updated supplements for some of the other languages have also be published.

AB13. Herbert, A. S. Historical Catalogue of Printed Editions of the English Bible, 1525-1961. Revised & expanded from the edition of T.H. Darlow & H.F. Moule, 1903. New York: American Bible Society, 1968.
Updates and expands vol. 1 of Darlow & Moule (see #AB12), covering up to 1961 and adding entries for editions in other libraries. Includes 2524 entries in publication date order.

Biblical Studies: Indexes

Indexed by: (i) translator, revisor, editor, etc.; (ii) printer and publisher; (iii) place of printing & publication; and (iv) general subjects.

AB14. Hills, Margaret T. The English Bible in America: a Bibliography of Editions of the Bible and the New Testament Published in America, 1777 - 1957. New York: American Bible Society, 1961.
Includes English-language Bibles printed in the U.S. and Canada. Based on the holdings of the A.B.S. library, but checked against other lists. Listed chronologically by publication date. Brief annotations; locations of some copies indicated.
Includes 6 indexes: (i) of geographical location of printers & publishers; (ii) of names of publishers and printers; (iii) of translators, revisors, and translations; (iv) of editors and commentators; (v) of edition titles; and (vi) a general index.

NOTE: See also items #160-180 (a selective annotated list of English versions), in John Bollier, The Literature of Theology (#A11).

**SPECIAL TOPICS

AB21. Vogel, Eleanor K. Bibliography of Holy Land Sites: Compiled in Honor of Dr. Nelson Glueck. Cincinnati: Hebrew Union College-- Jewish Institute of Religion, 1974.
Reprint from the 1971 issue (vol. 42) of the Hebrew Union College Annual. A 96-page bibliography, arranged alphabetically by place name, of materials about 200+ archeological excavation sites in the Holy Land. Includes cross-references from alternative names.

AB22. Henrichs, Norbert. Bibliographie der Hermeneutik und ihrer Anwendungsbereiche seit Schleiermacher. Düsseldorf: Philosophia Verlag, 1968.
A lengthy classified bibliography on modern

Biblical Studies: Indexes

hermeneutics. Two major sections: (i) general hermeneutics (including the philosophical, psychological, and epistemological discussions); and (ii) special hermeneutics -- see esp. section 1, "Theologische Hermeneutik" which has nearly 200 pages. Subject and person indexes.

AB23. Smith, Wilbur M. A Preliminary Bibliography for the Study of Biblical Prophecy. Boston: W. A. Wilde, 1952.
A selective, classified, annotated bibliography of books on biblical prophecy. Conservative evangelical perspective. A valuable list of older books about biblical prophecy & its application to contemporary events.

AB24. Gottcent, John H. The Bible as Literature: a Selective Bibliography. New York: G. K. Hall, 1979.
A selective annotated bibliography of materials on "the treatment of the Bible or any of its parts in the way critics and teachers of literature treat secular literary works."
   Covers primarily 1950 to mid-1978, listing only English-language materials. Includes books, articles, and dissertations. Arranged by the portion of the Bible covered, subdivided by subject. Author and limited subject index.

AB25. Warshaw, Thayer S. Bible-Related Curriculum Materials: a Bibliography. Nashville: Abingdon, 1976.
Lists secondary and college level curriculum materials. Divided into 30 chapters by the portion of the Bible covered. Under each, the items are subdivided: (i) Bible in Literature, (ii) Bible as Literature, (iii) Bible and Literature, and (iv) Bible in/and Other Media. Interesting but of questionable value.

Chapter 21
BIBLICAL STUDIES, O.T.: BIBLIOGRAPHIES/INDEXES

Most of the works listed here include both periodicals articles and books. Usually, they give access to the material by subject and author.

**O.T. PROPER

AC1. Old Testament Abstracts. Washington, DC: Catholic University of America, 1978-   . 3x a year.
The major indexing and abstracting tool for O.T. studies, similar in purpose and content to New Testament Abstracts. Includes abstracts (in English) of periodical articles in over 200 scholarly journals from many countries. Also includes a section of brief "Book Notices."
    Abstracts are grouped by broad subject classifications. The third issue of each year has cumulative author, Bible-passage, and semitic-word indexes. Good coverage, but only since 1978.

AC2. OT / ANE Permucite Index: an Exhaustive Interdisciplinary Indexing System for Old Testament Studies, Ancient Near Eastern Studies. Stellenbosch: Infodex, 1978-   .
A relatively new index offering author, subject, and citation indexing. Very extensive indexing in what has been published thus far, but the format is complex and is difficult to use.
    Current coverage includes c. 40 periodicals, although plans are to eventually cover ALL journal and "journal-like" publications in the field. Until its coverage expands significantly, its high price will be hard to justify.

AC3. Society for Old Testament Study. Booklist, 1946-   . London: the Society, 1946-   .
Lists only books. The annual booklist contains

O.T.: Biblios/Indexes

critical reviews (c. 150 words each) of the important O.T. books published in the preceding year. The reviews are signed and arranged by broad subject areas. Author index.

AC4. Society for Old Testament Study. Eleven Years of Bible Bibliography, 1946-1956. Edited by H. H. Rowley. Indian Hills, CO: Falcon's Wing Press, 1957.

AC5. Society for Old Testament Study. A Decade of Bible Bibliography, 1957-1966. Edited by G.W. Anderson. Oxford: Blackwell, 1967.

AC6. Society for Old Testament Study. Bible Bibliography, 1967 - 1973: Old Testament. Oxford: Blackwell, 1974.

These cumulative volumes reprint the annual lists (the reviews are not newly interfiled by subject) and provide a cumulative author index and a cumulative table of contents.

AC7. Buss, Martin J. Old Testament Dissertations, 1928-1958. Ann Arbor: University Microfilms, [1962?].

A privately printed list of O.T. dissertations. Arranged by author. Useful if Comprehensive Dissertation Index (#M11-M13) is not available.

AC8. North, Robert. Exégèse practique des petits prophètes postexiliens: bibliographie commentée, 950 titres. Rome: Biblico, 1969.

Covers Haggai, Zechariah, Joel, Jonah, & Malachi. The largest part of this work (c. 150 p.) is a passage-by-passage discussion of some of the problems of interpretation, with reference to works in the bibliography.

This section is followed by a bibliography of 950 books, journal articles, etc., arranged by author. The bibliography entry also gives the location in the essay where the item is discussed. Includes indexes by subject & persons and by scripture passages cited.

O.T.: Biblios/Indexes

**RELATED AREAS

AC21. Chicago. University. Oriental Institute. <u>Catalog of the Oriental Institute Library</u>. 16 vols. Boston: G. K. Hall, 1970.
Contains "all useful material on every aspect of the Near East." Includes 284,000 cards for 50,000 volumes & 220 journals; strengths in Assyriology, Egyptology, and Islam.

Includes all entry (author, title, & subject) cards, authority cards, series cards, and journal cards (which analyze the articles in relevant journals by subject & author).

AC22. Chicago. University. Library. <u>Catalog of the Middle Eastern Collection, formerly the Oriental Institute Library: First Supplement</u>. 1 vol. Boston: G.K. Hall, 1977.
Supplements the above. Now contains almost exclusively only main-entry (usually author) cards. Scope is somewhat broadened to all aspects of Middle East topics.

AC23. Hospers, J. H., ed. <u>A Basic Bibliography for the Study of the Semitic Languages</u>. 2 vols. Leiden: Brill, 1973-1974.
Vol. 1 forms the bulk of this work, covering most of the languages; Vol. 2 is restricted to material on the various facets of the Arabic language.

A lengthy bibliography of materials on the semitic languages. Arranged topically by language with numerous subdivisions. Indexed by author.

AC24. Grossfeld, Bernard. <u>A Bibliography of Targum Literature</u>. Cincinnati: Hebrew Union College Press, 1972.
Lists 1000+ items arranged by 10 major subject areas, subdivided by type of publication (books, chapters in books, articles in periodicals). Part 10 lists book reviews. Includes both texts of the targums and materials about them. Author/editor index.

O.T.: Biblios/Indexes

AC25. Grossfeld, Bernard. <u>A Bibliography of Targum Literature, Volume II</u>. Cincinnati: Hebrew Union College Press, 1977.
Supplements the above work with 1800 additional entries. Same basic subject & type-of-publication organization. In addition, this volume includes a section listing dissertations and theses and a brief specific subject index.

AC26. <u>A Classified Bibliography of the Septuagint</u>. By Sebastian P. Brock, Charles T. Fritsch, and Sidney Jellicoe. Leiden: Brill, 1973.
Covers 1900-1969, although "exceptional" earlier materials are included. See preface for the specific limitations of coverage. Includes some book reviews. Entries are arranged by a detailed subject classification, with cross-references and an author index. Very useful for Septuagintal studies.

Chapter 22
BIBLICAL STUDIES, N.T.: BIBLIOGRAPHIES/INDEXES

Most of the works listed here include both periodical articles and books. Usually, they provide access to the material by subject and author.

N.T. PROPER

AD1. Hurd, John C., Jr. *A Bibliography of New Testament Bibliographies*. New York: Seabury, 1966.
A classified list of bibliographies of literature about the N. T. Includes bibliographies that were published within books or as a periodical article, as well as those published separately.
 Includes some annotations but no indexes. Note esp. section IV: "N.T. Scholars: Biographies and Bibliographies."

AD2. *New Testament Abstracts: a Record of Current Periodical Literature*. Cambridge, MA: Weston College School of Theology, 1956- . 3x a year.
Provides brief English-language abstracts of articles on the N.T. and related areas, as well as brief "book notices." Uses a broad classified subject arrangement. Now indexes 500+ journals and lists 500+ books per year.
 Author, biblical-reference, book review, and book notice indexes are included in the 3rd issue of each year. A cumulative author and biblical-reference index is available for 1956-1971. Vols. 1-13 also contain a "biographical notes" section on N.T. scholars. Extremely valuable--the major indexing tool for N.T. studies.

AD3. Metzger, Bruce M. *Index of Articles on the New Testament and the Early Church Published in Festschriften*. Philadelphia:

N.T.: Biblios/Indexes

Society of Biblical Literature, 1951.

AD4. Metzger, Bruce M. **Supplement to Index of Articles ... in Festschriften**. Philadelphia: Society of Biblical Literature, 1955.
Indexes 2350 articles in 640 festschriften in various languages published before 1951. The entries are arranged in a detailed subject classification (see table of contents) with an author index.

The supplement includes those festschriften published in mid & late 1950. An important tool for access to otherwise little-known material.

AD5. **A Periodical and Monographic Index to the Literature on the Gospels and Acts: Based on the Files of the École Biblique in Jerusalem**. Pittsburgh: Clifford E. Barbour Library, Pittsburgh Theological Seminary, 1971.
A typewritten listing of the part of the shelflist of the École Biblique library covering the Gospels and Acts. Lists books and the articles from c. 80 periodicals. Arranged by biblical passage: book by book, chapter by chapter, etc. No indexes.

AD6. Metzger, Bruce M. **Index to Periodical Literature on Christ and the Gospels**. Leiden: Brill, 1966.
Indexes 10,090 items from 160 journals, covering from the beginning of each journal through 1961. Arranged by detailed subject classification (see the table of contents), with an author index.

Pages 112-162 & 208-370 form major parts that cover interpretation of passages in the Gospels. Indispensable for retrospective literature searching in this subject area.

AD7. Malatesta, Edward. **St. John's Gospel, 1920-1965**. Rome: Pontifical Biblical Institute, 1967.
"A Cumulative and Classified Bibliography of Books and Periodical Literature on the Fourth Gospel."

Has over 3100 entries for books, periodical articles, and parts of books about the fourth

N.T.: Biblios/Indexes

gospel. Arranged by a detailed subject classification. Includes cross-references, author index, and author of book reviews index.

Includes all relevant entries in the Elenchus Bibliographicus Biblicus (see #AB1), 1920-1966; and some additional material as well. Thorough for the period covered.

AD8. Mattill, A. J., & Mattill, Mary B. A Classified Bibliography of Literature on the Acts of the Apostles. Leiden: Brill, 1966.
Extensive coverage of periodical articles and books up through 1961. Arranged by subject with author index. Includes 6646 items, indexing 200+ journals as well as festschriften articles and monographs. Has an extensive chapter-by-chapter & verse-by-verse section.

AD9. Metzger, Bruce M. Index to Periodical Literature on the Apostle Paul. Grand Rapids: Eerdmans, 1960.
Indexes 2987 articles from 135 periodicals in 14 languages. Covers from the beginning of each journal through 1957. Arranged by a detailed classified subject scheme. A major section lists exegetical articles book-by-book, chapter-by-chapter, and verse-by-verse.

AD10. Kissinger, Warren S. The Parables of Jesus: a History of Interpretation and Bibliography. Metuchen, NJ: Scarecrow, 1979.
Includes 230 pages on the history of interpretation and 184 pages of a classified bibliography. Includes name and subject indexes. Well done, and very helpful when studying this topic.

AD11. Kissinger, Warren S. The Sermon on the Mount: a History of Interpretation and Bibliography. Metuchen, NJ: Scarecrow, 1975.
Similar in format to the above, with 126 pages on the history of interpretation and 148 pages of bibliography. Name/subject and biblical reference indexes. Very well done and very helpful.

N.T.: Biblios/Indexes

AD12. Metzger, Bruce M. Annotated Bibliography of the Textual Criticism of the New Testament, 1914-1939. Copenhagen: Munksgaard, 1955.
Includes nearly 1200 entries for books, dissertations, and articles from 236 periodicals and serials. Classified subject arrangement with good table of contents & author index. Brief descriptive annotations of some entries.

**RELATED AREAS

AD21. Nickels, Peter. Targum and New Testament: a Bibliography, Together with a New Testament Index. Rome: Pontifical Biblical Institute, 1967.
Part I, arranged by author, lists books and periodical articles on this topic. Part II indexes the books and articles by the N.T. passage(s) treated. Each citation in part II has a brief note explaining the article's relevance for the passage.

AD22. Delling, G. Bibliographie zur jüdisch-hellenistischen und intertestamentarischen Literatur, 1900 - 1970. 2., überarb. und bis 1970 fortgef. Aufl. Berlin: Akademie-Verlag, 1975.
A revision and expansion of the 1st ed. (1969). A bibliography of 2500+ items in classified subject order. Covers Apocrypha, Pseudepigrapha, Philo, Josephus, etc. Excludes Dead Sea Scrolls and Rabbinics. A large section lists items by apocryphal or pseudepigraphic text treated. Author index.

AD23. Charlesworth, James H. The Pseudepigrapha and Modern Research. Missoula, MT: Scholars Press, 1976.
A bibliographical report on the current state of study of the pseudepigrapha, listing 1618 items. Excludes pre-1960 materials, material on Qumran, and material on the N.T. apocrypha (see preface).
  Arranged topically -- each section includes a critical and descriptive bibliographical essay followed by a bibliography. Author index.

N.T.: Biblios/Indexes

AD24. Scholer, David M. <u>Nag Hammadi Bibliography, 1948-1969</u>. Leiden: Brill, 1971.
Includes all types of published materials, listing 2425 items--intends to be exhaustive. This bibliography is continued by the annual Nag Hammadi bibliography in <u>Novum Testamentum</u>. Under each book included, reviews of that book are noted.
Classified subject arrangement. Particularly valuable is the extensive listing of (i) the published texts of each tractate in the Nag Hammadi corpus, and (ii) publications about each tractate. Author index.

AD25. Schreckenberg, Heinz. <u>Bibliographie zu Flavius Josephus</u>. Leiden: Brill, 1968.
Lists materials by and about Josephus published between 1470 & 1968. Entries are arranged by year of publication. Beside each entry, one or more "subject code" numbers are given, see p. xvii for their meanings. Includes author, Josephus'-works-references, and Greek-word indexes.
Fairly complete, but difficult to use for material on specific subjects -- you must scan the pages looking for the correct "subject code."

AD26. Schreckenberg, Heinz. <u>Bibliographie zu Flavius Josephus: Supplementband mit Gesamtregister</u>. Leiden: Brill, 1979.
Updates & supplements the above for 1967 to early 1979. The major portion lists materials in a single alphabet, arranged by author. As in the above work, "subject codes" are indicated.
Part II of this work indexes the editions and translations of Josephus' works listed in both volumes, citing the editor & the page number where the full bibliographical entry is found. Includes an alphabetical author index for both volumes.

**THE DEAD SEA SCROLLS

AD41. Fitzmyer, Joseph A. <u>The Dead Sea Scrolls: Major Publications and Tools for Study; with an Addendum (January 1977)</u>. Missoula,

N.T.: Biblios/Indexes

MT: Scholars Press, 1977.
A very helpful guide to the primary sources (i.e. the published texts of the DSS) and to secondary materials. Topical arrangement, some entries have brief annotations. The addendum gives some updated entries beyond the original printing. Includes indexes by modern author and by biblical passage.

AD42. LaSor, William S. Bibliography of the Dead Sea Scrolls 1948-1957. Pasadena, CA: Fuller Theological Seminary Library, 1958.
Lists c. 3000 books, periodical articles, etc., arranged by a detailed subject classification (see pp. 4-6). Includes author index. Fairly comprehensive for the period covered.

AD43. Jongeling, B. A Classified Bibliography of the Finds in the Desert of Judah 1958-1969. Leiden: Brill, 1971.
Intended to be a continuation of LaSor's bibliography. Lists a large number of books & periodical articles in many languages. Entries listed under 13 broad subject headings, subarranged by author. Includes author index.

AD44. Burchard, Christoph. Bibliographie zu den Handschriften vom Toten Meer. 2 vols. Berlin: A. Töpelmann, 1957-1965.
A very extensive list of c. 4500 books and periodical articles on the Dead Sea Scrolls. Vol. 1 covers 1948-1956, vol. 2 covers 1956-1962. This bibliography is continued in Revue de Qumran.
   Both volumes are arranged the same: 3 major sections listing Roman, Greek, and Hebrew alphabet materials, each subarranged by author. At the back of each volume is a classified subject index.

AD45. Yizhar, Michael. Bibliography of Hebrew Publications on the Dead Sea Scrolls, 1948-1964. Cambridge: Harvard, 1967.
As title indicates, limited to Hebrew-language articles & books. Lists 703 items in a classified subject arrangement. Author & subject indexes.

Chapter 23
BIBLICAL STUDIES: ENCYCLOPEDIAS

GENERAL COVERAGE--MULTI-VOLUME

AE1. *Interpreter's Dictionary of the Bible.* 4 vols. New York: Abingdon, 1962.
"An Illustrated Encyclopedia Identifying and Explaining all Proper Names and Significant Terms and Subjects in the Holy Scripture, including the Apocrypha; with Attention to Archaeological Discussions and Researches into the Life and Faith of Ancient Times" (Subtitle).

Generally considered the best Bible encyclopedia available today. 250 scholars contributed the articles (most are signed), which have selective bibliographies and numerous illustrations. Moderate to extreme liberal viewpoint in most articles. A basic place to begin research on a biblical topic.

AE2. *Interpreter's Dictionary of the Bible: Supplementary Volume.* Nashville: Abingdon, 1976.
This volume updates the articles in the original volumes and adds new articles on important topics. Includes cross-references to articles in the main volumes.

AE3. *International Standard Bible Encyclopedia.* Fully rev. ed., ed. by Geoffrey Bromiley. 4 vols. Grand Rapids: Eerdmans, 1979- .
One volume published thus far. A "new, or at least a completely reconstructed," edition of the original "ISBE" (see below). Articles represent an attitude "of a reasonable conservatism," and the evangelical scholars who have contributed represent a variety of denominations & countries.

Its purpose is "to define, identify, and

Biblical Studies: Encyclopedias

explain terms and topics that are of interest for those who study the Bible." A mixture of short, unsigned entries and longer signed articles with selected bibliographies is used.

AE4. International Standard Bible Encyclopedia. [rev. ed.] Edited by James Orr. 5 vols. Chicago: Severance, 1930.
The 1st edition of this work was published in 1915. This rev. ed. revised some articles and added new ones. A few of the original articles are omitted or replaced. Same basic purpose and perspectives as the newest revision of this work listed above.

AE5. The Illustrated Bible Dictionary. 3 vols. Wheaton, IL: Tyndale House, 1980.
A revised and newly illustrated edition of the New Bible Dictionary (see #AE26). Has 2000+ entries by 165 leading biblical scholars with c. 1600 carefully chosen illustrations and selective bibliographies. Excellent layout and typography, with a comprehensive system of marginal references and cross-references. Vol. 3 includes a 6000-entry index.

AE6. Wycliffe Bible Encyclopedia. Charles F. Pfeiffer, Howard F. Vos, and John Rea, eds. 2 vols. Chicago: Moody Press, 1975.
Offers coverage of every personal and place name in the Bible, as well as important theological terms and doctrines. Conservative evangelical theological viewpoint.

AE7. Zondervan Pictorial Encyclopedia of the Bible. Merrill C. Tenney, ed. 5 vols. Grand Rapids: Zondervan, 1975.
Written by evangelicals, but other viewpoints are generally represented. Has received mixed reviews -- the quality of some articles is questionable. One place to come for a (but not the) evangelical viewpoint on biblical topics.

Brief bibliographies are included with most

Biblical Studies: Encyclopedias

articles. The 7500+ signed articles cover all places, objects, persons, customs, events, and teachings of the Bible. Well illustrated.

AE8. Biblisch-historisches Handwörterbuch: Landeskunde, Geschichte, Religion, Kultur, Literatur. Bo Reike & Leonhard Rost, eds. 3 vols. Göttingen: Vandenhoeck & Ruprecht, 1962-66.
A scholarly German Bible encyclopedia. Includes signed articles, short bibliographies, and illustrations. Places an emphasis on historical understanding of the Bible & its environment. An index volume is said to be in preparation.

AE9. Dictionnaire de la Bible. Fulcran Grégoire Vigouroux, ed. 5 vols. in 10. Paris: Letouzey, 1907-1912.

AE10. Dictionnaire de la Bible: Supplément. L. Pirot, ed. Paris: Letouzey, 1928-   .
"Contenant tous les noms de personnes, de lieux, de plantes, d'animaux mentionnés dans les Saintes Écritures, les questions théologiques, archéologiques, scientifiques, critiques relatives a l'Ancien et au Nouveau Testament et des notices sur les commentateurs anciens et modernes."
  Eleven volumes in supplement thus far (1979). The most extensive Bible encyclopedia, covering all topics named in the subtitle. Includes long signed articles by French Catholic scholars. Bibliographies and illustrations accompany each article.
  Note that this work includes biographical material about Bible commentators -- ancient and modern, regardless of religion. The supplement, not yet complete, stresses theological questions.

AE11. Dictionary of the Bible: Dealing with Its Language, Literature, and Contents, Including the Biblical Theology. Edited by James Hasting. 4 vols. & Supplement. New York: Scribners, 1898-1904.
An older standard work with long signed articles

Biblical Studies: Encyclopedias

and bibliographies. More moderate viewpoint than Cheyne (#AE12). Still valuable for its scholarly articles and representation of early 20th century biblical scholarship.
   The supplementary 5th volume includes 37 additional articles, maps, and indexes of (i) authors & their articles; (ii) subjects; (iii) Scripture texts; (iv) Greek & Hebrew terms; (v) illustrations, and (vi) the maps.

AE12. Encyclopaedia Biblica. Edited by T. K. Cheyne and J. S. Black. 4 vols. New York: Macmillan, 1899-1903.
"A Critical Dictionary of Literary, Political, and Religious History, the Archaeology, Geography, and Natural History of the Bible."
   Intended for the scholar & advanced student, its standpoint is that of the "advanced higher criticism" of the late 19th century. It is dedicated to W. Robertson Smith. Long signed articles with bibliographies by specialists.

**GENERAL COVERAGE--ONE VOLUME

   Used primarily for quick reference to find answers to specific questions. Thus, only English-language and relatively current titles are listed here.

AE21. Catholic Biblical Encyclopedia. John E. Steinmueller and Kathryn Sullivan, comps. 2 vols. in 1. New York: Wagner, 1956.
The first Catholic Bible encyclopedia in English. Intended for the educated layman. Includes material on geographical, biographical, archeological, and dogmatic subjects. Represents the more traditional pre-Vatican II Catholic scholarship.

AE22. Dictionary of the Bible. By James Hastings. rev. ed. Revised by F. C. Grant & H. H. Rowley. New York: Scribner, 1963.
A total revision of the 1st ed. done by Hastings in 1909. Includes contributions by 150+ American

Biblical Studies: Encyclopedias

and British biblical scholars. Protestant viewpoint, based on the Revised Standard Version. Has short signed articles without bibliographies.

AE23. <u>Dictionary of the Bible</u>. By John L. McKenzie. Milwaukee: Bruce, 1965.
Contains about 2000 scholarly but readable articles by this Jesuit priest who is an outstanding biblical scholar. Designed for the general reader. No bibliographies with the articles, but a general bibliography is included. Good system of cross-references. Has illustrations and maps.

AE24. <u>Encyclopedic Dictionary of the Bible</u>. Louis F. Hartman, trans. New York: McGraw-Hill, 1963.
"A Translation and Adaptation of A. van den Born's <u>Bijbels woordenboek</u> (2nd rev. ed., 1954-1957)." A "free adaption" of the Dutch original. Represents modern Catholic scholarship. Signed articles, with short bibliographies. The bibliographies have been updated & expanded, with English titles substituted wherever possible.

AE25. <u>Harper's Bible Dictionary</u>. By Madeleine S. and J. Lane Miller. 8th ed. New York: Harper, 1973.
A solid Protestant Bible encyclopedia. Extensively revised from the 1st ed. Treats biblical archeology, geography, chronology, etc. Short articles, numerous illustrations, and maps but no bibliographies.

AE26. <u>New Bible Dictionary</u>. James D. Douglas, ed. Grand Rapids: Eerdmans, 1962.
"The major product of the Tyndale Fellowship for Biblical Research." Written by evangelical scholars (primarily British) for Protestant laymen. Includes 2300 signed articles with short bibliographies. Strong on biblical archeology. A 3-vol. revision of this work has now appeared (#AE5).

Biblical Studies: Encyclopedias

AE27. New Westminster Dictionary of the Bible. Henry S. Gehman, ed. Philadelphia: Westminster Press, 1970.
A thorough reworking and updating of the 1st ed. (1944). Useful for pastors, students, and laymen; Protestant viewpoint. Includes about 4000 brief entries, indicates pronunciations where necessary, but has no bibliographies.

AE28. Zondervan Pictorial Biblical Dictionary. M. C. Tenney, ed. Grand Rapids: Zondervan, 1963.
A good single-volume Bible encyclopedia with 5000+ entries, 700 illustrations, & 40 maps. Written by 65 conservative evangelical scholars. Includes index to maps.

**"BIBLE TIMES"

AE41. Corswant, Willy A. A Dictionary of Life in Bible Times. Completed and illustrated by Édouard Urech. New York: Oxford, 1960.
Translation of Dictionnaire d'archéologie biblique (Paris, 1956). A popular-level dictionary covering the religious, private, and political life of Jews and Christians, as well as the natural phenomena of Israel. About 1200 brief articles, with extensive Bible references and numerous line drawings. No bibliographies.

AE42. Miller, Madeleine S., and Miller, J. Lane. Harper's Encyclopedia of Bible Life. 3rd rev. ed. Revised by Boyce M. Bennett & David H. Scott. New York: Harper, 1978.
Classified subject arrangement covering (i) the world of the Bible; (ii) how the people of the Bible lived, and (iii) how the people of the Bible worked. The appendix includes a selected bibliography, scriptural reference index, and name & subject index. Has illustrations and maps.

**ARCHEOLOGY

Biblical Studies: Encyclopedias

See also the topic "ATLASES" in section 25.

AE51. Archaeological Encyclopedia of the Holy Land. Edited by Avraham Negev. New York: Putnam's, 1972.
Brief articles on "the majority of the geographical names mentioned in the Bible, both places in the Holy Land and countries and cities in other parts of the Middle East, identifying them as far as possible, describing the excavations that have been carried out at or near them, and analysing the importance of the finds they have yielded." Written by 17 Israeli & 3 American archeologists. No bibliographies. Gives references to the Bible, Josephus, and other early writers.

AE52. Pfeiffer, Charles F. The Biblical World: a Dictionary of Biblical Archaeology. Grand Rapids: Baker, 1966.
The many short articles, often with bibliographies and a number of photographs, cover biblical topics as related to archeology. Includes major archeological terms & sites, and biblical personal & place names affected by archeology.

AE53. Encyclopedia of Archaeological Excavations in the Holy Land. English ed. 4 vols. Englewood Cliffs, NJ: Prentice-Hall, 1975-1978.
Intended as a "summary of excavation work in Israel," this edition covers work done through 1971. Includes, under the name commonly used in scholarly circles, articles on nearly 200 sites, each describing the history, excavations, and discoveries at that location. Vol. 4 has indexes of names & of places for the entire work.

AE54. Wright, G. E. Biblical Archaeology. New & rev. ed. Philadelphia: Westminster, 1962.
Its purpose is to briefly summarize archeological discoveries that help one to understand biblical

Biblical Studies: Encyclopedias

history. Arranged chronologically in 14 chapters, each with a bibliography.
Includes indexes by: modern names, biblical names, biblical places, subjects, and biblical references. Also has maps & numerous pictures.

**NEW TESTAMENT

AE61. Dictionary of Christ and the Gospels. Edited by James Hastings. 2 vols. New York: Scribner's, 1906-1908.
A complement to his Dictionary of the Bible, this work is intended to cover everything relating to Christ and the Gospels in the Bible and in world literature. Includes long signed articles with good bibliographies. Indexed by subject and by Greek terms. Dated but still useful.

AE62. Dictionary of the Apostolic Church. Edited by James Hastings. 2 vols. New York: Scribner's, 1916.
Designed to complement the above work. Covers the history of the early church from Christ's ascension to the end of the first century. Long signed articles with bibliographies. Includes indexes. Dated but still useful.

NOTE: The above two works were reprinted in 1973 by Baker Book House as a 4-volume set under the title: Dictionary of the New Testament.

AE63. Leon-Dufour, Xavier. Dictionary of the New Testament. New York: Harper, 1980.
Translation of Dictionnaire du Nouveau Testament. A compact, scholarly dictionary of c. 1000 N.T. terms needing historical, theological, literary, and/or archeological explanation, as well as important terms in N.T. study today.
Provides, with each entry, a listing of relevant biblical references. Has an excellent system of cross-references to other relevant articles in the dictionary, and an index of Greek words cited in the dictionary.

Biblical Studies: Encyclopedias

**SPECIAL TOPICS

AE71.   Payne, J. Barton. <u>Encyclopedia of Biblical Prophecy: the Complete Guide to Scriptural Prediction and their Fulfillment</u>. New York: Harper & Row, 1973.
Includes a long introduction followed by a listing of scriptural predictions (in canonical order) with accompanying summaries and comments on their meaning & fulfillments. Has 5 indexes & an 8-page bibliography. Evangelical Christian viewpoint.

Chapter 24
BIBLICAL STUDIES:
THEOLOGICAL DICTIONARIES & WORDBOOKS

**OT & NT

AF1. Allmen, Jean Jacques von, ed. A Companion to the Bible. New York: Oxford University Press, 1958.
A translation of Vocabulaire biblique (Delachaux & Niestlé, 2nd ed., 1956). Well known in Europe, written by French and Swiss Protestant scholars. Popular level but helpful.
A dictionary of 350 important biblical words, with the emphasis on their theology rather than linguistic backgrounds.

AF2. Bauer, Johannes B., ed. Sacramentum Verbi: an Encyclopedia of Biblical Theology. 3 vols. New York: Herder & Herder, 1970. Translation of the Bibeltheologisches Wörterbuch (3rd ed., 1967). Includes long signed articles with bibliographies by 53 European Catholic biblical scholars. Termed "an outstanding example of the renewal in Catholic biblical scholarship." Vol. 3 has a supplementary bibliography, an analytic index of the articles, a biblical reference index, and a Greek & Hebrew word index.

AF3. Leon-Dufour, Xavier, ed. Dictionary of Biblical Theology. 2nd rev. & enl. ed. Trans. by P. J. Cahill. New York: Seabury, 1973. Translation of Vocabulaire de théologie biblique (2nd ed., Paris: Ed. du Cerf, 1968). Intended primarily for Roman Catholic laity and clergy, it is "theological and pastoral in approach."
Arranged by broad topics, with extensive discussion and bibliographical references. Many cross-references, analytical table of contents.

Biblical Studies: Theo. Wordbooks

AF4. Richardson, Alan, ed. A Theological Word Book of the Bible. New York: Macmillan, 1951.
Includes biblical words of "theological" interest, and aims "to elucidate the distinctive meanings of the keywords of the Bible." Words are listed in the English form found in the 1885 English Revised Version, with the Greek and/or Hebrew words given in transliteration at the top of each article.

The clear, short, & well-organized articles are by 31 primarily British & Protestant scholars. Many short bibliographies are included. Useful, esp. to the "English-only" user, for its summaries of the theological import of biblical words.

**OLD TESTAMENT

AF11. Theological Dictionary of the Old Testament. Edited by G. Johannes Botterweck and Helmer Ringgren. Grand Rapids: Eerdmans, 1974- .
Known as "TDOT" or the "OT Kittel." Four volumes (--HMS) thus far. A translation of Theologisches Wörterbuch zum Alten Testament, Vols. 1 & 2 issued in 2 editions due to translation problems: 1st ed., 1974-75; rev. ed. 1977.

Includes extensive, well-documented articles on "theologically significant" Old Testament words, including information drawn from other Near Eastern languages. Written by recognized scholars with moderate to extreme critical viewpoints.

AF12. Jenni, Ernst. Theologisches Handwörterbuch zum Alten Testament. Unter Mitarbeit von Claus Westermann. 2 vols. München: Kaiser, 1971-1975.
Known as "THAT." A more compact and briefer wordbook than TDOT. Shorter, more "cryptic" entries, with numerous bibliographical and biblical references. Signed articles by O.T. scholars. Indexed by Hebrew words, by German words, and by the authors cited. A useful complement to TDOT.

Biblical Studies: Theo. Wordbooks

AF13. <u>Theological Wordbook of the Old Testament</u>. Edited by R. Laird Harris, Gleason L. Archer, & Bruce K. Waltke. 2 vols. Chicago: Moody Press, 1980.
Has 1400+ articles by 43 scholars that discuss every Hebrew word of theological significance in the O.T. Also provides the definitions of all other words. Articles stress theological, not linguistic, understanding & include bibliographies.

For the English-only user, a cross-index from the "Hebrew word number" in <u>Strong's Concordance</u> (#AG1) to entries in this wordbook is appended.

AF14. Unger, Merrill F., and White, William. <u>Nelson's Expository Dictionary of the Old Testament</u>. Nashville: Nelson, 1980.
Explains the root, use, and theological importance of 500 significant O.T. words, arranged by their English-language equivalents. Includes cross-index from alternative English words and phrases. Should be very helpful, especially for those who know little or no Hebrew.

**NEW TESTAMENT

AF21. <u>Theological Dictionary of the New Testament</u>. Edited by G. Kittel & G. Friedrich. 10 vols. Grand Rapids: Eerdmans, 1964-76.
Known as "Kittel" or "TDNT." Translation of the <u>Theologisches Wörterbuch zum Neuen Testament</u>, which began publication in 1932. Contributors are almost all German biblical scholars.

Older articles are somewhat dated, and the English edition does not update the German bibliography. The long, scholarly, and well-documented articles analyze the background and usage of many N.T. words. Indispensable for N.T. research.

Vol. 10, the Index, includes indexes for English key words, Greek words, Hebrew & Aramaic words, biblical references, and for contributors. The index also has brief biographical information on the contributors & a short "Pre-History of the the TDNT."

Biblical Studies: Theo. Wordbooks

Note: The 10th volume of the German edition is different and includes different indexes and additional bibliographical information.

AF22. <u>The New International Dictionary of New Testament Theology</u>. Edited by Colin Brown. 3 vols. Grand Rapids: Eerdmans, 1975-1978. Translated, with additions and revisions from the German <u>Theologisches Begriffslexikon zum Neuen Testament</u>. More concise, up-to-date, and conservative than the TDNT but not as extensive.
  Articles are arranged under English key words; vols. 1 & 2 have their own indexes of (i) Hebrew & Aramaic words; (ii) Greek words; and (iii) English words. Vol. 3 has cumulative indexes for all three volumes.
  The large bibliographies have been updated and enlarged from those of the German edition. A necessary complement to the TDNT.

AF23. Turner, Nigel. <u>Christian Words</u>. Edinburgh: T & T Clark, 1980.
"This book ... is but a sample of the speciality of Biblical and Christian language. By 'Christian words' I have in mind Greek terms which so far as I know the first believers devised for themselves .... the improvised 'Biblical' words in both LXX and NT."
  Words are arranged by their English translation, with Greek words given immediately below the English. An index by Greek words is included. For each word, the secular Greek and biblical Greek meanings are given. Indicates the applicable biblical references and scholarly literature for each word.

Chapter 25
BIBLICAL STUDIES: OTHER TOOLS

**CONCORDANCES & TOPICAL BIBLES

A few of the more widely used and important concordances and topical Bibles are listed below. Only concordances including both the Old Testament and the New Testament are listed. See the bibliographical guides listed in Chapter 19 for listings of concordances to the Old and New Testament and to their Greek and Hebrew texts.

Concordances arrange the words in the Bible alphabetically so that a user can find a particular verse by referring to one or more of the key words in it or can find where a given word occurs in a given translation.

Topical Bibles arrange small portions of the biblical text under specific topical headings so that the user can find the texts that relate to a given topic or theme even though the topic or theme itself may not be among the words used in the text.

AG1. Strong, James. <u>The Exhaustive Concordance of the Bible</u>. New York: Abingdon, 1890. Many editions and reprints have been published. The most complete English concordance of the King James Version, covering ALL words (occurrences of 47 of the most common, e.g. "the" & "and," are listed in an appendix). Totals c. 400,000 entries.

Under each English word, a single list of all its occurrences is given. Along side each occurrence, an entry number indicates the Greek or Hebrew word being translated. The entry numbers

Biblical Studies: Other Tools

refer to the numbered Hebrew & Chaldee dictionary and the biblical Greek dictionary at the back of the concordance.

AG2. Young, Robert. *Analytical Concordance to the Bible*. New York: Funk & Wagnalls, 1881.
Many editions and reprints have been published. Later editions include a variety of supplementary articles about the Bible.
  Includes 311,000 entries under the English words of the King James Version, subarranging the entries by the Greek and/or Hebrew word(s) being translated. Also includes a list of names of persons and places.
  At the back is an "index lexicon" which lists the Hebrew and Greek words of the original text, gives their meaning, and indicates the English word(s) used to translate each and the number of times it is used.

AG3. Ellison, John William. *Nelson's Complete Concordance of the Revised Standard Version Bible*. New York: Nelson, 1957.
Includes all the English words used in the RSV except for a few of high frequency. The original Hebrew and Greek words being translated are not indicated. Computer compiled -- does not analyze usage at all. Useful for study of the RSV but not as valuable for Bible study as either of the above two works.

AG4. Joy, Charles R. *Harper's Topical Concordance*. rev. & enl. ed. New York: Harper, 1962.
Lists 30,000+ verses under 2800+ topical headings. Not truly a concordance -- rather, it is a topical Bible for the person looking for biblical texts on a particular topic. A list of cross-references is appended to the main list.

AG5. Nave, Orville. *Nave's Topical Bible: a Digest of the Holy Scripture*. New York: International Bible Agency, 1897.

Biblical Studies: Other Tools

Reprinted numerous times under various titles, this is the most widely known topical Bible. Lists more than 100,000 references to Scripture under 20,000 topics and subtopics. Each entry tries to briefly bring together all that the Bible contains on a particular topic.

AG6. Viening, Edward. The Zondervan Topical Bible. Grand Rapids: Zondervan, 1969.
Although it does not say so, this work is based on Nave's Topical Bible, but is slightly revised and reorganized. Slightly preferable to Nave's.

**ATLASES

Only a few of the many available are listed below. See Chapter 23, items #AE51 & ff., for encyclopedias on biblical archeology.

AG11. Aharoni, Yohanan, and Avi-Yonah, Michael. The Macmillan Bible Atlas. rev. ed. New York: Macmillan, 1977.
One of the better Bible atlases, emphasizes the Holy Land. Contains 250+ maps arranged chronologically, covering from the Caananite period up to the 2nd Jewish revolt. Includes explanatory text, bibliographical references, and an index/gazeteer.

AG12. Baly, Denis, and Tushingham, A. D. Atlas of the Biblical World. New York: World, 1971.
A shorter atlas with 48 excellent maps (14 in color) and many illustrations. Covers the entire Middle East, concentrating on its geographical features, i.e. plant life, climate, and physical features. Includes bibliographies on the cartography, geography, and archeology of the area. Includes extensive indexes to the text and maps.

AG13. Grollenberg, Lucas Hendricus. Atlas of the Bible. Translated & edited by Joyce M. H. Reid & H.H. Rowley. New York: Nelson, 1956.
Translation of the Atlas van de Bibjel, 1954. A scholarly atlas with 37 excellent maps and many

151

Biblical Studies: Other Tools

illustrations. Includes a 26-page index of places & persons, including non-biblical names as applicable. The index entries give the etymology, map reference and Bible references.

AG14. Kraeling, Emil G. H. Rand McNally Bible Atlas. 3rd ed, Chicago: Rand McNally, 1966.
Designed for the general reader. Comprehensive, including extensive text, numerous illustrations, 51 maps, plans, and tables. Has a survey of the geographical and geological features of Palestine on both sides of the Jordan, a geographical introduction to the Bible book-by-book, and a geographical index of place names.

AG15. Negenman, Jan H. New Atlas of the Bible. Edited by H. H. Rowley. Garden City, NY: Doubleday, 1969.
Contains numerous maps and excellent photographs with accompanying text. Arranged so that it "traces in broad outline the growth of the Bible in the setting of the history out of which its papers came." Includes an index to the text, photographs, and maps.

AG16. May, Herbert Gordon. Oxford Bible Atlas. 2nd ed. New York: Oxford, 1974.
A small, inexpensive, but helpful atlas. Includes physical, historical, and archeological maps; a well-illustrated text; and a gazeteer with notes.

AG17. Wright, George E., and Filson, F. V. The Westminster Historical Atlas to the Bible. rev. ed. Philadelphia: Westminster, 1956.
A scholarly, if now somewhat dated, work that includes a great deal of archeological information. Has 33 colored maps, 88 illustrations, and a table of dates.
The indexes included are (i) an index to the text, (ii) an index/gazetteer ("topographical concordance of all places mentioned in the Bible"), and (iii) an index to Arabic names (identifying Arabic names with biblical place names).

Biblical Studies: Other Tools

AG18. Atlas of Israel: Cartography, Physical Geography, Human and Economic Geography, History. Jerusalem: Survey of Israel, Minister of Labor; Amsterdam: Elsevier, 1970.
An extensive atlas of Israel useful for the study of the Bible. Includes maps covering geology, climate, botany, zoology, land use, history, etc.
  Covers both the current times and the past. Originally published in Hebrew in the early 1960s. Includes explanatory text and selective bibliographies.

**MISCELLANEOUS

AG31. Finegan, Jack. Handbook of Biblical Chronology. Princeton, NJ: Princeton University Press, 1964.
"Principles of Time Reckoning in the Ancient World and Problems of Chronology in the Bible." Part 1 covers the calendars of Egypt, Babylon, Israel, etc., as well as early Christian chronologies.
  Part 2 is a discussion of some of the major problems of biblical chronology. Includes full footnoting & bibliographies. Indexed by Scripture references and by subject. Very helpful book.

AG32. The Cambridge History of the Bible. 3 vols. New York: Cambridge University Press, 1963-1970.
Editors: v.1--P. R. Ackroyd & C. F. Evans; v.2--C. W. H. Lampe; v.3--S. L. Greenslade. Volumes were published in reverse order.
  Gives "accounts of the texts and versions of the Bible used in the West, of its multiplication in manuscript and print, and its circulation; of attitudes toward its authority and exegesis; and of its place in the life of the Western church."
  Has well-done bibliographies for each chapter, & each volume has bibliographical appendices. Good indexes and plates. Material is written by a wide range of scholars. A good source for a brief summary & further bibliography on these topics.

General Church History

Chapter 26
CHURCH HISTORY: GENERAL COVERAGE

**GENERAL HISTORY--BIBLIOGRAPHIES, GUIDES, INDEXES

BA1. Poulton, Helen J. The Historian's Handbook: a Descriptive Guide to Reference Works. Norman, OK: Univ. of Oklahoma Press, 1972.
"Surveys a wide variety of the major reference works in all fields of history," as well as relevant general and related-discipline tools.
   A good basic introduction to the reference tools of historical study. No distinct church history section. Lists c. 1000 items with running commentary, emphasis on American studies. Includes a general index and an index of titles.

BA2. American Historical Association. Guide to Historical Literature. New York: Macmillan, 1961.
A selective, briefly annotated bibliography of c. 20,000 items, emphasizing English-language materials. Items listed include important periodical articles. Arranged by time period, then geographical area, then by subject.
   See esp. pp. 65-74, "Christianity," but also be certain to use the extensive subject index to locate many other pertinent items. Includes author index. A valuable tool.

BA3. International Bibliography of Historical Sciences. Edited for the International Committee of Historical Sciences, 1926- . Oxford: Oxford University Press, 1930- . Annual.
Publisher varies. Vol. 15, to cover 1940-46, never published. An extensive, useful, and important bibliography of historical publications, including periodical articles.

General Church History

Classified arrangement by time period and geographical location. Includes author/proper name index and geographical index. The 1976 issue included c. 6000 items.

**CHURCH HISTORY--BIBLIOGRAPHIES, GUIDES, INDEXES

BA11. Chadwick, Owen. The History of the Church: a Select Bibliography. 3rd ed. London: Historical Association, 1973.
A valuable selective bibliography arranged by subject. Lists both reference works and major works in the field, giving brief annotations for many of them. An excellent beginning point for research, but lacks both subject & author indexes. Stronger on the Reformation and the British churches, weak on American church history.

BA12. Case, Shirley Jackson, ed. A Bibliographical Guide to the History of Christianity. Chicago: University of Chicago, 1931.
An extensive and still useful, although somewhat dated, annotated bibliography. Entries are arranged by broad geographical areas, then by time period and/or topical subjects. Lists 2500+ books and periodical articles. Somewhat difficult to use due to its limited subject index and its lack of a table of contents.

BA13. "Bibliographie" in Revue d'histoire ecclésiastique. Louvain: Université catholique de Louvain, 1900- . 3x a year.
Now issued as a separately paged section of the journal. An extensive bibliography, this is the major indexing work for church history. Indexes over 900 periodicals and also lists numerous books & other types of printed material.

Entries are arranged by a detailed subject scheme (see the table of contents which appears at the end of the last issue for each year). Difficult to search retrospectively since there are now 240+ separate issues of the bibliography which are NOT cumulated in any way. Includes author index.

General Church History

NOTE: There is no other periodical index devoted to church history in general. You will need to use either one of the more specialized indexes listed below, one of the general or humanities indexes (chapter 15), or one of the general religious/theological indexes.

For English-language materials, Religion Index One (see #T12 & T13 above) and the Catholic Periodical and Literature Index (#T14 & T15) are particularly helpful.

**CHURCH HISTORY--ENCYCLOPEDIAS

There is a fine line between what is a "theological" encyclopedia and what is a "church history" encyclopedia. Listed here are some of those encyclopedias oriented more obviously to church history. Remember though that the theological encyclopedias (listed in Chapter 3) certainly also include a great deal of church history material.

BA21. Oxford Dictionary of the Christian Church. F. L. Cross & E. A. Livingstone, eds. 2nd ed. New York: Oxford University Press, 1974.
First published in 1957, this is the standard 1-volume reference work for church history. Its broad coverage includes many biographies, as well as definitions of ecclesiastical terms & customs. Includes c. 6000 entries, most with good, & often extensive, bibliographies.
Emphasis on Christianity in Western Europe, esp. Great Britain, stressing the Anglican and Catholic churches. Relatively poor coverage of American Christianity.

BA22. The New International Dictionary of the Christian Church. J. D. Douglas, ed. rev. ed. Grand Rapids: Zondervan, 1978.
Similar in scope to the Oxford work, but c. 2/3 as long and with much less extensive bibliographies.

General Church History

Offers better coverage of North American and world Christianity.
Has 4800+ brief signed articles which include bibliographies, written by 150 contributors from the perspective of evangelical Protestantism. 2nd ed. is not substantially different from the first.

BA23. Westminster Dictionary of Church History. Jerald C. Brauer, ed. Philadelphia: Westminster, 1971.
Offers brief unsigned articles "concerning the major men, events, facts, and movements in the history of Christianity." Emphasizes modern church history and the American scene. Some articles have brief bibliographies.

BA24. Corpus Dictionary of Western Churches. Thomas C. O'Brien, ed. Washington, DC: Corpus, 1970.
Primarily by Catholic scholars, but ecumenically oriented. The 2300+ concise unsigned articles are "a convenient source of biographies, beliefs, practices, and history of the churches of Western Christendom," stressing the North American church.

BA25. Baudrillart, Alfred. Dictionnaire d'histoire et de géographie ecclésiastiques. Paris: Letouzey, 1912- .
19 vols. (-Francois) published thus far. Covers the history of the Roman Catholic church from the beginning to the present and other churches as they affect the Roman Catholic church. Has signed articles with bibliographies. Esp. good coverage of the Byzantine period, medieval theology, and Catholic biography and ecclesiastical data.

BA26. Moyer, Elgin S. Who Was Who in Church History. rev. ed. Chicago: Moody Press, 1968.
Offers brief information on c. 1700 individuals in church history. Helpful as a source for biographical information on lesser known evangelicals and fundamentalists not listed elsewhere.

General Church History

**CHURCH HISTORY--MAJOR WORKS

BA31. Jedin, H., and Dolan, J., eds. History of the Church. Translated from the 3rd rev. German ed. 10 vols. Somers, CT: Seabury, 1980-   .
Translation of the Handbuch der Kirchengeschichte, 1962-79. Vols. 1, 3, & 4 originally published by Herder & Herder, 1965-1970, under the title Handbook of Church History. A long scholarly history of the church from a Catholic perspective. Each volume is indexed separately and includes bibliographies for each chapter.

BA32. Latourette, Kenneth Scott. A History of Christianity. rev. ed. 2 vols. New York: Harper & Row, 1975.
A successful attempt to summarize all of church history (totals over 1500 pages in length) by a major church historian. Each chapter has selected bibliographies, and the detailed index includes over 6000 entries. First published in 1954.
The rev. ed. includes a "Supplementary Bibliography" (found just before the index) listing additional books published since 1950, and a chapter 62, "The World Christian Movement, 1950-1975." The supplementary bibliographies and the 62nd chapter are by Ralph Winter.

BA33. Schaff, Philip. History of the Christian Church. 7 vols. in 8. New York: Scribner, 1882-1910.
An older, extensive, detailed, and documented history by a major church historian. While now dated, it still offers a wealth of information. Includes bibliographies and a name/subject index in each volume.

**CHURCH HISTORY--ATLASES

BA41. Atlas zur Kirchengeschichte: die christlichen Kirchen in Geschichte und Gegenwart. Hrsg. von Hubert Jedin, Kenneth Latourette,

General Church History

und Jochen Martin. Freiburg: Herder, 1970. An excellent and detailed atlas, useful whether or not one reads German. Contains 257 colored maps & charts covering most aspects of church history, with 80 pages of documented text and commentary on those maps and charts.

A very detailed (36 6-column pages) index/gazeteer gives good access to the maps and text. Finally, bibliographical references are given for each map and chart at the end of the commentary on the map or chart.

BA42. Littell, Franklin H. <u>The Macmillan Altas History of Christianity</u>. New York: Macmillan, 1976.
Not as detailed or as extensive as the above work. Includes 197 maps with text. Emphasis on the intellectual, ethical, and moral development of Christianity in relation to times and places. Has name and subject index.

Chapter 27
ANCIENT CHURCH HISTORY & PATRISTICS

**BIBLIOGRAPHICAL GUIDES/HANDBOOKS

BB1. Altaner, Berthold. <u>Patrology</u>. 2nd ed. Translated by Hilda C. Graef. New York: Herder & Herder, 1960.
A handbook briefly summarizing the lives, writings, and teachings of the church fathers up to 636 (West) and 749 (East). Gives extensive bibliographies, with descriptive commentary, of works by and about each person. Catholic orientation. Patristic name and title index.
  The 8th German edition (<u>Patrologie</u>, 8. Aufl. von Alfred Stuiber, Freiburg: Herder, 1978) has updated bibliographies.

BB2. Quasten, Johannes. <u>Patrology</u>. 3 vols. Westminster, MD: Newman Press, 1951-1960.
Similar to Altaner (above) but has more extensive treatment of each person. Bibliographies are less cryptic, more extensive, and better arranged. Extensive name and subject indexes in each volume.
  Three volumes have been published (v.1: The Beginnings of Patristic Literature; v.2: The Ante-Nicene Literature after Ireneaus; v.3: The Golden Age of Greek Patristic Literature from the Council of Nicaea to the Council of Chalcedon). Two more projected volumes will probably never appear.
  This work and (where Quasten is incomplete) Altaner's are indispensable for patristic studies.

BB3. Bardenhewer, Otto. <u>Patrology: the Lives and Works of the Fathers of the Church</u>. Trans. from the 2nd German ed. St. Louis: Herder, 1908.
Dated and intended primarily for Catholic seminarians, but still helpful. For each person it gives

Ancient Church History

(i) a biographical sketch, (ii) a statement on his writings and theology, and (iii) a bibliography of works by & about the individual. Includes index.

>BB4. Sample, Robert L. *Pre-Nicene Syrian Christianity: a Bibliographic Survey*. Evanston, IL: Garrett-Evangelical Theological Seminary Library, 1977.

A classified & selectively annotated bibliography of "modern scholarly works on the various facets of Syrian Christianity." Covers up to the council of Nicea in 325.

**BIBLIOGRAPHIES/INDEXES

>BB11. Stewardson, J. L. *A Bibliography of Bibliographies on Patristics*. Evanston, IL: Garrett Theological Seminary Library, 1967.

"The purpose of this bibliography is to list and describe as completely as time and resources permit the main bibliographical sources for the field of patristics."

Lists 195 books and periodical articles, arranged in 14 major sections. Includes fairly lengthy annotations. Somewhat helpful, esp. in explaining the usefulness of some of the more esoteric tools. No indexes.

>BB12. *Bibliographia Patristica; Internationale patristische Bibliographie, 1956-   *. Berlin: de Gruyter, 1959-   . Annual.

Somewhat slow in appearing, vol. 15 (1970) published in 1977. An extensive bibliography of books and periodical articles. Covers up to A.D. 657 (West) and 787 (East).

Entries are arranged by subject with detailed table of contents and author index. Includes a major section arranged by the names of the church fathers, a section on patristic biblical exegesis, and a listing of reviews of relevant books. No annotations.

Ancient Church History

BB13. Bulletin de théologie ancienne et médiévale. Louvain: Abbaye du Mont César, 1929- . Annual.
Frequency varies. A detailed and critical bibliography of materials on ancient and medieval theology, listing works in many languages. Includes name, doctrine, and manuscript indexes.

**ENCYCLOPEDIAS

BB21. Pauly, August Friedrich von. Pauly's Real-Encyclopädie der classischen Altertumswissenschaft. Stuttgart: Druckenmüller, 1893- .
Publisher varies. Known as "Pauly-Wissowa." A major authoritative German work covering classical history, antiquities, literature, biography, and all other aspects of the period. Now includes over 80 physical volumes.
The overall arrangement and alphabetizing are complex, with a number of series and supplements. Includes signed articles with extensive bibliographies, written by specialists on each topic.

BB22. Cabrol, Fernand, and Leclercq, Henri. Dictionnaire d'archéologie chrétienne et de liturgie. Publié sous la direction de Henri Marrou. 15 vols. in 30. Paris: Letouzey, 1907-1953.
An important scholarly work on all aspects of ancient Christianity down to the time of Charlemagne. Lengthy documented articles with major bibliographies appended.
Covers the architecture, art, ceremonies, customs, epigraphy, iconography, institutions, liturgy, numismatics, rites, symbols, etc., of the early church.

BB23. Klauser, Theodor, ed. Reallexikon für Antike und Christentum; Sachwörterbuch zur Auseinandersetzung des Christentums mit der antiken Welt. In Verbindung mit Franz J. Dölger & Hans Lietzmann. Stuttgart: Hier-

Ancient Church History

semann, 1950- .
Up to Lief. 84 (-Gnosis) in Sept. 1980. A basic German work on Christianity and the ancient world, covering up to the 6th century A.D. Includes long signed articles by specialists with selected bibliographies.

BB24. Smith, William, and Cheethan, Samuel. Dictionary of Christian Antiquities. 2 vols. Boston: Little, 1876-1880.
Intended to complement the Dictionary of Christian Biography (#BB25 below), it excludes biography but treats subjects connected with the organization of the church (e.g. officers, architecture, music, discipline, sacred days, etc.).
Covers down to the time of Charlemagne (c. A.D. 800). Contains long, signed articles with bibliographies. Not up-to-date but still helpful.

BB25. Smith, William, and Wace, Henry, eds. Dictionary of Christian Biography, Literature, Sects and Doctrine. 4 vols. London: Murray, 1877-1887.
Covers down to the time of Charlemagne (c. A.D. 800). Its object is "to supply an adequate account, based upon original authorities, of all persons connected with the History of the Church within the period treated concerning whom anything is known, of the Literature connected with them, and the controversies respecting Doctrine or Discipline in which they were engaged."
Includes long, valuable, signed articles with good bibliographies. While 100 years old, often the only or major source for information on minor figures in church history. Special attention is given to names and subjects in the church history of the British Isles.

BB26. Wace, Henry, & Piercy, William. Dictionary of Christian Biography and Literature to the End of the Sixth Century, A.D., with an Account of the Principal Sects and Heresies. Boston: Little, 1911.

Ancient Church History

An abridgement of Smith & Wace (#BB25 above) by cutting off two centuries and by omitting many insignificant names included in the original work. Does include more recent bibliographical entries.

**PATRISTIC WRITINGS--BIBLIOGRAPHIES

BB31. Dekkers, Eligius. <u>Clavis patrum latinorum: qua in novum corpus Christianorum edendum optimas quasque scriptorum recensiones a Tertulliano ad Bedam.</u> Ed. altera, aucta et emendata. Steenbrugis: In Abbatia Sancti Petri, 1961.
An extensive index to the published texts of the Latin church fathers -- whether in books, sets, or periodicals. Arranged chronologically by the date of the person. Includes indexes by personal names & works, by subject, and by first lines.

BB32. Geerard, Mauritius. <u>Clavis patrum graecorum: qua optimae quaeque scriptorum patrum graecorum recensiones a primaeuis saeculis usque ad octavum commode recluduntur.</u> Turnhout: Brepols, 1974- .
Thus far, vols. 2-4 have been published. Arranged chronologically by when the Greek church father lived. Each entry includes a brief bibliography of material about the person & then lists each of his works with bibliographies of published texts.
   Notes in the margins indicate where the texts can be found in Migne's <u>Patrologiae</u>. An appendix cross-indexes Migne volume and page numbers to the entry numbers in this work. Also has alphabetical index of persons included.

BB33. Parks, George B., and Temple, Ruth Z. <u>The Literatures of the World in English Translation. Vol. I: The Greek and Latin Literatures.</u> New York: Ungar, 1968.
Valuable in patristics for its fairly complete (up to 1968) listings of translations of the Greek and Latin writings of the church. See pp. 54-58, 138-145, & 243-268 which cover Christian literature.

Ancient Church History

Also use the index to locate additional listings for individual authors.
Helpful for its author-by-author analysis of the contents of translation sets which are not indexed elsewhere and/or analyzed in the card catalog; as well as for its listings of individually published translations.

**PATRISTIC WRITINGS--LEXICONS AND CONCORDANCES

BB41. Lampe, G. W. H. A Patristic Greek Lexicon. Oxford: Clarendon Press, 1961.
"The object of this work is primarily to interpret the theological and ecclesiastical vocabulary of the Greek Christian authors from Clement of Rome to Theodore of Studium" (preface). Helpful for the study and reading of the Greek Fathers.
Excludes the common meanings of words given in Liddell-Scott-Jones, and usages found in the LXX and N.T. biblical materials. Includes some bibliography and cites numerous examples of use as well as analyzing meanings.

BB42. Biblia Patristica: Index des citations et allusions Bibliques dans la littérature patristique. Paris: Éditions du Centre national de la recherche scientifique, 1975- .
Two volumes thus far. Vol. 1 covers from the beginnings to Clement of Alexandria & Tertullian. Vol. 2 covers the third century except for Origen. Gives, in Bible passage order, the locations in the patristic writings where the Bible is used.
Each location is identified by the patristic work's name and the book, chapter, paragraph, page, & line (as applicable). A section at the beginning of each volume lists the exact edition of each patristic work which is indexed in the book. Based on an extensive new project to identify and index all such usages.

Ancient Church History

BB43. Kraft, Henricus. Clavis patrum apostolicorum: catalogum vocum in libris patrum qui dicuntur apostolici non raro occurrentium. München: Kösel, 1963.
Lists the Greek and Latin words that appear in the writings of the apostolic fathers; gives a brief (German or Latin) definition, and a list of where that word occurs. Thus serves as a limited lexicon and concordance to the very early patristic writings. Arranged in 2 sections: Greek words (c. 470 pages) and Latin words (c. 30 pages).
Supersedes E. J. Goodspeed, Index Patristicus sive Clavis Patrum Apostolicorum Operum (Leipzig: Hinrichs', 1907).

BB44. Sieben, Hermann Josef. Voces: eine Bibliographie zu Wörtern und Begriffen aus der Patristik (1918-1978). Berlin: de Gruyter, 1980.
Arranged in two sections: Greek words and Latin words. In each section words are listed alphabetically, and under each word are bibliographical citations to articles and/or books discussing patristic usage of that word. Indexed by the patristic authors referred to and by the modern authors cited.

**OTHER

BB51. Meer, Frederik van der & Mohrmann, Christine. Atlas of the Early Christian World. Translated & edited by Mary F. Hedlund & H. H. Rowley. London: Nelson, 1958.
Translation of the Atlas van de oudchristelijke wereld (Amsterdam, 1958). Covers down to the 7th century. Has 42 6-color maps with commentary. More extensive is the section with 620 plates and commentary on the sculpture, architecture, cities, mosaics, etc., of early Christianity.
Includes a geographical index to the plates and maps, and an index to author and "things" mentioned in the text. Particularly helpful for locating early cities, etc., by their old names.

Ancient Church History

BB52. <u>Cambridge Ancient History</u>. 12 vols. & 5 vols. of plates. Cambridge, Eng.: University Press, 1923-39.
3rd ed., 1970- in progress. An authoritive and extensive standard history covering from the time of Egypt and Babylonia to 324 A.D. The essays included were contributed by top scholars in each area. Each section also includes a bibliography, usually found at the end of the volume.

Chapter 28
MEDIEVAL CHURCH HISTORY

There are few specialized tools for the study of medieval church history. What is listed below is, for the most part, a highly selective list of some general tools for the study of medieval history. Those working extensively in this area will need to consult the bibliographical guides listed below for more information.

**BIBLIOGRAPHIES/INDEXES

>   BC1. Caenegem, R. C. van. <u>Guide to the Sources of Medieval History</u>. With the collaboration of F. L. Ganshof. Amsterdam: North Holland, 1978.

Revised & enlarged ed. of a guide earlier done in German (1964) & Dutch (1962). Five major sections: (i) The sources of medieval history; (ii) Archives & libraries (where source material can be found); (iii) Great collections & repertories of sources; (iv) Reference works; and (v) Bibliographical introduction to the auxiliary historical sciences.

Each section explains its topic in some detail listing and describing the many materials available for medieval studies. Good table of contents. Name and limited title index.

>   BC2. Paetow, Louis John. <u>A Guide to the Study of Medieval History</u>. rev. ed. New York: F.S. Crofts, 1931.

An older (but still useful), standard, scholarly guide for medieval studies. Classed arrangement, listing original source materials and secondary works in the field.

Has annotated entries and each section has an explanatory introduction. Complete index of authors, editors, titles of large collections, and subjects. Critical and scholarly, but now dated.

Medieval Church History

BC3. Boyce, Gray Cowan. Literature of Medieval History 1930-1975: a Supplement to Louis John Paetow's "A Guide to the Study of Medieval History." 5 vols. Millwood, NY: Kraus, 1981.
An extensive supplement to Paetow listing 55,000+ works on all aspects of medieval life and culture. Classified subject arrangement. Part 1 is a listing of reference works for the study of medieval history. Author & subject-name indexes.

BC4. Rouse, Richard H. Serial Bibliographies for Medieval Studies. Berkeley: Univ. of California Press, 1969.
Lists 283 serials (i.e. continuing publications) with bibliographies of help in medieval studies. Entries are arranged topically and include annotations. Has title and editor indexes.

BC5. Pontifical Institute of Medieval Studies. Library. Dictionary Catalogue of the Library of the Pontifical Institute of Medieval Studies, Toronto, Canada. 5 vols. Boston: G. K. Hall, 1972.
Includes nearly 90,000 author, title, and subject catalog cards of the library. A strong source of information on the medieval period.

BC6. Pontifical Institute of Medieval Studies. Library. Dictionary Catalogue of the Library of the Pontifical Institute of Medieval Studies, Toronto, Canada. Supplement. Boston: G. K. Hall, 1979-   .
Updates the above work with new entries.

BC7. Chevalier, Cyr Ulysse J. Répertoire des sources historiques du moyen age. Nouv. éd. refondue, corr. et augm. 2 volumes in 4. Paris: Picard, 1894-1907.
An important bibliography indexing a large amount of the source material and secondary literature of medieval history.
   Two major parts: (i) Bio-bibliographie --

which lists individuals from the period (by the French form of name) and gives brief biographical data and references to materials about them; and (ii) Topobibliographie -- which is a similar list for places and topics.

NOTE: See also the Bulletin de théologie ancienne et médiévale (#BB13 above) which indexes material on medieval theology.

MAJOR WORKS

BC11. Cambridge Mediaeval History. 8 vols. Cambridge, Eng.: University Press, 1911-36. 2nd ed., 1966- in progress. An extensive and authoritative work by specialists in the field. Covers from A.D. 324 up to the Renaissance.

SPECIAL TOPICS

BC21. Constable, Giles. Medieval Monasticism: a Select Bibliography. Toronto: University of Toronto Press, 1976.
Intended "to provide a guide to the secondary literature of Christian monasticism from its origins to the end of the Middle Ages." A valuable, selected, classified bibliography of c. 1000 items in French, German, English, Italian, Latin, and Spanish.

BC22. Atiya, Aziz S. The Crusade: Historiography and Bibliography. Bloomington, IN: Indiana University Press, 1962.
A classified bibliography of the source material and of the secondary material in periodicals and books. Includes non-English materials. Also has a chapter on the historiography of the Crusades.

Chapter 29
THE REFORMATION

**GENERAL--BIBLIOGRAPHICAL GUIDES

BD1. Walt, B. J. van der. <u>Contemporary Research on the Sixteenth Century Reformation</u>. Potchefstroom, S. Africa: Potchefstroomse Univ. for Christian Higher Education, 1979.
A brief survey of current-day research activity, country-by-country. Includes numerous bibliographical entries.

BD2. Wood, A. Skevington. "A Bibliographical Guide to the Study of the Reformation. Part 1: Beginnings." <u>Themelios</u> 2 (Jan. 1977): 52-57; "... Part 2: Development." <u>Themelios</u> 3 (Jan. 1978): 24-27.
A good basic bibliographical survey of the literature on the Reformation. Suggests a few of the better English-language works in each area. Needs to be supplemented, but a good starting point.

BD3. Bainton, Roland H., and Gritsch, Eric W. <u>Bibliography of the Continental Reformation; Materials Available in English</u>. 2nd rev. & enl. ed. Hamden, CT: Archon, 1972.
1st ed. (1935) much less extensive. Provides good coverage with a topical arrangement. No indexes, but has a detailed table of contents. Most entries have brief annotations. Includes many periodical articles, and has a large section on the individual reformers. Intended to supplement Read (#BD41 below) and Schottenloher (#BD31 below).

BD4. Selinger, Suzanne. <u>Renaissance/Reformation Bibliography: a Guide to Research</u>. Chico, CA: Scholars Press, [forthcoming].
Announced as forthcoming but not yet published.

The Reformation

**GENERAL--BIBLIOGRAPHIES/INDEXES

BD11. International Committee of Historical Sciences. Commission internationale d'histoire ecclésiastique comparée. <u>Bibliographie de la Réforme, 1450-1648; ouvrages parus de 1940 à 1955</u>. Leiden: Brill, 1958- .
Fascicules 6-7 read ". . . parus de 1940 a 1960." Thus far, 7 fascicules have been published with (evidently) only a few remaining to be done.
    Lists books, dissertations, and periodical articles published between 1940 and 1955 (1960 for fasc. 6-7). Subdivided into fascicules by the country where the material was published. Each fascicule includes indexes of authors, subjects, etc., but no overall index exists.

BD12. Center for Reformation Research. <u>Microform Holdings from All Periods: a General Finding List</u>. 8 vols. St. Louis: the Center, 1977-1979.
The Center, which has major holdings on microform of some 10,000 printed works from the Reformation period, will lend microform copies of its holdings to researchers.
    This work lists all those printed works held (i) except for the Newberry French political pamphlets (indexed elsewhere) and (ii) works listed in earlier numbers (#2, 3, 6, & 7) of the series <u>Sixteenth Century Bibliography</u> (see #BD13 below).
    Entries are arranged by author, subarranged by title and then by publication date. A valuable bibliographic tool for Reformation research, particularly since copies of works listed here can generally be borrowed from the Center.

BD13. <u>Sixteenth Century Bibliography, v. 1-</u> . St. Louis: Center for Reformation Research, 1975- .
A series of small separately published bibliographies covering many topics of Reformation

studies. All are well done, many are annotated. For a listing of those available, consult the card catalog in your library. Several of these are listed individually below.

BD14. Archiv für Reformationsgeschichte: Beiheft, Literaturbericht; Archive for Reformation History: Supplement, Literature Review. Gütersloher: Mohn, 1972- . Annual.
Provides, since 1972, fairly comprehensive coverage of literature on the Reformation, covering 1450-1650 in Eastern Europe, Western Europe, and the British Isles.

Detailed subject arrangement (see table of contents) but no indexes. A volume of cumulative indexes of authors, names, & places for vols. 1-5 was published in 1978. The editorial apparatus is in German, the critical & descriptive annotations are in German, English, or French.

BD15. Bibliographie internationale de l'Humanisme et de la Renaissance, 1965- . Geneva: Droz, 1966- . Annual.
The volume covering 1975 appeared in 1980. An extensive bibliography (in 1975 c. 6400 items) of the literature on all aspects of life in the 15th and 16th centuries. An important scholarly tool for the study of the Reformation and its setting.

Classified subject arrangement with two major sections: (1) materials on individuals, arranged by name of the person (e.g. Calvin, Bucer); and (2) material on subjects (see esp. part II, "Religion et vie religieuse"). Author index.

**GENERAL--OTHER WORKS

BD21. Encyclopedia of the Middle Ages, Renaissance and Reformation. Edited by Nicholas Mann, Guillaume P. Meyjes, & Gerhard Verbeke. Leiden: Brill, [forthcoming].
First fascicle to be published in 1981; will eventually include 20+ volumes. Intended "to

The Reformation

become the standard scholarly work of reference for the culture of Western Christendom in the millennium AD 600-1600."

BD22. Anderson, Charles S. Augsburg Historical Atlas of Christianity in the Middle Ages and Reformation. Minneapolis: Augsburg, 1967.
Designed to be a "working atlas for the study of Medieval and Reformation Church History," this work illustrates that history with maps and texts from Gregory the Great (590 A.D.) to the Peace of Westphalia (1648 A.D.). Has 32 colored maps with texts. Two indexes: of the plates by place & subject, of the text by subject.

BD23. The Reformation. Edited by G. R. Elton. Cambridge: Cambridge Univ. Press, 1958.
Vol. 2 of the New Cambridge Modern History. A well-received carefully structured set of essays by authorities in the field, both church and "secular" historians.

**IN GERMANY AND SWITZERLAND

BD31. Schottenloher, Karl. Bibliographie zur deutschen Geschichte im Zeitalter der Glaubensspaltung: 1517-1585. 7 vols. Leipzig: Hiersemann, 1933-1940; Supplement, 1966.
A very comprehensive bibliography (primarily of German materials) of books and periodical articles published up through 1960. Detailed subject arrangement with extensive indexes.
Contents: v.1-2--Personen, A-Z; v.3--Reich und Kaiser, Teritorien und Landesherren; v.4--Gesamtdarstellungen der Reformationszeit, Stoffe; v.5--Nachträge und Ergänzungen Zeittafel; v.6--Verfasser- und Titelverzeichnis; and v.7--Das Schrifttum von 1938 bis 1960 [i.e., Supplement].

BD32. Center for Reformation Research. Early Sixteenth Century Roman Catholic Theologians and the German Reformation; a Finding List

The Reformation

of CRR Holdings. St. Louis: the Center, 1975.
Lists the microfilm holdings at the Center of early (1520-1550) anti-Reformation writings by 21 Catholic theologians. For each theologian, a brief vita is given, followed by a listing of available writings (in publication date order). The Center will lend copies of its holdings to researchers.

BD33. Center for Reformation Research. *Evangelical Theologians of Wurttemberg in the Sixteenth Century: a Finding List of CRR Holdings*. St. Louis: the Center, 1975.
Lists the microfilm holdings at the Center of the writings of 5 major theologians from Wurttemberg (Jacob Andreae, Johannes Brenz, Jakob Heerbrand, Lucas Osiander, & Dietrich Schnepf) and of the official publications by Wurttemberg (a center of Lutheran thought in the 16th century).
Under each author, works are listed by date of publication. The Center will lend microfilm copies of its holdings to researchers.

**IN GREAT BRITAIN

BD41. Read, Conyers, ed. *Bibliography of British History, Tudor Period, 1485-1603*. 2nd ed. Oxford: University Press, 1959.
A selective 6543-item bibliography of pamphlets, books, periodical articles, etc., up to Jan. 1957. Strong on church history, but covers all aspects of the history of the period. Stresses English-language materials. Includes some annotations, detailed table of contents, author/subject index.

BD42. Davies, Godfrey. *Bibliography of British History, Stuart Period, 1603-1714*. 2nd ed., edited by Mary F. Keeler. Oxford: Clarendon Press, 1970.
Complements the above, covering another century. This work includes 4350 items, arranged topically. Detailed table of contents, includes an author and subject index. Some annotations are included.

The Reformation

BD43. Baker, Derek. The Bibliography of the Reform, 1450-1648, Relating to the United Kingdom and Ireland for the Years 1955-1970. Oxford: Blackwells, 1975.
Sponsored by the Commission internationale d'histoire ecclésiastique comparée, British sub-commission of the International Committee of Historical Sciences.
    Serves as a complement to #BD11 (above) for materials on the Reformation in Great Britain. In three major sections: (i) England & Wales, (ii) Scotland, and (iii) Ireland.
    Subdivided by type of material (book, periodical article, review, thesis) and then listed alphabetically by author. Given this arrangement and NO subject index, subject access is difficult. NO author index.

BD44. Union Theological Seminary, New York. Library. Catalogue of the McAlpin Collection of British History and Theology. Compiled & edited by Charles R. Gillett. 5 vols. New York: the Library, 1927-1930.
Includes 15,000+ titles published between 1501 and 1700 that were in the collection through 1926. Arranged by date of publication, then by author. Vol. 5 is an author index. Especially important for its listing of pre-1700 publications.

BD45. Union Theological Seminary, New York. Library. Catalogue of the McAlpin Collection of British History and Theology; Acquisitions, 1924-1978. 1 vol. New York: G. K. Hall, 1979.
Supplement to the above. Lists 3000+ additional titles. Unlike the main set above, this work reproduces the author, title, & subject cards for each title, arranged in a single alphabet.

BD46. Early Nonconformity, 1566-1800: a Catalogue of Books in Dr. William's Library, London. 12 vols. Boston: G.K. Hall, 1968.
The collection consists of books on early noncon-

formity in Great Britain and Ireland which were printed between 1566 and 1800.

The 12 volumes form 3 distinct subsets, each reproducing catalog cards for the same books in different ways: (i) Author arrangement (5 vols., 32,200 cards); (ii) Subject arrangement (5 vols., 33,500 cards); (iii) Date of publication arrangement (2 vols., 14,300 cards).

BD47. Macgregor, Malcolm B. The Sources and Literature of Scottish Church History. Glasgow: J. McCallum, 1934.
A classified and briefly annotated bibliography of primary & secondary material, with emphasis on the Reformation period. Includes a detailed "chronological table," a subject index, and an author and "biographical subject" index. Good coverage of pre-1930 materials.

**CALVIN/CALVINISM--MAIN SEQUENCE

The following four works form a continuous bibliography of Calviniana up to the present. Listed in the following section are some additional bibliographies which may supplement these works.

BD51. Erichson, D. Alfredus. Bibliographia Calviniana: Catalogus chronologicus operum Calvini, catalogus systematicus Operum quae sunt de Calvino. reprint ed. Nieuwkoop: de Graaf, 1960.
Reprint of vol. 59 of the Calvini Opera volumes of the Corpus Reformatorum. Includes two parts: (1) editions of Calvin's works up to 1898 & (2) books about Calvin up to 1898.

Entries in part 1 are listed three times, in three different sequences: (i) in order of the edition, (ii) in alphabetical order, and (iii) in chronological order (includes all known subsequent editions and versions). Part 2 is arranged topically, subdivided geographically. Emphasis on German, Latin, & French materials. Author index.

The Reformation

BD52. Niesel, Wilhelm. Calvin-Bibliographie, 1901-1959. München: Kaiser, 1961.
Intended to supplement the above work up through 1959. Classified arrangement, author index.

BD53. Tylenda, Joseph. "Calvin Bibliography: 1960-1970," ed. by Peter De Klerk. Calvin Theological Journal 6 (1971): 156-193.
Supplements the above work through 1970. Includes French, English, German, Dutch, and Italian books and periodical literature, as well as some dissertations. Classified arrangement (an outline is on p. 193). Pages 190-191 list other bibliographies.

BD54. De Klerk, Peter, ed. "Calvin Bibliography, 1972-   ." in Calvin Theological Journal 7- (1972-   ). Annual.
An annually published continuation of the above bibliography. Classified arrangement. Includes books, journal articles, dissertations, encyclopedia articles, parts of books, etc. The author is librarian at Calvin Seminary.

**CALVIN/CALVINISM--OTHER BIBLIOGRAPHIES

BD57. De Koster, Lester R. "Living Themes in the Thought of John Calvin: a Bibliographical Study." PhD dissertation, University of Michigan, 1964.
An extensive (563 pp.) study of the literature on Calvin. Each chapter covers a different topic and discusses the relevant bibliography. Includes a thematic index and an author index. Very helpful for its thematic approach.

BD58. Kempff, Dionysius. A Bibliography of Calviniana 1959-1974. Leiden: Brill, 1975.
Updates & supplements Niesel (#BD52). Lists 3000+ titles, divided into 4 major areas: (i) Calvin's works, (ii) General works about Calvin, (iii) specialized works about Calvin, and (iv) Calvinism and later development. Classified subject arrangement under each topic. Includes author index.

**LUTHER

There is no major retrospective bibliography devoted to material about Luther. However, since Schottenloher's bibliography (#BD31) includes extensive coverage of Luther bibliography, as well as related topics, this is not a major problem.

In Schottenloher, see vol. 1, pp. 458-631, and vol. 7, pp. 114-161, for the listing of materials by and about Luther.

BD61. Aland, Kurt. *Hilfsbuch zum Lutherstudium*. Dritte, neubearb. und erw. Aufl. Witten: Luther-Verlag, 1970.

An extensive work which lists, indexes, and cross-indexes the various published editions of Luther's writings. Invaluable for study of the text and/or editions of Luther's works.

Part I is a classified alphabetical list of his works, arranged by the first significant word in the title of the work. It tells where the work is found in the modern editions and translations listed in part II (19th & 20th century editions) and part III (16th-18th century editions). Parts II & III are cross-indexed to the other parts.

BD62. Bigane, Jack, & Hagen, Kenneth. *Annotated Bibliography of Luther Studies, 1967-1976*. St. Louis: Center for Reformation Research, 1977.

"This bibliography is a scholarly survey of representative and significant literature on Luther to appear during the last decade."

Selection is based on a poll of a number of Luther scholars. Lists c. 160 items with substantial descriptive annotations. Arranged by author. An appendix lists "Surveys of Modern Research."

The Reformation

BD63. "Lutherbibliographie 1925- ." In Luther-jahrbuch. Göttingen: Vandenhoeck und Ruprecht, 1926- . Annual.
Publisher varies. The bibliographies for 1940-1953 were published as a single listing in the 1957 volume. Now a fairly comprehensive bibliography covering materials by and about Luther and about closely related topics. Includes books, periodical articles, dissertations, etc., as well as a listing of reviews of significant books in Luther studies. Classified subject arrangement with author index.

**ZWINGLI

BD71. Finsler, Georg. Zwingli-Bibliographie: Verzeichnis der gedruckten Schriften von und über Ulrich Zwingli. Zürich: Stiftung von Schnyder von Wartensee, 1897.
Covers up to 1895. Two major parts: 1. Writings of Zwingli & 2. Writings about Zwingli. Part 1 lists editions of his works (arranged chronologically) with a title index. Part 2 lists secondary materials by author and has a classified subject index and a date-of-publication index. Includes brief annotations.

BD72. Pipkin, H. Wayne. A Zwingli Bibliography. Pittsburgh: Clifford E. Barbour Library, Pittsburgh Theological Seminary, 1972.
Designed to extend and supplement the above work. Part 1 lists works about Zwingli alphabetically by author; Part 2 lists new editions and translations of Zwingli's works. Entries include book reviews, as well as items of fiction, drama, poetry, and music. Two indexes: of reviews and of subjects.

BD73. Gäbler, Ulrich. Huldrych Zwingli im 20. Jahrhundert: Forschungsbericht und annotierte Bibliographie, 1897-1972. Zürich: Theologischer Verlag, 1975.
Designed to complement Finsler (#BD71). Part 1 reviews 20th century research on Zwingli. Part 2

lists materials by and about Zwingli. Arranged by year, subdivided into "by" and "about" items, then subarranged by author. Includes 1679 items with brief annotations. Indexed by author, writings & letters of Zwingli, proper names, and subjects.

THE RADICAL REFORMATION

BD81. Horst, Irvin B. *A Bibliography of Menno Simons, ca. 1496-1561, Dutch Reformer: with a Census of Known Copies*. Nieuwkoop: de Graaf, 1962.

Lists "all printed books devoted entirely or in part to the writings of Menno Simons." An appendix selectively lists books and pamphlets about him. Arranged by titles of collected works and of individual works. Includes many title page facsimilies and a name index.

BD82. Hillerbrand, Hans J. *A Bibliography of Anabaptism, 1520-1630*. Elkhart, IN: Institute of Mennonite Studies, 1962.

Intends to be exhaustive. Listing c. 4500 items, it includes books, periodical articles, parts of books, and dissertations. Uses a detailed subject arrangement very similar (deliberately so) to that of Schottenloher (#BD31). Has author & short-title index.

Gives limited information on the locations of pre-1940 titles; has only a few brief annotations. Coverage of the Mennonites is continued by Springer & Klassen (#BE25).

BD83. Hillerbrand, Hans J. *A Bibliography of Anabaptism, 1520-1630: a Sequel, 1962-1974*. St. Louis: Center for Reformation Research, 1975.

Supplement to the above work. Classified subject arrangement with same structure as original work. Lists 500+ items without annotations or index. Excludes material on Thomas Müntzer.

The Reformation

BD84. Hillerbrand, Hans J. Thomas Müntzer: a Bibliography. St. Louis: Center for Reformation Research, 1976.
Intended to be a comprehensive bibliography of material by & about Müntzer from the 16th century to the present.
 Entries divided into four groups: (i) Primary works; (ii) General assessments; (iii) Specific studies; and (iv) Belles Lettres. Within each section, entries are arranged by date of publication. Includes c. 280 books & periodical articles. Author index.

**SPECIAL TOPICS

BD91. Zeman, Jarold K. The Hussite Movement and the Reformation in Bohemia, Moravia and Slovakia (1350-1650). Ann Arbor: Michigan Slavic Pub., 1977.
"A Bibliographical Study Guide (with Particular Reference to Resources in North America)." Published under the auspices of the Center for Reformation Research. A classified bibliography with brief introductions to each section but no annotations.
 Lists most (up to 1972) manuscripts, rare books, microfilms, and modern critical editions of primary source material. Gives locations of the materials in N. America.
 Extensive coverage of materials in English, moderate coverage of other western European languages, selective for Slavic and eastern European materials. See esp. Part IV, "Aids to Study." Includes author/editor index.

BD92. Hammer, Wilhelm. Die Melanchthonforschung im Wandel der Jahrhunderte; ein beschreibendes Verzeichnis. 2 vols. Gütersloh: Gerd Mohn, 1967-1968.
Lists 4136 items by & about Melanchthon. Includes all types of printed material & gives annotations for each item. Arranged by date of publication, subdivided into "by" & "about" sections. No index.

Chapter 30
POST-REFORMATION CHURCH HISTORY

**GENERAL

BE1. Cambridge Modern History. 13 vols. & altas. Cambridge, England: University Press, 1902-1912.
Covers from the Renaissance to the present. An extensive authoritative work by specialists in the field. Vol. 13 includes a long general index. Is now being superseded by the following work.

BE2. New Cambridge Modern History. 14 vols. Cambridge, England: University Press, 1957-1979.
Vol. 12 issued in a 1st (1960) & rev. ed. (1968). Similar to the original, but entirely rewritten and updated. Does not include the footnotes or the extensive bibliographies found in its predecessor. For the bibliographies, see Roach (#BE3).

BE3. Roach, John. A Bibliography of Modern History. Cambridge: University Press, 1968.
Intended to serve as the bibliography for the New Cambridge Modern History. Arranged in 3 sections by date (1493-1648, 1648-1793, 1793-1945); then by subject within each section. Highly selective--mainly monographs are listed (few periodical articles are included), emphasis on English & Western-European languages. Cutoff date: 1961. Includes personal name and country index.

BE4. Historical Abstracts, 1775-1945: Bibliography of the World's Periodical Literature. Santa Barbara, CA: Clio Press, 1955- . Quarterly.
Published in two parts since v.17 (1971): (A, Modern History Abstracts, 1775-1914; and B, Twentieth

Post-Reformation Church History

Century Abstracts, 1914-   ) with the expanded coverage indicated in the new subtitles.
Up to 1964 included the U.S. & Canada, since then the U.S. & Canada are excluded and covered in America: History and Life (see #BF2). Includes English abstracts of articles from 2000+ periodicals, festschriften, proceedings, & transactions. Arranged in classified order, with quarterly, annual, and 5-year subject & author indexes.

BE5. Latourette, Kenneth Scott. Christianity in a Revolutionary Age: a History of Christianity in the Nineteenth and Twentieth Centuries. 5 vols. New York: Harper, 1958-1962.
Covers all aspects of Christianity (Roman Catholic, Orthodox, & Protestant) throughout the world (e.g., organization; devotional life; and social, political, & educational influences) since 1815. Includes numerous footnotes and selected annotated bibliographies. Detailed index in each volume.

**THE ECUMENICAL MOVEMENT

BE11. Rouse, Ruth, and Neil, Stephen C., eds. A History of the Ecumenical Movement. 2nd ed. with rev. bibliography. 2 vols. Philadelphia: Westminster Press, 1967-1970.
A survey covering from the Reformation to 1968, this is an authoritative work with essays by many scholars in the field. Each volume includes an extensive classified bibliography, an analytical subject index, and an author index. Vol. 1 covers 1517-1948; & vol. 2 covers 1948-1968. Vol. 2 was edited by Harold Fey.

BE12. Crow, Paul A. The Ecumenical Movement in Bibliographical Outline. New York: Dept. of Faith and Order, National Council of the Churches of Christ, 1965.
A classified but NOT annotated bibliography, mainly of English-language materials. Intended to

update and supplement the earlier bibliographies of Auguste Senaud (Christian Unity, a Bibliography. Geneva: World's Committee of Y.M.C.A., 1937) and Henry R. T. Brandreth (Unity and Religion, a Bibliography. London: A & C Black, 1945).

BE13. Lescrauwaet, Josephus F. Critical Bibliography of Ecumenical Literature. Nijmegen: Bestel Centrale V.S.K.B., 1965.
A classified, annotated bibliography from a post-Vatican II Catholic perspective. Includes two types of materials: (i) "general description of the interested parties in the ecumenical area," & (ii) "the history and the problems of the present-day ecumenical movement." Lists c. 350 items, indexed by author.

BE14. World Council of Churches, Geneva. Library. Classified Catalog of the Ecumenical Movement. 2 vols. Boston: G. K. Hall, 1972.
Includes 25,000 catalog cards, representing about 11000 titles, arranged by subject using a modified dewey classification (outlined at the front of the first volume). The catalog includes cards for relevant periodical articles.
   An extensive collection of ecumenical material, international in scope, primarily English in language. Lists only the printed materials in the collection, not the mss. or mimeographed items. Has an alphabetical index by author & editor.

BE15. Internationale ökumenische Bibliographie: International Ecumenical Bibliography, 1962/63-   . München: Kaiser, 1967-   . Annual.
An important classed bibliography of books and periodical articles which deal with the ecumenical movement, inter-church relations, and controversial theology. Some brief annotations, author index. Includes a section listing book reviews.

Post-Reformation Church History

BE16. Ecumenism Around the World: a Directory of Ecumenical Institutes, Centers, and Organizations. 2nd ed. Rome: the Friars of the Atonement, for Centro pro Unione, 1974.
A directory of 300+ bodies concerned with ecumenism. Arranged by continent and then by country. Indexed by country. Appendix I lists bulletins, newsletters, & reviews which deal with ecumenism.

**DENOMINATIONAL BIBLIOGRAPHIES

   Bibliographies that are limited to inclusion of material by and/or about members of a particular denomination.

BE21. Starr, Edward C. A Baptist Bibliography: Being a Register of Printed Materials by and about Baptists; Including Works Against the Baptists. 25 vols. Rochester: American Baptist Historical Society, 1947-1976.
Publisher varies. Lists books by & about Baptists. Arranged alphabetically by author. Each volume has indexes of co-editors & co-authors, titles, subjects, and Baptist publishers. NO cumulative index. Gives locations of copies of each title.
   Supersedes William T. Whitely, A Baptist Bibliography (2 vols., London: Kingsgate Press, 1916-1922).

BE22. Rowe, Kenneth E. Methodist Union Catalog: Pre-1976 Imprints. Metuchen, NJ: Scarecrow, 1975- .
Five vols. thus far, to be c. 20 vols. Will list c. 50,000 books, pamphlets, and theses by & about Methodists. Gives locations of each work in c. 200 U.S., Canadian, and British libraries. Arranged by author. The set will eventually include cumulative title, added-entry, and subject indexes.
   When complete will replace: Brooks B. Little, Methodist Union Catalog of History, Biography, Disciplines, and Hymnals. Prelim. ed. Lake Junaluska, NC: Assoc. of Methodist Hist. Soc., 1967.

Post-Reformation Church History

BE23. Dexter, Henry M. "Collections toward a Bibliography of Congregationalism." In <u>The Congregationalism of the Last 300 Years; as Seen in Its Literature</u>. New York: Harper, 1880.
This bibliographical appendix contains 326 pages, has 7250 entries, and is one of the most extensive bibliographies on Congregationalism.

BE24. Spencer, Claude E. <u>An Author Catalog of Disciples of Christ and Related Religious Groups</u>. Canton, MO: Disciples of Christ Historical Society, 1946.
A catalog of works written BY members of the denomination. For each person, the dates and places of birth and death are given when known.

BE25. Springer, Nelson P., and Klassen, A. J. <u>Mennonite Bibliography, 1631-1961</u>. 2 vols. Scottsdale, PA: Herald Press, 1977.
Designed to supplement Hillerbrand's <u>Bibliography of Anabaptism, 1520-1630</u> (see #BD82). Intends to comprehensively list all types of published materials by and about Mennonites. The 28,000 entries are arranged geographically, then by type of publication or topic. Includes author, subject, and book review indexes. A valuable complement to Hillerbrand's work.

BE26. Durnbaugh, Donald F., and Schultz, Lawrence W. <u>A Brethren Bibliography, 1719-1963: Two Hundred Fifty Years of Brethren Literature</u>. Elgin, IL: Brethren Press, 1964.
Issed as vol. 9, no. 1 & 2 (Winter/Spring 1964) of <u>Brethren Life and Thought</u>. A nearly comprehensive compilation of publications by (NOT about) brethren authors. Tries to list all such literature published prior to 1900. Post-1900 material was selected for its "relevance to the life, history, or teaching of the Church of the Brethren."
   Omits unpublished material (e.g. theses and dissertations). Arranged by publication date, subarranged by author. Author/editor/compiler index.

Post-Reformation Church History

BE27. Jones, Charles E. *A Guide to the Study of the Holiness Movement*. Metuchen, NJ: Scarecrow, 1974.
A major bibliography of material by and about the Holiness churches arranged in 6 parts: (1) General works; (2) The Holiness Movement -- subdivided by specific movements and denominations; (3) The Keswick Movement; (4) The Holiness-Pentecostal Movement; (5) Schools [of the Movement]; and (6) Biography. Subarranged in each area by specific subjects. Includes an author & subject index.

**SPECIAL TOPICS

BE31. Dollen, Charles. *Vatican II: a Bibliography*. Metuchen, NJ: Scarecrow, 1969.
Lists 2500+ English-language articles & books from 1959 to 1968. Designed to "introduce the student and the scholar to the intellectual ferment of that era." Arranged by author with subject index.

BE32. Ollard, Sidney, L.; Crosse, Gordon; & Bond, M. F. *Dictionary of English Church History*. 3rd rev. ed. New York: Morehouse, 1948.
A standard work that covers only England proper (i.e. Canterbury and York), and limited mainly to coverage of the Church of England. Includes signed articles with brief bibliographies on the history, beliefs, etc., of the church. Includes numerous biographies. High church point of view.

BE33. Wardin, Albert W. *Baptist Atlas*. Cartography by Don Fields. Nashville: Broadman, 1980.
A combination atlas and history of the Baptists. Each of the five chapters has excellent maps and useful statistical tables. Topics covered are: (i) origins in Netherlands and England; (ii) U.S.A. Baptists (3 chapters); and (iii) Baptist movements of the world.

Chapter 31
AMERICAN CHURCH HISTORY

**GENERAL AMERICAN HISTORY

BF1. Harvard Guide to American History. rev. ed. 2 vols. Edited by Frank Freidel. Cambridge: Harvard University Press, 1974.
The major selective bibliographical guide for American history. Vol. 1 arranged topically, vol. 2 chronologically. Vol. 1 also includes some valuable methodological essays. See esp. chapter 24 (1:512-530), "Religion," which has 7 major topical sections. The 7th section lists material by denomination or religious group.
Be sure (i) to read "How to Use the GUIDE to Locate Historical Materials" found on the inside cover, and (ii) to use the separate name & subject indexes to find additional material.

BF2. America: History and Life: A Guide to Periodical Literature. Santa Barbara: Clio Press, 1964-   . Quarterly.
Covers the history of the U.S. & Canada. Abstracts articles from 2000+ periodicals, festschriften, proceedings, and annuals from many countries.
Since 1974, published in 4 parts: A. Article abstract & citations (Spring, Summer, & Fall); B. Book reviews (Spring & Fall); C. American history bibliography (annual, includes all materials in A & B, as well as dissertations); & D. Annual index. Five-year indexes are also published.

**BIBLIOGRAPHICAL GUIDES/BIBLIOGRAPHIES

BF11. Sandeen, Ernest R., and Hale, Frederick. American Religion and Philosophy: A Guide to Information Sources. Detroit: Gale, 1978.

American Church History

Contains 1639 entries with brief descriptive and critical annotations. Entries are arranged topically in some detail, with a functional overall structure. Separate author, title, and subject indexes. Does not supersede the bibliography below but is easier to use and more up-to-date.

BF12. Burr, Nelson R. A Critical Bibliography of Religion in America. 2 vols. Princeton: Princeton University Press, 1961.
Published as vol. 4, parts 1-5 of Religion in American Life. A valuable and comprehensive bibliography of "select titles which seemed to be essential and illustrative of movements and influences" covering all religions in America.
  Arranged by subject with citations in a running commentary that also incorporates historical and critical notes. Extensive table of contents but NO subject index. Author index is included.

BF13. Burr, Nelson R. Religion in American Life. New York: Appleton-Century-Crofts, 1971.
A very selective classified bibliography with brief annotations listing books, journal articles, dissertations, etc. Emphasis on 20th century research and the sociological aspects of American religion. Author index.

BF14. Mode, Peter G. Source Book and Bibliographical Guide for American Church History. Menasha, WI: Banta, 1921.
An older but still useful tool. Includes 29 chapters, each with a bibliography & selected source documents. Covers from the 17th to the early 20th century. The bibliographies are actually short bibliographical essays which discuss the relevant bibliography for each chapter. Subject index.

**MAJOR WORKS

BF21. Ahlstrom, Sydney E. A Religious History of the American People. New Haven: Yale University Press, 1972.

American Church History

A major comprehensive survey by a leading American church historian. Includes nearly 1100 pages of text, an extensive classified bibliography, and a detailed index. An authoritative work, useful (through the index) for reference consultation.

BF22. Handy, Robert T. A History of the Churches in the United States and Canada. Oxford: Clarendon Press, 1976.
About 1/2 the length of Ahlstrom, but oriented toward the institutional, rather than the cultural & intellectual, aspects of American religious history. Gives particularly good coverage to Canada. Includes an excellent bibliographical essay and a detailed subject index.

**ATLASES

BF31. Gaustad, Edwin S. Historical Atlas of Religion in America. rev. ed. New York: Harper, 1976.
1st ed. published in 1961. Uses maps, tables, and charts with accompanying text to show the expansion & development of churches & their membership in America. Covers 1650 through the early 1970s with 70+ maps and 60+ charts & tables. Indexed by place, religious bodies, names, and subjects.
   Helpful for an overview of the development of a religious group and for demographical and geographical information on religion.

BF32. Halvorson, Peter L., & Newman, William M. Atlas of Religious Change in America; 1952-1971. Washington, DC: Glenmary Research Center, 1978.
Consists primarily of 144 maps in 36 sets of 4 maps each. Also contains an introduction and brief commentaries on each set of maps.
   Each set gives, for a denomination or group of churches, maps of county-by-county data on: (i) 1952 adherents; (ii) 1971 adherents; (iii) % of change in 1952-1971; and (iv) "shift-share, 1952-1971." (The 36th set is for "all denominations.")

American Church History

**SPECIAL TOPICS

BF41. "The Black Church in the United States: A Resource Guide." Renewals, a Bibliographic Newsletter of the B.T.I. Libraries 2:4 (Feb. 1979): 1-6.
Lists 33 such resources, including bibliographies, bibliographical guides, etc. Classed arrangement with annotations. A good point at which to start if you are working in this area.

BF42. Ellis, John T. A Guide to American Catholic History. Milwaukee: Bruce, 1959.
A classified list of c. 800 titles, including dissertations, with critical annotations. Author, title, & subject index. A supplementary section lists relevant manuscript depositories, historical associations, and periodical titles. Now somewhat dated but still helpful.
   For other reference works on American Catholic church history, see McCabe, Critical Guide to Catholic Reference Books (#A13 above).

BF43. Trinterud, Leonard J. A Bibliography of American Presbyterianism During the Colonial Period. Philadelphia: Presbyterian Historical Society, 1968.
Intended "to identify the printed sources available for the study of American Presbyterianism in the Colonial Period, or, more precisely, up to that year in which each particular Presbyterian body terminated its colonial pattern by some form of reorganization prior to 1800."
   Material is arranged by the 12 distinctive bodies covered, subarranged by author. Lists only American imprints. Includes author & major cross-reference indexes.

BF44. Sprague, William Buell. Annals of the American Pulpit. 9 vols. New York: Carter, 1859-69.
"Commemorative Notices of Distinguished American Clergymen of Various Denominations, from the

American Church History

Earliest Settlement of the Country to the Close of the Year 1855, with Historical Introductions." Provides biographical information on many individuals not listed elsewhere.

Divided into sections and volumes by denomination. Within each section, the individuals are listed by when they began their ministry. Includes a 2-5 page sketch of each individual with (where applicable) a bibliography of materials by that person. Has a name index for each denomination but no cumulative index.

Chapter 32
SYSTEMATIC THEOLOGY

**CURRENT STATE

CA1. Hall, Thor. Systematic Theology Today: the State of the Art in North America. Washington, DC: Univ. Press of America, 1978- .
One volume published thus far. An analytic summary of material found in the Directory of Systematic Theologians. Presents a detailed analysis of the current state of systematic theology, focusing on the activities, training, careers, research interests, & publications of 560 theologians.

CA2. Hall, Thor. A Directory of Systematic Theologians in North America. Chattanooga: University of Tennessee, 1977.
Lists, with brief biographical information, 500+ individuals who are considered "systematic theologians" in North America today.

**BIBLIOGRAPHIES

CA11. Cottrell, Jack. "Systematic Theology [a Bibliography]." Seminary Review 26 (March 1980): 9-34.
Lists c. 300 books with brief annotations. Codes are given to indicate usefulness and theological viewpoint. Conservative evangelical perspective, but many books from other positions are included. Classed subject arrangement under 25 headings.

CA12. Pinnock, Clark H. A Selective Bibliography for the Study of Christian Theology. [Madison, WI: Theological Students Fellowship, 1974?].
A very short selective list by a well-known evangelical scholar. Lists, without annotations and

Systematic Theology

with only minimal bibliographical information, about 400 works under 15 categories. "A few titles in each section are marked with an asterisk to indicate books of particular importance."

CA13. Princeton Theological Seminary. Library. Bibliography of Systematic Theology for Theological Students. Princeton, NJ: the Library, 1949.
Now somewhat dated but still of use. Intended to be "a convenient hand list of the most important works of theological study." Not annotated. Classified subject arrangement.

NOTE: No periodical index is devoted exclusively to systematic theology. However, of the general religious/theological indexes, the "Elenchus Bibliographicus" in Ephemerides Theologicae Lovanienses (#T15) has the most extensive coverage.

**ENCYCLOPEDIAS--PROTESTANT

There is a fine line between what is a "general theological" encyclopedia and what is a "systematic theology" encyclopedia. Thus, the general theological encyclopedias in Chapter 3 include much material on dogmatic theology. Listed here are those works more closely confined to explaining the terms of systematic theology.

CA21. Baker's Dictionary of Theology. Everett F. Harrison, ed. Grand Rapids: Baker, 1960.
Includes brief signed articles by a number of evangelical American and British scholars. Conservative evangelical perspective. Some articles have brief bibliographies.

CA22. A Dictionary of Christian Theology. Alan Richardson, ed. Philadelphia: Westminster Press, 1969.
"Emphasis is laid upon developments of thought

rather than upon biographical details or events of church history .... The main thrust of this Dictionary is in the interlocking areas of theology and philosophy."

Includes c. 700 brief signed articles by 36 contributors, mainly British. The longer articles include brief bibliographies.

CA23. A Handbook of Christian Theology: Definition Essays on Concepts and Movement of Thought in Contemporary Protestantism. New York: World Books, 1958.
Contains 101 brief essays by American and European Protestant scholars. Most have bibliographies. Intended to be a source book for the understanding of Protestant thinking, emphasizing the new directions of Protestant thought.

CA24. A Handbook of Theological Terms. By Van A. Harvey. New York: Macmillan, 1964.
Has c. 300 short articles on Christian theological terms aiming "to indicate how such terms, ancient and modern, have been variously used in differing circumstances and what is at issue in these various uses." Intended for the layman.

**ENCYCLOPEDIAS--CATHOLIC

CA31. Sacramentum Mundi: an Encyclopedia of Theology. Karl Rahner, ed. 6 vols. New York: Herder, 1968-70.
A very important work for the study of Catholic theology, now published in six languages. Post-Vatican II viewpoint. Has 1000+ lengthy articles by 600+ Catholic scholars from many countries. Most of the articles have bibliographies & vol. 6 includes a general index & a list of contributors.

CA32. Encyclopedia of Theology: the Concise Sacramentum Mundi. Karl Rahner, ed. New York: Seabury, 1975.
"Contains revised versions of the major articles ... from Sacramentum Mundi, together with a large

Systematic Theology

number of articles translated from the major German works Lexikon für Theologie und Kirche and Theologisches Taschenlexikon, and entirely new articles on topics of major importance written for the occasion." Intended for the student and layperson, no bibliographies.

CA33. A Catholic Dictionary of Theology. H. F. Davis, ed. New York: Nelson, 1962- .
To be 4 volumes. Has signed, scholarly articles with bibliographies. Produced with the approval of the Catholic hierarchy in England and Wales, it is intended to be a companion to A Catholic Commentary on Holy Scripture. Has been criticized for being too uncritical for scholars while too difficult for laymen.

**THE CREEDS

CA41. Schaff, Philip. The Creeds of Christendom: with an History and Critical Notes. 6th ed. 3 vols. New York: Harper, 1919.
Vol. 1 contains essays on the history of creeds, church by church, with many bibliographies. Vol. 2 contains the creeds of the Greek & Latin churches; Vol. 3 includes the creeds of the Evangelical Protestant churches. Each creed is given in its original language with an accompanying English translation. Each volume has an index of subjects.

CA42. Curtis, William A. A History of Creeds and Confessions of Faith in Christendom and Beyond. Edinburgh: Clark, 1911.
A major survey of the creeds, with extensive representative quotes. Includes bibliographies, an index, & appendices containing historical tables.

**SPECIAL TOPICS

CA51. Abbot, Ezra. The Literature of the Doctrine of a Future Life. New York: W. S. Waddleton, 1871.
"A catalogue of works relating to the nature, ori-

gin, and destiny of the soul; the titles classified, and arranged chronologically, with notes, and indexes of authors and subjects." Originally an appendix to: William Alger, Critical History of the Doctrine of a Future Life, 1860.

An extensive (234 p.) classified bibliography with brief annotations. Has author and subject indexes. Covers the older literature on this subject extensively, including all types of printed material. Valuable for historical study of this topic.

CA52. Ayres, Samuel G. Jesus Christ Our Lord: an English Bibliography of Christology Comprising Over Five Thousand Titles Annotated and Classified. New York: Armstrong 1906.
Includes 5000+ books on Christ, arranged topically under c. 70 headings. Each section has a brief introduction and short list of recommended titles, followed by an extensive bibliography in author order. Includes subject and author indexes. Dated but valuable for its pre-1905 inclusivensss.

CA53. Ehlert, Arnold D. A Bibliographic History of Dispensationalism. Grand Rapids: Baker, 1965.
Intended "to provide a basis for the study of the doctrinal history of the subject of ages and dispensations." Consists primarily of a well done bibliographical essay discussing the literature. At the end is an "additional bibliography" (that lists only material not discussed in the text) and an index of authors cited in the essay.

CA54. Kwiran, Manfred. Index to Literature on Barth, Bonhoeffer and Bultmann. Basel: F. Reinhardt, 1977.
An extensive bibliography (5645 items) of the secondary literature on three major theologians of the 20th century. Includes books, periodical articles, theses, and dissertations.

Divided into 3 major sections, one for each

Systematic Theology

theologian. Within each section are found: (i) a brief vita for the man; (ii) a listing of the secondary literature, arranged alphabetically by author; (iii) an index by persons; (iv) an index by subjects; and (v) an index which lists the major works of the individual and indicates which entries in the bibliography discuss those works.

CA55. Gill, Athol. *A Bibliography of Baptist Writings on Baptism, 1900-1968*. Rüschlikon-Zürich: Baptist Theological Seminary, 1969.
A classified bibliography of 1250 books and periodical articles on baptism & its various aspects. Has author index and an index of book reviews.

CA56. Martin, Ira Jay. *Glossolalia, the Gift of Tongues: a Bibliography*. Cleveland: Pathway Press, 1970.
A useful and fairly comprehensive list of English-language materials on the topic (few foreign-language items are included). No annotations. Arranged by type of material (books, periodical articles, tracts, dissertations & theses, articles in encyclopedias, etc.), subarranged by author.

NOTE: On third world theology in general, and liberation theology in particular, see Chapter 37.

Christian Ethics

Chapter 33
CHRISTIAN ETHICS

**BIBLIOGRAPHIES

There is no important or extensive bibliography for Christian ethics as such. A few of the more recent and helpful of a number of specialized bibliographies are listed below.

However, both the general theological bibliographies & periodical indexes (See Chapters 8 & 16) and the general philosophical bibliographies and indexes (see Chapter 34) have reasonable coverage of the bibliography of Christian ethics.

CB1. Cottrell, Jack. "Ethics [a Bibliography]." Seminary Review 26 (March 1980): 35-51. Lists c. 200 books with brief annotations. Codes are given to indicate usefulness and theological viewpoint. Conservative evangelical perspective, but many books from other positions are included. Covers ethics in general, Christian ethics, and specific issues in ethics. Classified subject arrangement under 11 headings.

CB2. "Bibliographie" in Zeitschrift für evangelische Ethik, 1957-   . Quarterly. Covers all aspects of Christian ethics including politics, the family, anthropology, psychology, medicine, etc. Up to 1968, it included both books and periodical articles, since then only books are listed. Primarily German material, but books in other languages, esp. English, are included.

CB3. Blondel, Jean-Luc. "Recherches éthiques aux États-Unis." Études théologiques et religieuses 54 (1979): 647-657.

Christian Ethics

A helpful survey of recent (c. 1974 to 1979) work on Christian ethics in the United States, discussing 29 particular books and their context. A good starting point for surveying contemporary thought.

CB4. Garber, Glen. "A Critical Bibliography of Recent Discussions of Religious Ethics by Philosophers." Journal of Religious Ethics 2 (1974): 53-80.

A bibliographical essay on "religious ethics in recent Anglo-American philosophical literature, organized in terms of a critical analysis of the main lines of argument." Emphasis on metaethics. The essay is followed by an alphabetical bibliography of all works discussed.

CB5. Gustafson, R. K. "The Literature of Christian Ethics, 1932-1956." ThM Thesis, Union Theological Seminary in Virginia, 1957.

Discusses in some detail c. 200 major English-language works on Christian ethics. A good survey, although now dated. Works included are also rated as to "value."

CB6. Suttle, Bruce B. Selected Bibliography on Moral Education. Parkland College, Champaign, IL: the author, 1980.

A helpful 46-page unannotated bibliography. Arranged by publication format, NOT by subject. Includes a section on "Sources with Major Bibliographies" on the topic.

**DICTIONARIES AND ENCYCLOPEDIAS

CB11. Baker's Dictionary of Christian Ethics. Carl F. H. Henry, ed. Grand Rapids: Baker, 1973.

Contains moderate length essays and numerous short entries on all aspects of Christian ethics by 263 well-known evangelical scholars. All articles are signed but only occasionally have bibliographies, and those are short.

Christian Ethics

CB12. <u>Concise Dictionary of Christian Ethics</u>. Bernhard Stoeckle, ed. New York: Seabury, 1979.
Has 100+ central articles plus supplementary definitions, written by 30 leading moral theologians. Attempts to provide the latest information available for ethical decision-making in a Christian context. Includes short bibliographies.

CB13. <u>A Dictionary of Christian Ethics</u>. John MacQuarrie, ed. Philadelphia: Westminster, 1967.
Brief signed articles by 80 scholars and theologians, some with short bibliographies. Contributors are from the Protestant, Anglican, Orthodox, Catholic and Jewish traditions. Includes material on all aspects of Christian ethics & related ethical systems and issues.

CB14. <u>Encyclopedia of Morals</u>. Vergilius Ferm, ed. New York: Philosophical Library, 1956.
Covers both ethical theory and moral behavior. Has moderate length articles, most with bibliographies. Also has numerous cross-references and a personal name index.

CB15. <u>Evangelisches Soziallexikon</u>. Im Auftrag des Deutschen Evangelischen Kirchentages. Hrsg. F. Karrenberg. 6. Aufl. Stuttgart: Kreuz, 1969.
Includes numerous signed articles by over 230 contributors on a wide variety of social and ethical topics. Protestant German viewpoint. Most articles have bibliographies. This work is well cross-indexed and also has a subject index.

**BIOETHICS

CB21. Walters, LeRoy. "Information Retrieval in the Field of Bioethics." <u>American Theological Library Association Proceedings</u> 29th (1975): 151-162.
Includes a discussion of the scope of the field,

Christian Ethics

coverage of the various bibliographical control tools and their use, and a basic bibliography for further work. A good introductory survey.

CB22. Walters, LeRoy. Bibliography of Bioethics. Detroit: Gale, 1975- .
New volumes published at irregular intervals. The four volumes published through 1978 list over 5600 documents. Each entry includes full bibliographical information as well as a list of subject terms summarizing the item.
   Each volume has 6 sections: (i) introduction; (ii) a list of journals cited; (iii) the Bioethics thesaurus; (iv) subject entry section; (v) title index; and (vi) author index. Read the introduction in order to use this work effectively.

CB23. Encyclopedia of Bioethics. Warren T. Reich, ed. in chief. 4 vols. New York: Free Press, 1978.
A widely acclaimed major work in the field, dealing with the major issues in the area as well as specifics. The 300 articles, each with a bibliography, include the latest scholarship and give thorough coverage to this topic. Fully cross-referenced & indexed. Indispensable when working in bioethics.

**SPECIFIC ISSUES

CB31. Anglemyer, Mary; Seagreaves, Eleanor; and LeMaistre, Catherina. A Search for Environmental Ethics: an Initial Bibliography. Washington, DC: Smithsonian Inst. Press, 1980.
A selective annotated bibliography of c. 400 books and articles on ethics & the natural environment. Covers English-language material from 1945-1979. Arranged by author with subject and name indexes. Includes a good number of works from a religious, usually Christian, perspective.

Christian Ethics

CB32. Hexham, Irving. "Christianity and Apartheid: an Introductory Bibliography." <u>Reformed Journal</u> 30 (April 1980): S2-S11. Published as special supplementary pages at the center of the journal.

An excellent bibliographical essay with sections on: basic works about South Africa; Christianity & race relations with particular reference to S. Africa; the Christian Institute of S. Africa & Spro-Cas; Christianity in S. Africa; background studies; journals; and works in Afrikaans.

CB33. Institute on the Church in Urban-Industrial Society. <u>An ICUIS Working Bibliography on World Hunger</u>. Chicago: the Institute, 1974. "With Special Attention to Food and Population, the Green Revolution, Energy, Land, and Organizing." A selective annotated bibliography of items about these problems and the Church's response to them. Author index.

CB34. Muldoon, Maureen. <u>Abortion: an Annotated Indexed Bibliography</u>. New York: E. Mellin Press, 1980.

Includes 3400 N. American English-language items, primarily from 1970-1980. Lists other bibliographies; studies of the ethical, theological, medical, social, & legal aspects of abortion; and studies on abortion in various states & countries.

Arranged by author with a classified subject index at the front of the volume. Some entries have brief annotations.

Phil. of Religion, Apologetics

Chapter 34
PHILOSOPHY OF RELIGION & APOLOGETICS

**GENERAL PHILOSOPHY--BIBLIOGRAPHICAL GUIDES

CC1. De George, Richard T. The Philosopher's Guide to Sources, Research Tools, Professional Life, and Related Fields. Lawrence, KS: Regents Press of Kansas, 1980.
Arranged in 3 major parts: (1) An introduction to the research and reference tools in philosophy. (Contents of this section are arranged by subject and type of tool. Also includes lists of philosophical journals, associations, research centers, etc.); (2) A survey of general reference tools; and (3) basic research & reference tools in fields related to philosophy. Each bibliographical entry has a brief annotation.

CC2. Jordak, Francis Elliott. A Bibliographical Survey for a Foundation in Philosophy. Washington, DC: University Press of America, 1978.
An extensive classified bibliography designed to direct the user to the best available works. The first 16 pages list reference tools, the rest of the book lists important works on various topics in philosophy, e.g. the major philosophers, logic, ethics, oriental philosophy, etc.
Most entries include descriptive and critical annotations. The "index" is actually a detailed table of contents. A helpful guide.

CC3. Tobey, Jeremy L. The History of Ideas: a Bibliographical Introduction. Santa Barbara, CA: Clio, 1975-   .
Two vols. thus far. "This bibliography surveys the most important bibliographical guides and writings on the history of philosophy, science, aesthetics,

Phil. of Religion, Apologetics

and religious thought."
   The books are discussed in the well organized and carefully written bibliographical essay. Full bibliographical citations are given in the index/bibliography at the end of each volume. See vol. 1, pp. 160-74 and vol. 2, pp. 146-182 for coverage of Christianity.

**GENERAL PHILOSOPHY--BIBLIOGRAPHIES/INDEXES

CC11. Guerry, Herbert. A Bibliography of Philosophical Bibliographies. Westport, CT: Greenwood Press, 1977.
A bibliography of 2400+ other bibliographies that cover philosophy in general or specific topics.
   Arranged in two major A to Z sections: (i) bibliographies of individual philosophers, listed alphabetically by the name of the philosopher, and (ii) bibliographies on specific philosophical subjects arranged alphabetically by specific subject. Author index.

CC12. Bechtle, Thomas C., and Riley, Mary F. Dissertations in Philosophy Accepted at American Universities, 1861-1975. New York: Garland, 1978.
Lists 7500+ doctoral dissertations done in North American universities. Arranged by author with a detailed subject index. Very helpful for locating such dissertations.

CC13. The Philosopher's Index: an International Index to Philosophical Periodicals. Bowling Green, OH: Philosophical Documentation Center, Bowling Green State University, 1967- . Quarterly.
Annual cumulations. Indexes all the major English-language philosophy journals and selected foreign-language titles. An important tool.
   Now includes 2 major sections: (i) a subject index and (ii) an author listing with the full bibliographic entries & abstracts. A 3rd section indexes book reviews found in the journals.

Phil. of Religion, Apologetics

CC14. The Philosopher's Index: a Retrospective Index to U. S. Publications from 1940. 3 vols. Bowling Green, OH: Philosophical Documentation Center, Bowling Green State University, 1978.
Indexes books (c. 6000) from 1940 to 1976 & periodicals (c. 15,000 articles) from 1940 to 1966. Note the limitation to U.S. publications. Vol. 3 is a listing by author, vols. 1 & 2 are a listing by specific subject.

CC15. The Philosopher's Index: a Retrospective Index to non-U.S. English Language Publications from 1940. 3 vols. Bowling Green, OH: Philosophical Documentation Center, Bowling Green State University, 1980.
Indexes books (c. 5000) from 1940 to 1978 & journal articles (c. 12,000) from 1940 to 1966. Vol. 3 is a listing by author, vols. 1 & 2 are a listing by specific subject.

**GENERAL PHILOSOPHY--ENCYCLOPEDIAS

CC21. Encyclopedia of Philosophy. Edited by Paul Edwards. 8 vols. New York: Macmillan, 1967.
The major English-language work in the field, this work covers the whole of philosophy. A good starting point when researching a topic in philosophy.
The 1400+ articles are generally on broad subject areas -- you must use the index to find specific topics. The long signed articles include bibliographies, many with annotations.

CC22. Dictionary of the History of Ideas: Studies of Selected Pivotal Ideas. Philip P. Wiener, ed. 5 vols. New York: Scribners, 1973-74.
Includes over 300 long signed articles covering a wide range of topics in intellectual history. Concentrates on concepts which can be traced historically. Includes bibliographies, a good index, and an analytical table of contents.

Phil. of Religion, Apologetics

CC23. Dictionary of Philosophy and Psychology, Including Many of the Principal Conceptions of Ethics, Logic, Aesthetics, Philosophy of Religion. James M. Baldwin, ed. 3 vols. in 4. New York: Macmillan, 1901-1905.
The first two volumes are an A-Z sequence of articles on philosophy. Articles are generally fairly short summaries of a topic. Vol. 3, which is bound in two parts, is an extensive bibliography of philosophy and psychology.
The first encyclopedia of philosophy in English, this work is now largely superseded by The Encyclopedia of Philosophy (#CC21), but is still of importance historically.

**GENERAL PHILOSOPHY--OTHER

CC31. Directory of American Philosophers, 1980-81. 10th ed. Ed. by Archie J. Bahm. Bowling Green, OH: Philosophical Documentation Center, Bowling Green State University, 1980.
New edition published every 2 years. Arranged by country (U.S. or Canada); then by state/province; then by institution. Under each institution is a list of its philosophy faculty members. Includes name indexes to philosophers and institutions.

CC32. International Directory of Philosophy and Philosophers, 1978-81. 4th ed. Bowling Green, OH: Philosophical Documentation Center, Bowling Green State University, 1978.
Provides up-to-date information on worldwide philosophical activities. Part I gives brief information on international philosophical organizations.
Part II is arranged country by country. Under each country, brief information is given about its universities & colleges, institutions & research, associations & societies, journals, and publishers of interest to philosophers.
Indexed by the names of (i) societies, (ii) philosophers, (iii) universities, (iv) centers & institutions, (v) journals, and (vi) publishers.

**PHILOSOPHY OF RELIGION, APOLOGETICS

CC41. Pinnock, Clark H. A Selective Bibliography for Christian Apologetics. Madison, WI: Theological Students Fellowship, [1974?].
A classified bibliography of c. 150 items divided into 9 subject areas, prepared by a leading evangelical theologian. A minimum of bibliographical information is given and only a few entries have brief annotations. "An asterisk indicates primary books of particular value" in each subject area.

CC42. Wainwright, William J. Philosophy of Religion: an Annotated Bibliography of Twentieth-Century Writings in English. New York: Garland, 1978.
Contains 1135 entries with fairly long descriptive and critical annotations. Addressed primarily to those working in the analytic tradition and interested in "the solution of philosophical problems," not systems or history.
"Items have been included which either make a significant contribution to our understanding of the relevant problem or have proved to be influential." Thus, it is highly selective -- only works by analytic philosophers are included.

CC43. McLean, George F. A Bibliography of Christian Philosophy and Contemporary Issues. New York: Ungar, 1967.
A selective bibliography of books and periodical articles, 1937 to 1966, on Christian philosophical perspectives. Wide coverage with emphasis on Catholic authors. Topical arrangement, author index.
Topics covered: Christian Philosophy, Contemporary Philosophies, Philosophy and Technology, Philosophy of Man and God, The Problem of God in a Secular Culture, Religious Knowledge & Language, Moral Philosophy, and Teaching Philosophy.

Practical Theology

Chapter 35
PRACTICAL THEOLOGY

**GENERAL WORKS

DA1. Princeton Theological Seminary. Library. Bibliography of Practical Theology. Princeton: the Library, 1949.
Intended to be a helpful list for the student and pastor. Lists suggested titles in most areas of practical theology, arranged by subject. No author index. A helpful list, but now dated.

DA2. Resources for Christian Leaders: a Guide for Churches, Denominations, Missions, Service Agencies. [5th ed.] Monrovia, CA: Missions Advanced Research and Communication Center, 1980.
A selective, classified, annotated bibliography of books and other materials to help the Christian leader. Includes both "Christian" works on management (marked with an *) and helpful "secular" works. Author and title indexes.

DA3. Baker's Dictionary of Practical Theology. Edited by Ralph G. Turnbull. Grand Rapids: Baker, 1967.
Intended to be "a source book for pastors and students." Ten major topical sections: preaching, homiletics, hermeneutics, evangelism & missions, counseling, administration, pastoral, stewardship, worship, and education. Under each heading are a number of essays on aspects of the topic, complete with bibliographies. Indexed by subject and by persons. Conservative and American orientation.

DA4. Répertoire bibliographique des institutions chrétiennes, 1967-   . Strasbourg: Centre de recherche et de documentation des insti-

Practical Theology

tutions chrétiennes, 1968-   . Semiannual. English name: <u>Repertory of Christian Institutions</u>. Published annually 1967-1976. "RIC" is a computer-produced continuing bibliography of materials on the life and work of the church. Includes books and periodical articles in 5 languages with international and ecumenical coverage.

The arrangement and structure of this index is somewhat unusual -- be sure to read its preface for use information. Provides good subject access but has no author indexing.

DA5. RIC [Répertoire bibliographique des institutions chrétiennes]. Supplement, 1-   . Strasbourg: Cerdic, 1973-   .
An on-going series of computer-compiled bibliographies on various special topics of concern to the church today.

Various formats are used, see the preface of each work for a clear explanation of its use. In general, the more recent ones have better coverage and easier to use formats.

Listed below are the numbers, the titles, and the dates of the included material for each of these bibliographies:
1. Marriage and Divorce, 1970-1972.
2. Church and State, 1972.
3. Armed Forces and Churches, 1970-1972.
4. Jesus Movement, 1972.
5. Evangelization and Mission, 1972.
6. Liberation and Salvation, 1972-1973.
7. Politics and Faith, 1972-1973.
8. Religious Life, 1972-1973.
9. Baptism, 1971-1973.
10. Eucharist and Eucharistic Hospitality, 1971-1973.
11. Mixed Marriage, 1960-1974.
12. Development and Justice, 1972-1973.
13. Christianism and Religions, 1972-1974.
14. Holy Spirit, 1972-1974.
15. Evangelization and Mission, 1973-1974.
16. Christian Communities, 1972-1974.
17. Eucharist, 1971-1974.

Practical Theology

18. War, Peace and Violence, 1973-1974.
19. Participation in the Church, 1968-1975.
20. Abortion, 1973-1975.
21. The Women in the Church, 1973-1975.
22. Christianity in Latin America, 1973-1974.
23-26. Marriages in Sub Saharan Africa, 1945-1975.
27. Authority in the Church, 1972-1975.
28. Religious Liberty, 1968-1975.
29. Revision of the Code of Canon Law, 1965-1977.
30. African Theology, 1968-1977.
31-34. Oecumene 1, 1975-1976.
35-38. Church and State, 1973-1977.
39-40. Cultes et enseignement en Alsace et en Moselle, 1801-1977.
41-42. Marriage and divorce, 1975-1977.
43-44. Oecumene 2, 1977.
45-46. Church and State in France, Book Repertory, 1801-1979.
47-49. Religious Liberty, 1918-1978.
50-52. Book Publishers Directory in the Field of Religion, 1980.

**CHURCH AND SOCIETY

DA11. Sociological Abstracts. San Diego: Sociological Abstracts, 1952- . Bimonthly.
Sixth issue is cumulative index for the year. The major American abstracting and indexing tool in sociology. Classified arrangement. Indexes and abstracts a large number of U.S. and foreign periodicals, covering a wide range of sociological research.

DA12. Institute on the Church in Urban-Industrial Society. Abstract Service. Chicago: the Institute, 1970- . Monthly.
Now prepared by the ICUIS and published by the Urban-Rural Mission Office, Commission on World Mission and Evangelism, World Council of Churches.

Practical Theology

Indexes & abstracts material on the urban church, church ministries to minorities, etc.
Also provides information on where copies of the abstracted items may be obtained. An annual author, title, and subject index is available.

DA13. Institute on the Church in Urban-Industrial Society. *Forming a Theology of Urban-Industrial Mission*. Chicago: the Institute, 1975.
A classified annotated bibliography of materials treating the theology of the church's mission in modern urban society. Author index. Also lists addresses of sources of the materials listed.

DA14. Institute on the Church in Urban-Industrial Society. *Mission Beyond Survival: the Task for the Urban Church in the Eighties*. Chicago: the Institute, 1980.
A classified annotated bibliography of materials about the church's mission in the city. Fairly long descriptive annotations.

DA15. James, Gilbert, & Wickens, Robert G. *Town and Country Church: a Topical Bibliography*. Wilmore, KY: Asbury Theological Seminary, 1968.
A classified bibliography of 1000+ books, articles, and pamphlets on the topic. No annotations or index. A useful guide on the topic.

DA16. Byers, David M., & Quinn, Bernard. *Readings for Town and Country Church Workers: an Annotated Bibliography*. Washington, DC: Glenmary Research Center, 1974.
"An attempt to bring together recent material of significant value on the peoples, places, problems, and prospects of rural America." A highly selective list of 425 primarily non-religious items which will provide a background for church work in rural areas. Has descriptive and critical annotations. Indexed by author and by particular states discussed in the various materials.

Practical Theology

**CHURCH AND STATE

DA21. Buzzard, Lynn Robert. <u>Law and Theology: an Annotated Bibliography</u>. Oak Park, IL: Christian Legal Society, 1979.
Lists books and periodical articles which are of major importance when exploring legal-theological questions. Selections are limited to (i) English-language material and (ii) materials of particular interest to the Judeo-Christian tradition.
Includes moderate-length descriptive annotations. Arranged by author, limited subject index. Also has a list of additional works that "may be appropriate to the purpose of this volume." The Society intends to issue supplements to this work.

DA22. Menendez, Albert J. <u>Church-State Relations: an Annotated Bibliography</u>. New York: Garland, 1976.
"Includes only English language, full-length books which treat the subject in some depth or completeness." Emphasis on the situation in the U.S. and Great Britain. Classified arrangement, brief annotations, author index.

DA23. LaNoue, George R. <u>Bibliography of Doctoral Dissertations on Politics and Religion, Undertaken in American and Canadian Universities (1940-1962)</u>. New York: National Council of Churches, 1963.
Lists 649 dissertations on the topic in a simple classified arrangement. No annotations or indexes are included. Citations give author, title, area of concentration, school granting, & year granted for each item.

DA24. Drouin, Edmond G. <u>The School Question: a Bibliography on Church-State Relationships in American Education, 1940-1960</u>. Washington, DC: Catholic Univ. of America, 1963.
Lists 1300+ books, pamphlets, periodical articles, book reviews, dissertations, and court decisions. Classified subject arrangement with author/title

Practical Theology

index. Note esp. the lists of other earlier bibliographies on pp. 2-3, 26-27, 72, 132, and 166. A helpful bibliography, for the time covered, on all aspects of the topic.

DA25. Gianna, Andrea. Religious Liberty: International Bibliography 1918-1978. (RIC Supplement, 47-49). Strasbourg: Cerdic, 1980. Lists books and periodical articles "on religious liberty treated under juridical, sociological or historical aspects. Works that are specifically theological have been left out."

A wide variety of countries and languages are represented in the material. Classified subject arrangement -- the detailed table of contents is at the back of the volume. Note on pp. 112-114 the list of other bibliographies on this topic.

Psychology & Pastoral Counseling

Chapter 36
PASTORAL PSYCHOLOGY AND COUNSELING

**PSYCHOLOGY--SURVEYS/GUIDES

DB1. Elliott, Charles K. <u>A Guide to the Documentation of Psychology</u>. Hamden, CT: Shoestring, 1971.
Both a "how to do research" guide and a basic bibliography. Ten appendices list (for psychology) associations & societies, journals, newsletters, reference sources, etc.

DB2. Gottsegen, Gloria B., & Gottsegen, Abbey J. <u>Humanistic Psychology: a Guide to Information Sources</u>. Detroit: Gale, 1980.
Lists English-language books about alternatives to behaviorism and psychoanalysis, giving brief annotations. Has author, title, & subject indexes. Topics covered include humanistic psychology's historical, philosophical, and theoretical origins; texts; affective education; encounter, sensitivity, & T-groups; experiential techniques & activities; industrial & organization applications; general applied settings; interpersonal behaviour reference sources; periodicals; and organizations & associations.

DB3. <u>American Handbook of Psychiatry</u>. 2nd ed. 6 vols. Edited by Silvano Arieti, et al. New York: Basic Books, 1974-75.
An extensive guide by leading authorities in the field. Each essay is accompanied by a bibliography. Each volume has name & subject indexes.
Contents: v.1--Foundations of Psychiatry; v.2--Child and Adolescent Psychiatry, Sociocultural and Community Psychiatry; v.3--Adult Clinical Psychiatry; v.4--Organic Disorders and Psychosomatic Medicine; v.5--Treatment; and v.6--New Frontiers.

Psychology & Pastoral Counseling

DB4. Basic Handbook of Child Psychiatry. Joseph D. Noshpitz, ed. 4 vols. New York: Basic Books, 1979-1980.
An extensive survey of and guide to child psychiatry containing essays by 250 authorities in the field. Each essay includes a bibliography. Each volume has a name and subject index.
Contents: v.1--Development; v.2--Disturbances of Development; v.3--Therapeutic Interventions; and v.4--Prevention & Current Issues.

**PSYCHOLOGY--INDEXES

DB11. Psychological Abstracts. Washington, DC: American Psychological Association, 1927- . Monthly.
The major indexing and abstracting work in the field. Includes new books, journal articles, and reports, each with a signed abstract. Classified arrangement in 17 major sections, some subdivided. Includes author and subject indexes which are cumulated annually. Indispensable.

DB12. Psychological Abstracts. Cumulated Subject Index to "Psychological Abstracts," 1927-1960. 2 vols. Boston: G. K. Hall, 1966.
DB13. Psychological Abstracts. Cumulated Subject Index to "Psychological Abstracts;" Supplement, 1961-65. Boston: G. K. Hall, 1968.
DB14. Psychological Abstracts. Cumulated Subject Index to "Psychological Abstracts;" Supplement, 1966-68. 2 vols. Boston: G.K. Hall, 1971.
The original set plus its two supplements include over 650,000 entries. A detailed alphabetical subject index to the first 34 years of Psychological Abstracts. Gives reference to the year & the number of the relevant abstracts.

DB15. Columbia University. Psychological Library. Author Index to "Psychological Index," 1894-1935, and "Psychological Abstracts," 1927-1958. 5 vols. Boston: G.K. Hall, 1960.

DB16. __Psychological Abstracts: Cumulative Author Index, Supplement, 1959-63__. Boston: G.K. Hall, 1965.

DB17. __Psychological Abstracts: Cumulative Author Index, Supplement, 1964-68__. 2 vols. Boston: G.K. Hall, 1970.

The original volumes plus the supplements include nearly 450,000 entries. Together, they provide easier multiple-year author access to the bulk of __Psychological Abstracts__.

**PSYCHOLOGY--BIBLIOGRAPHIES

DB21. Watson, Robert I. __Eminent Contributors to Psychology__. 2 vols. New York: Springer, 1974-76.

An extensive bibliography arranged by the name of 500 individuals from 1600 to 1967 who contributed to psychology, although they were not necessarily psychologists. Volume 1 lists materials written by the individuals (c. 12,000 items), vol. 2 lists materials about them (c. 50,000 items).

DB22. __Inventory of Marriage and Family Literature__. Minneapolis: Univ. of Minnesota, 1967- .

Title varies: vols. 1-2 covering 1900-1972 are titled: __International Bibliography of Research in Marriage and the Family__. The first 4 volumes list 25,000+ articles from major journals in the field of marital and family relations. Includes subject, author, & key-word-in-title indexing. An extensive and valuable tool for this topic.

DB23. Freeman, Ruth St. John, and Freeman, Harrop A. __Counseling: a Bibliography (with Annotations)__. New York: Scarecrow, 1964.

Has 9 major sections, one of which is "Religion (Clergy)." Uses a strange indexing system, be sure to read the preface. Covers 1950 to 1964.

Psychology & Pastoral Counseling

**PSYCHOLOGY--ENCYCLOPEDIAS

DB31. International Encyclopedia of Psychiatry, Psychology, Psychoanalysis & Neurology. Edited by B.B. Wolman. 12 vols. New York: Van Nostrand Reinhold, 1977.
A major new international encyclopedia intended to give "an authoritative, complete, and up-to-date description of research, theory, and practice in sciences and professions dealing with man's mind and its ills."
Definitely aimed at professionals & graduate students. Includes 1900+ articles by over 1500 specialists. All articles are signed, most have bibliographies. Vol. 12 includes: (i) a complete list of all articles; (ii) a name index; and (iii) an extensive subject index.

DB32. Encyclopedia of Psychology. H. J. Eysenck, ed. 3 vols. New York: Herder & Herder, 1972.
An earlier well-done but much less extensive work, less technical in content. Includes concise definitions and 282 articles, many with selective bibiographies. No index.

DB33. Goldenson, Robert M. The Encyclopedia of Human Behavior: Psychology, Psychiatry, and and Mental Health. 2 vols. Garden City, NY: Doubleday, 1970.
Intended "to present essential information on ... man's knowledge of himself ... in a form that will be readily understood by the student and the interested layman, yet useful to the professional worker."
Begins with a "category index" (i.e., a classified list of articles) and ends with a selected bibliography & a detailed subject index. Includes 1000+ articles, some with illustrative cases.

Psychology & Pastoral Counseling

**PASTORAL PSYCHOLOGY/COUNSELING

DB41. Stokes, G. Allison. "Bibliographies of Psychology / Religion Studies." Religious Studies Review 4 (1978): 273-279.
An annotated list of 34 past bibliographies on the subject. Helpful for its list of past bibliographies (particularly those that are part of larger works).

DB42. Capps, Donald; Rambo, Lewis; & Ransohoff, Paul. Psychology of Religion: a Guide to Information Sources. Detroit: Gale, 1976.
See esp. section G, "Directional Dimension of Religion." A classified bibliography with author, title, and subject indexes. Includes only post-1950 items, no unpublished materials, and very few foreign titles.

DB43. Meissner, William W. Annotated Bibliography in Religion and Psychology. New York: Academy of Religion and Mental Health, 1961.
An older but still important annotated bibliography of 2900+ books and journal articles on the topic. Author index. Entries are listed under one of 47 subject categories. Covers up through 1960.

DB44. Pastoral Care and Counseling Abstracts. 7 vols. National Clearinghouse, Joint Council on Research in Pastoral Care and Counseling, 1972-1978.

DB45. Abstracts of Research in Pastoral Care and Counseling. National Clearinghouse, Joint Council on Research in Pastoral Care and Counseling, 1979-   . Annual.
Lists known published, unpublished, & in-progress research for the year. Gives abstracts in a classified arrangement. Author index. Abstracts vary considerably in quality and length.

DB46. Menges, Robert J., & Dittes, James E. Psychological Studies of Clergymen: Abstracts of Research. New York: Nelson, 1965.

Psychology & Pastoral Counseling

Lists 700+ books, articles, reports, etc., in a classified and annotated bibliography. Covers, for the most part, only 1955-1965. Indexed by author, instruments & methods, samples, and subjects.

DB47. Beit-Hallahmi, Benjamin. *Psychoanalysis and Religion: a Bibliography.* Norwood, PA: Norwood Editions, 1978.

A selective bibliography of books judged to be "attempts to relate religion and psychoanalysis in a meaningful way." Arranged in two major sections: (i) a classifed subject arrangement under 39 subject headings; (ii) the same articles in author order. Note esp. subject section #39: "Psychoanalytic Influences on Pastoral Counseling."

DB48. American Association of Pastoral Counselors. *1979-1980 Directory.* Washington, DC: the Association, 1979.

Published at irregular intervals. The main portion of this work is an alphabetical list of members which gives the exact name, academic degrees, full address, phone number, relation to the AAPC, and church affiliation of each. Also has a directory of institutional members, a list of affiliate members, and a geographical directory for the U.S. and Canada.

Chapter 37
MISSIONS, THE THIRD WORLD CHURCH

BIBLIOGRAPHIES/INDEXES

DC1. Missionary Research Library, New York. <u>Dictionary Catalog</u>. 17 vols. Boston: G.K. Hall, 1968.
A major resource of the study of missions. Now located at Union Theological Seminary in New York, this collection began as a result of action of the 1910 Edinburgh world missionary conference.

This printed catalog includes 273,000 author, title, & subject cards (in a single A-Z sequence) which represent c. 100,000 titles. Includes cards for c. 800 mission periodicals (in vol. 17), as well as for reports of missions, pamphlets, etc.

DC2. Streit, Robert. <u>Bibliotheca Missionum</u>. 30 vols. Freiburg: Herder, 1916-1974.
Imprint varies. The monumental Catholic bibliography of the literature on missions, covering from the 16th century to the present. Estimated to contain entries for more than 60,000 items. Arranged first by country, then by year, then by author.

Each volume has author, person, subject, and place indexes. Appendix 2 lists 701 relevant periodicals. Gives, for each entry: full bibliographical information, a critical annotation, and some locations in European libraries.

DC3. <u>Bibliografia missionaria</u>. Rome: Pontificia Universita' Urbaniana, 1933- . Annual.
Publisher varies; first few issues covered several years. Four-year cumulated indexes are available. A continuing bibliography of Catholic missions but also includes some Protestant material. Classified arrangement with author and subject indexes.

Missions, The Third World Church

DC4. Vriens, Livinus, ed. Critical Bibliography of Missiology. English ed., trans. from the Dutch Ms by Deodatus Tummers. Nijmegen: Edition Bestel Centrale V.S.K.B., 1960.
Contains 206 items on all aspects of Catholic missions, but does not include Protestant missions or Protesant work in the mission field. Classified arrangement, annotated entries, and author index.

DC5. Jackson, Samuel Macauley. "A Bibliography of Foreign Missions." In: The Encyclopedia of Missions [#DC23] 1:575-661.
"Being a List of Books and Pamphlets upon Missionary Work and Workers, and upon the Religions, Ethnology, Topography and Geography of Missionary Lands Down to the Close of 1890."
An extensive classified bibliography on the topics indicated in the subtitle. Its compressed and abbreviated form is difficult to use.

DC6. "Bibliography of World Mission and Evangelism." In: The International Review of Mission, 1912- . Quarterly.
Title varies, previously titled "International Missionary Bibliography." Appears in each issue of the journal. Includes about 1000 books, dissertations, and articles a year. Arranged by a fairly detailed classed system, using 8 main sections. A good way to keep current on missions bibliography.

**SPECIALIZED BIBLIOGRAPHIES

DC11. Amistad Research Center. Author and Added Entry Catalog of the American Missionary Association Archives, with References to Schools and Mission Stations. 3 vols. Westport, CT: Greenwood, 1970.
A major archival collection which, along with the missions materials, includes substantial material for the study of Black history and the abolition movement. The archives includes 105,000+ items, primarily letters. The last volume has an index of "References to schools and mission stations."

Missions, The Third World Church

DC12. Tippett, A. R. *Bibliography for Cross-Cultural Workers*. Pasadena, CA: William Carey Library, 1971.
Includes all types of materials. Arranged by subject without annotations or indexes. Covers two major areas: "The Anthropological Dimensions" and "The Religious Dimensions" of cross-cultural work. The second section covers only Animism.

DC13. Anderson, Gerald H. *Bibliography of the Theology of Missions in the Twentieth Century*. 3rd ed., rev. & enl. New York: Missionary Research Library, 1966.
A bibliography of about 1000 items, stressing the Protestant and Anglican literature, with representative Catholic works.
Divided topically into 4 major sections: (i) biblical studies; (ii) historical studies; (iii) Christianity and other faiths; and (iv) theory of missions. Arranged by author within each section. Indexed by names & by corporate/conference names.

DC14. *Studies in Missions: an Index of Theses on Missions*. Monrovia, CA: Missions Advanced Research & Communication Center, 1974.
Lists 200 graduate theses from 21 schools, including Fuller Seminary, Wheaton College, and Trinity Evangelical Divinity School. Gives an abstract of each; has author and key-word title indexing.

DC15. Nelson, Marlin L. *Bibliography of Third World Missions with Emphasis on Asia*. Pasadena, CA: School of World Mission, Fuller Theological Seminary, 1976.
A helpful introduction to the topic with c. 300 briefly annotated items. Includes books, articles, and theses. Items are coded "most important," "important," and "informative."

DC16. Sims, Michael. *United States Doctoral Dissertations in Third World Studies, 1869-1978*. Waltham, MA: Crossroads Press, 1980.
Lists c. 19,000 dissertations done at U.S. univer-

Missions, The Third World Church

sities between 1869 and 1978 on topics pertaining to the Third World (Africa, Latin America, Asia, and the Middle East).
Arranged geographically by region & country, then alphabetically by author. Includes extensive indexes of: topical subjects, personal names, place names, languages, and ethnic groups.

NOTE: The International Bulletin of Missionary Research (formerly the Occasional Bulletin of Missionary Research, and the Occasional Bulletin from the Missionary Research Library) often publishes helpful bibliographies on many aspects of missions research.

**ENCYCLOPEDIAS & DIRECTORIES--GENERAL

DC21. Concise Dictionary of the Christian World Mission. Edited by Stephen Neill, Gerald H. Anderson, and John Goodwin. Nashville: Abingdon, 1971.
An international & ecumenical dictionary covering from 1492 to the present. Covers all aspects of the extension of the church and its evangelistic work. The brief articles are signed and include bibliographies. Entries for persons and organizations are included. A valuable, if brief tool.

DC22. The Encyclopedia of Modern Christian Missions: the Agencies. Edited by Burton L. Goddard, et al. Camden, NJ: Nelson, 1967.
Prepared by the Gordon Divinity School faculty. Gives primary coverage to Protestant missions with survey articles on missions in other traditions. Focuses on mission organizations, describing their history, activities, organization, etc.
Most of the 1400+ articles have bibliographies. Includes an index by country and area, and a supplementary index by organization names.

DC23. The Encyclopedia of Missions: Descriptive, Historical, Biographical, Statistical. Edwin M. Bliss, ed. 2 vols. New York: Funk

Missions, The Third World Church

and Wagnalls, 1891. Covers mission organizations, the countries where missions were located, mission stations, missionaries, special topics, etc. A-Z dictionary format with numerous (and sometimes extensive) entries. Of importance in studying the history of missions. The appendices are (i) an extensive bibliography (see #DC5); (ii) a list of Bible versions; (iii) a list of mission societies & addresses; (iv) a list of mission stations; (v) an extensive set of statistical tables; & (vi) a general index.

DC24. Missions Advanced Research & Communication Center. *Mission Handbook: North American Protestant Ministries Overseas.* 11th ed. Monrovia, CA: the Center, 1976.
Titles of earlier editions vary. Its purpose is "to provide in a single volume a convenient reference to descriptive and statistical data on all North American Protestant overseas ministries." Includes brief essays on some major mission topics, information concerning the many agencies listed, a mass of statistics, and indexes that are useful in locating specific information. A new edition was announced for early 1981.

DC25. McCurry, Don M., ed. *World Christianity: Middle East.* Monrovia, CA: MARC, 1979.
DC26. Liao, David C. E., ed. *World Christianity: Eastern Asia.* Monrovia, CA: MARC, 1979.
DC27. Hedlund, Roger E., ed. *World Christianity: South Asia.* Monrovia, CA: MARC, 1980.
The "World Christianity" series is a project of the Strategy Working Group of the Lausanne Committee for World Evangelization. Each regional list is arranged by country, with some larger countries (e.g., India) subdivided.
Gives a brief profile of Christianity among the peoples of each country, including information on unreached peoples, national churches, foreign missions, major Christian activities, and the nation & its people in general. Each chapter also includes a selected bibliography.

Missions, The Third World Church

DC28. Unreached Peoples '79-   . C. Peter Wagner and Edward R. Dayton, eds. Elgin, IL: D.C. Cook, 1978-   . Annual.
A few numbers published before 1978 with somewhat different titles and formats. "Each book in [this] series will contain in-depth articles by recognized missiologists on reaching the unreached, detailed case studies of some specific unreached peoples, general descriptions of eight to a hundred other unreached peoples with some indication of their receptivity to the gospel, and a cumulative index [for the series]."

**ENCYCLOPEDIAS & DIRECTORIES--U.S. & CANADA

DC41. The Native American Christian Community: a Directory of Indian, Aleut, and Eskimo Churches. R. Pierce Beaver, ed. Monrovia, CA: MARC, 1979.
Includes an introductory essay; directories of denominational agencies, nondenominational agencies, & independent churches working with native Americans; a list of native American churches in cities over 30,000; a directory of councils, service agencies, & educational ministries; Christian population reports; and statistical tables.
  A valuable source of information & statistics difficult, if not impossible, to find elsewhere.

DC42. Turner, Harold W. Bibliography of New Religious Movements in Primal Societies. Vol. II: North America. Boston: G.K. Hall, 1978.
Includes "those [religious movements] which arise in the interaction of a primal society with another society where there is a great disparity of power or sophistication."
  Covers the Indians of North Mexico, the U.S., Canada, & Alaska and the Eskimos of Greenland, Canada, & Alaska. Lists and selectively annotates 1607 books, articles, and dissertations. Arranged geographically, subarranged by name of the religious movement. Includes religious movement/Indian name and author indexes.

DC43. *Harvard Encyclopedia of American Ethnic Groups*. Stephan Thernstrom, ed. Cambridge: Harvard University Press, 1980.
Includes long articles on major ethnic groups and short sketches of many other smaller and lesser known groups. Treats their cultural, social, economic, religious, and political history.
   Also includes 29 general essays on general themes such as education, health, religion, etc. Lacks index and cross-references. An important, scholarly, and authoritative work.

**OTHER TOOLS

DC51. Latourette, Kenneth S. *A History of the Expansion of Christianity*. 7 vols. New York: Harper, 1937-1945.
An extensive authoritative work on the missionary work of the church from its beginnings up to the present. Covers Catholic, Protestant, and Orthodox mission work in a comprehensive scholarly survey. Each volume includes an index, extensive bibliographies, and maps.

DC52. Freitag, Anton, ed. *The Twentieth Century Atlas of the Christian World: the Expansion of Christianity Through the Ages*. New York: Hawthorne, 1964.
Contains a series of 29 colored maps, along with illustrations and explanatory text, showing the growth of the church through its mission work. Indexed by proper name.

DC53. *Directory of Christian Work Opportunities*. U.S. & International ed. Seattle: Intercristo, 1977- . Semiannual.
A listing, giving brief information, of Christian service opportunities available worldwide (including the U.S.), both long and short term. Arranged by job category; with indexes by agency, geographical location, and length of service.

Missions, The Third World Church

**ASIA

DC61. Anderson Gerald H. Christianity in Southeast Asia: a Bibliographical Guide. New York: Missionary Research Library, 1966.
"An Annotated Bibliography of Selected References in Western Languages." A selective classified list with brief annotations. Intended to be representative of the scholarly literature on the topic. Lists books, articles, dissertations, and relevant periodical titles.

DC62. Anderson, Gerald H. "A Selected Bibliography in Western Languages." In Asian Voices in Christian Theology, pp. 261-321. Edited by Gerald H. Anderson. Maryknoll, NY: Orbis, 1975.
Lists books & periodical articles on Asian Christian theology, giving brief annotations. Arranged by country, subarranged by author.

DC63. Elwood, Douglas J. "A Selected Bibliography in Western Languages, Classified and Annotated." In What Asian Christians are Thinking, pp. 458-497. Edited by Douglas J. Elwood. Quezon City, Philippines: New Day Publishers, 1976.
Lists, for the most part, the same materials as Anderson's bibliography (#DC62) but arranges the materials by subject. Classified arrangement with specific subject index. Note the list of other bibliographies on Asian Christianity at the beginning of this bibliography.

DC64. Bong, Rin Ro, ed. 1978 Directory of Theological Schools in Asia. Taipei, Taiwan: Asia Theological Association, 1978.
Part I lists c. 500 theological schools and Bible colleges in Asia and the South Pacific. Entries are arranged by country, subarranged by name of the school. Part II gives brief statistics for 176 schools in Asia.

Missions, The Third World Church

DC65. Bong, Rin Ro, ed. <u>1979 Directory of Theologians in Asia</u>. Taipei, Taiwan: Asia Theological Association, 1979.
Gives short biographical information on 350+ evangelical theological scholars in Asia. Entries are arranged by country, then by theological school to which the person is attached. Includes a picture of each person.

**LATIN AMERICA

DC71. Sinclair, John H. <u>Protestantism in Latin America: a Bibliographical Guide</u>. Pasadena, CA: William Carey Library, 1976.
"An Annotated Bibliography of Selected References Mainly in English, Spanish, and Portuguese and Useful Bibliographical Aids to Assist the Student and Researcher in the General Field of Latin American Studies."
Lists 3000+ works in two major sections: (i) a reprint of the 1967 edition & (ii) a supplement of new material. Classified arrangement with an author index.

DC72. Wagner, C. Peter, ed. <u>Catalog of the C. Peter Wagner Collection of Materials on Latin American Theology of Liberation</u>. Pasadena, CA: Fuller Theological Seminary, 1974.
A 70-page annotated bibliography of "(1) materials directly addressed to Latin American theology of liberation, (2) other writings of the principal figures in the Latin American theology of liberation ... and (3) background materials published in Spanish and/or Portuguese...."
Arranged by author, with entries under each person subarranged by date. Includes books, periodical articles, and circulated but unpublished materials.

NOTE: On Latin American liberation theology, see also RIC Supplements #6 (covering 1972-73) and #22 (covering 1973-74).

Missions, The Third World Church

**AFRICA

DC81. Ofori, Patrick E. Christianity in Tropical Africa: a Selective Annotated Bibliography. Nendeln: KTO Press, 1977.
Lists 2859 books, articles, theses, etc., on the history of Christianity in Africa south of the Sahara. Materials are arranged topically by the regions and countries discussed, subarranged by author. Includes author index.

DC82. Turner, Harold W. Bibliography of New Religious Movements in Primal Societies. Vol. 1: Black Africa. Boston: G.K. Hall, 1977.
Supersedes Turner's earlier work, A Comprehensive Bibliography of Modern African Religious Movements (Northwestern Univ. Press, 1966).
Lists materials on religious movements "which arise in the interaction of a primal society with another society where there is a great disparity of power or sophistication." Movements derived from or connected with Christianity receive extensive coverage.
Covers all sub-Saharan Africa, listing 1906 books, articles, dissertations, and theses. Many items have brief annotations. Arranged geographically by country. Indexed by author and subject.

DC83. Facelina, Raymond, and Rwegera, Damien. African Theology: International Bibliography, 1968-1977, Indexed by Computer. (RIC Supplement #30). Strasbourg: Cerdic, 1977.
Lists 393 books & articles on the modern "Africanisation" of Christianity and theology. Stresses material produced in Africa, primarily in French & English. Arranged by author, no subject index.

NOTE: See also the section on "Christian Church and Africa," as well as other relevant items, in E. L. Williams, Howard University Bibliography of African and Afro-American Religious Studies (#H64).

Chapter 38
CHRISTIAN EDUCATION

**EDUCATION

DD1. Berry, Dorothea M. A Bibliographic Guide to Educational Research. 2nd ed. Metuchen, NJ: Scarecrow, 1980.
"A concise guide to assist students in education courses to make effective use of the resources of the library of their college or university." Lists 772 items with annotations. Arranged by type of material (journals, research studies, government documents, reference tools, etc.), subarranged by subject. Author, title, & subject indexes.

DD2. Education Index. New York: Wilson, 1929- . 10x a year.
"A cumulative author subject index to a selected list of educational periodicals, proceedings, and yearbooks." Published monthly except for July and August; annual cumulations.
Provides author and subject entries for articles from c. 250 educational periodicals, arranged in a single A-Z sequence. From mid-1961 to mid-1969 had only subject indexing. An established periodical index in the field, its format is similar to Reader's Guide.

DD3. CIJE: Current Index to Journals in Education. New York: CCM Information Sciences, 1969- . Monthly.
Semiannual & annual cumulations. Currently indexes 700+ publications. Each issue has four parts: (i) main section (with full bibliographic information and an abstract) arranged by "document number," (ii) subject index; (iii) author index; and (iv) journals' contents index. Provides wide coverage with good indexing.

Christian Education

DD4. Resources in Education. Syracuse, NY: Educational Resources Information Clearinghouse, 1966-   . Monthly.
Formerly titled: Research in Education. Known as "ERIC." Published monthly with semiannual and annual cumulative indexes. Gives bibliographical information & descriptive abstracts of unpublished materials "of interest to the education community" -- reports, papers, etc., that have been submitted for listing.
   Entries are arranged by "document number." To locate relevant abstracts, there are indexes by subject, author, & institutions. Contains a great variety of useful material, of varying quality, most of which is available on paper or microfiche from the ERIC reproduction service (see preface to any issue).

DD5. Encyclopedia of Education. Edited by Lee C. Deighton. 10 vols. New York: Macmillan, 1971.
Treats all aspects of educational activity in over 1000 articles by specialists, most with bibliographies. Given the relatively few & long articles, be sure to use the index (vol. 10) to locate material on specific topics. For additional tips on use, see the "Guide to Articles" in vol. 9.

**CHRISTIAN EDUCATION--BIBLIOGRAPHIES

DD11. Taylor, Marvin J., ed. "A Selected Bibliography." In Religious Education: a Comprehensive Survey, pp. 418-430. New York: Abingdon, 1960.
DD12. Taylor, Marvin J., ed. "A Selected Bibliography Since 1959." In An Introduction to to Christian Education, pp. 383-98. New York: Abingdon, 1966.
DD13. Taylor, Marvin J., ed. "A Selected Bibliography Since 1966." In Foundations of Christian Education in an Era of Change, pp. 271-83. Nashville: Abingdon, 1976.
Combined together, these three bibliographies list

c. 1000 post-1950 books important to this field. All 3 use nearly the same outline for arranging the entries, which are not annotated.

Major areas covered are: The nature, principles, & history of religious education; religious growth & the learning-teaching process; the organization and administration of religious education; curriculum for religious education; methods in religious education; and prayer & worship.

DD14. Wyckoff, DeWitte Campbell. Bibliography in Christian Education for Seminary and College Libraries. New York: Program Agency, Mission in Education Unit, United Presbyterian Church in the U.S.A., 1960- . Annual.

Publisher & title varies. Issued in loose mimeographed (and later printed) format. Intended to be a selective, annotated guide to the most important materials for training church workers in Christian education. Primarily of material on Christian education, but also lists representative & important secular works.

Subjects covered include Christian education; education theory; the theology, philosophy, & history of education; the behavioral foundations of religion & education; administration; curriculum; religion and higher education; religion and the public school.

DD15. Little, Lawrence C. Researches in Personality, Character and Religious Education; a Bibliography of American Doctoral Dissertations, 1885 to 1959. With an index by Helen-Jean Moore. Pittsburgh: University of Pittsburgh Press, 1962.

Preliminary ed. in 1960. Lists 6304 dissertations "of possible value to students who do research in personality, character, religious education, and closely related fields." Arranged alphabetically by author with minimal bibliographic information. An extensive subject index provides detailed specific subject access to the material.

Christian Education

DD16. Kasch, Wilhelm F., ed. Ökumenische Bibliographie: Religionsunterricht, Religionspadagogik, Christliche Erziehung. Paderborn: Schöningh, 1976.

An extensive bibliography of both material about religious education and materials for use in religious instruction. Covers the reference works, theory, & practice of Christian education. Almost exclusively German-language materials in a very brief bibliographical form. Includes author index.

DD17. "Doctoral Dissertation Abstracts in Religious Education." In Religious Education, 1906- .

Title varies somewhat. Now appears in the journal annually, but it appeared less frequently in its early days. It contains "selected abstracts of doctoral dissertations of interest to religious educators" condensed from Dissertation Abstracts (#M15), arranged by major subject areas.

"Criteria for inclusion have been: inclusion of studies from the major religious groups in the country; representation from as large a group of schools as possible; relevance to the concerns and problems of religious education."

**CHRISTIAN EDUCATION--OTHER TOOLS

DD21. Westminster Dictionary of Christian Education. Kendig B. Cully, ed. Philadelphia: Westminster, 1963.

An ecumenical dictionary of the theory & practice of Christian education with short signed articles by c. 400 contributors. At the back of this work is a 42-page bibliography of books with 1277 numbered entries.

Preceding this bibliography is a "table of subject headings and bibliographical references" which lists the encyclopedia articles by title and then gives the number(s) of the bibliography items that are relevant.

Christian Education

DD22. <u>Annual Review of Research: Religious Education, vol. 1-   </u>. Ed. by John H. Peatling. Schenectady, NY: Character Research Press, 1980-   . Annual.
Published in cooperation with the Religious Education Association. Vol. 1, for 1980, contains abstracts of 134 studies in religious education from 7 nations. Also includes several other lists of research & a general review of the year's work.

NOTE: On the question of Christian education and the state, see #DA24 above.

Worship, Music, Preaching

Chapter 39
WORSHIP & LITURGY, CHURCH MUSIC, AND PREACHING

WORSHIP & LITURGY

DE1. <u>The Westminster Dictionary of Worship</u>. J. G. Davies, ed. Philadelphia: Westminster, 1979.
First edition had title: <u>A Dictionary of Liturgy and Worship</u>. Covers the liturgy and worship of the major & minor Christian groups with brief accounts of other major religions. Articles give a definition of each item, its historical background, its interpretation, and its current significance.
   Most of the articles, written by a wide variety of scholars, have bibliographies. Articles on topics of widely varying opinion have two or more sections by representatives of various viewpoints.

DE2. Vismans, T. A., and Brinkhoff, Lucas. <u>Critical Bibliography of Liturgical Literature</u>. English ed. Nijmigen: Bestelcentrale, der V.S.K.B., 1960.
A classified annotated bibliography of 278 items. Primarily Roman Catholic in purpose & orientation, but some Eastern and Protestant works are listed. Includes author & anonymous title index.

DE3. Spencer, Donald H. <u>Hymn and Scripture Selection Guide</u>. Valley Forge, PA: Judson, 1977.
Section 1 lists 380 hymns arranged by title. Under each hymn, brief phrases identify its subject and selected relevant Scripture passages are listed.
   Section 2 is a listing of Scripture passages in canonical order. Under each passage, the number(s) of the more appropriate hymn(s) are listed. Useful for appropriate selection of hymns to go with a sermon on a particular text.

Worship, Music, Preaching

**CHURCH MUSIC

DE11. Grove, George, ed. The New Grove Dictionary of Music and Musicians. 6th ed., edited by Stanley Sadie. 20 vols. New York: Grove's Dictionaries of Music, Inc., 1979.
A major revision of an established authoritative encyclopedic work on music. Includes 22,500 articles, long bibliographies, 7500 cross-references, 3000 illustrations, and 16,500 biographies on all aspects of music & musicians. Has a great deal of material of use in the study of church music.

DE12. Clark, Keith C. A Selective Bibliography for the Study of Hymns, 1980. Springfield, OH: Hymn Society of America, 1980.
Revision of the 1964 ed. A well done 42-page classified bibliography of significant works for the study of hymnology. Includes books, periodical articles, & unpublished materials. No annotations or index. Titles particularly valuable in a basic collection are indicated.

DE13. Key Words in Church Music: Definition Essays on Concepts, Practices, and Movements of Thought in Church Music. Ed. by Carl Schalk. St. Louis: Concordia, 1978.
"Intended to provide the practicing church musician with information, largely historical, that may be helpful in addressing matters of contemporary practice in church music." Has 76 articles, each about five pages long, which include selected bibliographies.

DE14. Julian, John. A Dictionary of Hymnology Setting Forth the Origin and History of Christian Hymns of All Ages and Nations. rev. 2nd ed., with new supplement. New York: Scribners, 1907.
Still the most comprehensive and authoritative work on the Christian hymns of all ages. Includes signed articles with bibliographies on hymnology, hymn writers, and individual hymns.

Besides the main A-Z dictionary section, the work includes (i) a cross-reference index to first lines in English, French, German, Latin, etc.; (ii) an index of authors and translators of hymns; and (iii) various supplements to the main work.

DE15. Routley, Erik. *An English-Speaking Hymnal Guide*. Collegeville, MN: Liturgical Press, 1979.

Intended to be a companion to a hymnal, this work lists 888 hymns that are found 4 or more times in 26 major 20th century hymnals.

For each hymn, it gives (as applicable) the first line, length & meter, author's name, original sources, notes of interest, and the hymnals in which the hymn appears. Includes chronological & author indexes, as well as brief bibliographies.

DE16. Diehl, Katharine Smith. *Hymns and Tunes: an Index*. New York: Scarecrow, 1966.

Indexes the hymns from 78 English-language hymnals by (i) first lines; (ii) variant first lines; and (iii) authors. Indexes hymn tunes by names & variants and by composer. Also includes a systematic index to the melodies and other useful appendices.

DE17. McDormand, Thomas B., & Crossman, Frederic S. *Judson Concordance to Hymns*. Valley Forge, PA: Judson, 1965.

Provides a subject approach to 2342 hymns from 27 major denominational hymnals in the U.S. & Canada. The hymns included are listed alphabetically in the "table of first lines."

In the "line index" section, lines from hymns are arranged by key word and refer the user to the correct entry in the table of first lines.

**STUDY OF PREACHING

DE21. Cleary, James W., & Haberman, Frederick W. *Rhetoric and Public Address: a Bibliography, 1947-1961*. Madison, WI: University of Wisconsin Press, 1974.

Worship, Music, Preaching

"A comprehensive listing of important publications on the subject of rhetoric and public address which have appeared in the major languages of Western civilization."
Includes 8035 books, periodical articles, & dissertations. Arranged by author with an extensive subject index. See esp. the heading "Preaching" where numerous works, subarranged by narrower topics, are listed.

DE22. "Bibliography of Rhetoric and Public Address for the Year: 1951-1968." In Speech Monographs v.19-36, 1952-1969. Annual.
Lists books, journal articles, dissertations, and book reviews from the major fields of interest to scholars in rhetoric & public address. Classified subject arrangement, no indexes. Note the section on "Pulpit Address."

DE23. "Graduate Theses: an Index of Graduate Work in Speech." In Speech Monographs v.2-36, 1935-1969. Annual.
In total lists 20,002 theses. Each annual list is arranged by the school where the thesis was done, subarranged by type of degree. Lists all type of theses -- MA, MS, MFA, ThM, PhD, etc. Each list also has a classified subject index, see esp. the subdivision "Homiletics-Preaching" under the division "Public Address."
In addition, most years of this journal also include an "Abstracts of Dissertations in the Field of Speech" section which has abstracts for a limited number of recent theses.

DE24. Bibliographic Annual in Speech Communication, 1970-   . Falls Church, VA: Speech Communications Association, 1971- . Annual.
Lists and abstracts masters theses and doctoral dissertations in speech communication. Also offers a number of specialized bibliographies on aspects of communication.

DE25. Toohey, William, & Thompson, William, eds. *Recent Homiletical Thought: a Bibliography, 1935-1965*. Nashville: Abingdon, 1967.
A listing of 2100+ books, articles, theses, and dissertations on preaching and on Protestant and Roman Catholic homiletics. Most entries have brief annotations.
Divided into four major sections by type of material (book, article, etc.), then arranged topically under 15 subject headings. An appendix lists periodicals of interest. Author index.

DE26. Caplan, Harry, and King, Henry H. "Pulpit Eloquence: a List of Doctrinal and Historical Studies in English." *Speech Monographs* 22, Special Issue (1955): 5-159.
Lists all types of materials on the history & doctrine of preaching -- excludes sermon collections, homiletical aids, and material on hermeneutics. Divided into sections by century of publication, subarranged by author. Unfortunately, no subject index (or any other subject access) is provided.
Seventh in a series of 8 bibliographies: the other 7 list material in Latin, Italian, French, Spanish, Scandinavian, Dutch, and German. For bibliographical citations for these works, see the footnote on p. 5 of this bibliography, or see Toohey (#DE25), pp. 222-223.

DE27. Knower, Franklin H. "Bibliography of Communications Dissertations in American Schools of Theology." *Speech Monographs* 30 (1963): 108-136.
Lists 913 doctoral, masters, and baccalaureate theses done before 1960 at 45 schools belonging to the American Association of Theological Schools. Theses are listed by school, then subarranged by type of degree and author. A classified subject index is also provided.

DE28. Fant, Clyde E., and Pinson, William M. *20 Centuries of Great Preaching: an Encyclopedia of Preaching*. 13 vols. Waco, TX:

Worship, Music, Preaching

Word Books, 1971.
Has chapters on 90+ Christian preachers from many denominations, countries, religious vocations, and theological positions. For each preacher, the chapter includes a portrait, a brief chronology, a concise biography, a sample of his sermons, and a selected bibliography of material by & about him. Individuals covered are arranged chronologically.
   Vol. 13 contains an alphabetical list of the preachers included and excellent indexes of (i) subjects, (ii) Scripture references, (iii) persons, (iv) sermon names, (v) homiletical style and usage, and (vi) illustrations used in the sermons.

**HOMILETICAL AIDS

DE41. Bartlett, John. <u>Familiar Quotations: a Collection of Passages, Phrases and Proverbs Traced to Their Sources in Ancient and Modern Literature.</u> 15th rev. and enl. ed. Emily M. Beck, ed. Boston: Little, Brown, & Co., 1980.
A standard tool for finding apt quotations on a given topic or for tracing the origin of known sayings. Quotations are arranged chronologically by the author's dates. Access to these is provided by an extensive 100,000-entry key-word index.

DE42. Granger, Edith. <u>Granger's Index to Poetry.</u> 6th ed., completely rev. & enl., indexing anthologies published through Dec 31, 1970. Edited by William J. Smith. New York: Columbia University Press, 1973.
An extensive index to poetry by title and first line. Also gives a location in an anthology where the entire poem may be found. Includes author index and subject index.

DE43. Woods, R. L., comp. <u>The World Treasury of Religious Quotations: Diverse Beliefs, Convictions, Comments, Dissents, and Opinions from Ancient and Modern Sources.</u> New York: Hawthorn, 1966.

Worship, Music, Preaching

Arranged 10,000 quotations under 1500 subject headings, subarranged by date. Provides wide coverage, but only 2 of the quotations are taken from the Bible. Author index. NO key-word index.

DE44. Mead, Frank S., comp. Encyclopedia of Religious Quotations. Westwood, NJ: Revell, 1965.
A collection of around 10,000 religious quotations arranged under 170 subject headings. Contains Christian & non-Christian sources. Includes index of authors and topics.

INDEX

To authors, editors, titles,
& alternative titles

A.L.A. Index; N1
Abbaye du Mont César; BB13
Abbot, Ezra; CA51
Abortion; CB34
Abstract Service; DA12
Abstracts of Research in Pastoral Care and
  Counseling; DB45
Academy of Religion and Mental Health; DB43
Ackroyd, P. R.; AG32
Adams, Charles; H1
ADRIS Newsletter; A22
African Theology; DC83
Afro-American Religious Studies; H64
Aharoni, Yohanan; AG11
Ahlstrom, Sydney; BF21
Aids to a Theological Library; H21
Aland, Kurt; BD61
Alger, William; CA51
Allmen, Jean Jacques von; AF1
Alphabetical Arrangement of the Main Entries
  (Union Theological Seminary Library); H11
Alphabetical Subject Index to Periodical Articles
  on Religion; T31
Altaner, Berthold; BB1
America: History and Life; BF2
American Association of Bible Colleges; E14
American Association of Pastoral Counselors; DB48
American Association of Theological Schools; E17
American Baptist Historical Society; BE21
American Bibliography; J64
American Book Publishing Record; J35
American Book Publishing Record Cumulative; J62-63
American Council of Learned Societies; F24
American Doctoral Dissertations; M14
American Handbook of Psychiatry; DB3
American Heritage Dictionary of the English
  Language; V3
American Historical Association; BA2
American Library Association; N1

251

American Library Directory; E31
American Missionary Association Archives; DC11
American Psychological Association; DB11
American Reference Books Annual; A4
American Religion and Philosophy; BF11
American Theological Library Association; H21, J53, M41, N11-13, T12-12
American Theological Library Association Proceedings; CB21
Amistad Research Center; DC11
Analytical Concordance to the Bible; AG2
Anderson, Charles; BD22
Anderson, G. W.; AC5
Anderson, Gerald; DC13, DC21, DC61-62
Anglemyer, Mary; CB31
Annals of the American Pulpit; BF44
Année philologique; AB6
Annotated Bibliography in Religion and Psychology; DB43
Annotated Bibliography of Luther Studies, 1967-1976; BD62
Annotated Bibliography of the Textual Criticism of the New Testament; AD12
Annuaire protestant; D4
Annual Review of Research: Religious Education; DD22
Archaeological Encyclopedia of the Holy Land; AE51
Archer, Gleason; AF13
Archiv für Reformationsgeschichte: Beiheft, Literaturbericht; BD14
Archive for Reformation History: Supplement, Literature Review; BD14
Arieti, Silvano; DB3
Arnim, Max; F2-3
Articles on Antiquity in Festschriften; AB7
Arts and Humanities Citation Index; S43
Asbury Theological Seminary; DA15
Ash, Lee; E32
Asia Theological Association; DC64-65
Asian Voices in Christian Theology; DC62
Association for the Development of Religious Information Systems; A22
Association of Baptist Professors of Religion; P12
Association of Methodist Historical Societies; BE22
Association of Research Libraries; M14
Association of Theological Schools; E17, DD14
Atiya, Aziz; BC22
Atlas of Israel; AG18
Atlas of Religious Change in America; 1952-1971; BF32
Atlas of the Bible; AG13

Atlas of the Biblical World; AG12
Atlas of the Early Christian World; BB51
Atlas van de oudchristelijke wereld; BB51
Atlas van den Bibjel; AG13
Atlas zur Kirchengeschichte; BA41
Augsburg Historical Atlas of Christianity in the Middle Ages & Reformation; BD22
Author and Added Entry Catalog of the American Missionary Assoc. Archives; DC11
Author Catalog of Disciples of Christ and Related Religious Groups; BE24
Author Index to "Psychological Index," and "Psychological Abstracts; DB15
Avi-Yonah, Michael; AG11
Ayres, Samuel; CA52

B.T.I. Union List of Periodicals; U11
Baer, Eleanora; U31
Bahm, Archie; CC31
Bainton, Roland; BD3
Baker, Derek; BD43
Baker's Dictionary of Christian Ethics; CB11
Baker's Dictionary of Practical Theology; DA3
Baker's Dictionary of Theology; CA21
Baldwin, James; CC23
Baly, Denis; AG12
Baptist Atlas; BE33
Baptist Bibliography; BE21
Baptist Theological Seminary; CA55
Barber, Cyril; H41-42
Bardenhewer, Otto; BB3
Barker, Kenneth; AA12
Barrow, John; G21
Basic Bibliographic Guide for New Testament Exegesis; AA21
Basic Bibliography for the Study of the Semitic Languages; AC23
Basic Books for a Minister's Library; H43
Basic Handbook of Child Psychiatry; DB4
Basic Tools of Bibical Exegesis; AA1
Batson, Beatrice; H30
Baudrillart, Alfred; BA25
Bauer, Johannes; AF2
Beaver, R. Pierce; DC41
Bechtle, Thomas; CC12
Beck, Emily; DE41
Beit-Hallahmi, Benjamin; DB47
Bennett, Boyce; AE42
Berkowitz, Morris; H61
Berlin, Charles; N14
Berry, Dorothea; DD1
Besterman, Theodore; G11-12

Bibeltheologisches Wörterbuch; AF2
Bible as Literature; AB24
Bible Bibliography, 1967-1973; AC6
Bible Related Curriculum Materials; AB25
Bible: Texts and Translations of the Bible from
 Pre-1956 Imprints; AB11
Biblia Patristic; BB42
Biblica; AB1
Biblical Archaeology; AE54
Biblical Bibliography; AB3
Biblical Bibliography II; AB4
Biblical World; AE52
Bibliografia missionaria; DC3
Bibliographia academica; H27
Bibliographia Calviniana; BD51
Bibliographia Patristica; BB12
Bibliographic Annual in Speech Communication; DE24
Bibliographic Guide to Educational Research; DD1
Bibliographic History of Dispensationalism; CA53
Bibliographic Index; G13
Bibliographic Newsletter of the B.T.I.; A21, BF41
Bibliographical Guide to New Testament Research;
 AA22
Bibliographical Guide to the History of
 Christianity; BA12
Bibliographical Guide to the Study of the
 Reformation; BD2
Bibliographical Repertory of Christian
 Institutions; DA4
Bibliographical Survey for a Foundation in
 Philosophy; CC2
Bibliographie Biblique; AB3
Bibliographie Biblique II; AB4
Bibliographie de la Réforme, 1450-1648; BD11
Bibliographie der deutschen Zeitschriften-
 literatur; S34
Bibliographie der Fest- und Gedenkschriften; N15
Bibliographie der fremdsprachigen Zeitschriften-
 literatur; S35
Bibliographie der Hermeneutik und ihrer
 Anwendungsbereiche; AB22
Bibliographie des sciences théologiques; H28
Bibliographie internationale de l'Humanisme et de
 la Renaissance; BD15
Bibliographie zu den Handschriften vom Toten Meer;
 AD44
Bibliographie zu Flavius Josephus; AD25-26
Bibliographie zu Wörtern und Begriffen aus der
 Patristik; BB44
Bibliographie zur deutschen Geschichte im
 Zeitalter der Glaubensspaltung; BD31

Bibliographie zur jüdisch-hellensistischen und
  intertest. Literature; AD22
Bibliographies of Psychology/ Religion Studies;
  DB41
Bibliographies, Subject and National; G1
Bibliographische Nachschlagewerke zur Theologie
  und ihren Grenzgebieten; A15
Bibliographisches Beiblatt der Theologischen
  Literaturzeitung; H74
Bibliography for Cross-Cultural Workers; DC12
Bibliography for Old Testament Exegesis and
  Exposition; AA12
Bibliography in Christian Education for Seminary
  and College Libraries; DD14
Bibliography of American Presbyterianism During
  the Colonial Period; BF43
Bibliography of Anabaptism, 1520-1630; BD82-83
Bibliography of Baptist Writings on Baptism; CA55
Bibliography of Bible Study for Theological
  Students; AA5
Bibliography of Bibliographies in Religion; G21
Bibliography of Bibliographies on Patristics; BB11
Bibliography of Bioethics; CB22
Bibliography of British History, Stuart Period,
  1603-1714; BD42
Bibliography of British History, Tudor Period,
  1485-1603; BD41
Bibliography of Calviniana, 1959-1974; BD58
Bibliography of Christian Philosophy and
  Contemporary Issues; CC43
Bibliography of Communications Dissertations in
  American Schools of of Theology; DE27
Bibliography of Doctoral Dissertations on Politics
  & Religion; DA23
Bibliography of Foreign Missions; DC5
Bibliography of Hebrew Publications on the Dead
  Sea Scrolls; AD45
Bibliography of Holy Land Sites; AB21
Bibliography of Jewish Bibliographies; G23
Bibliography of Menno Simons; BD81
Bibliography of Modern History; BE3
Bibliography of New Religious Movements in Primal
  Societies: Black Africa; DC82
Bibliography of New Religious Movements in Primal
  Societies: North America; DC42
Bibliography of New Testament Bibliographies; AD1
Bibliography of Philosophical Bibliographies; CC11
Bibliography of Post-Graduate Master's Theses in
  Religion; M41
Bibliography of Practical Theology; DA1
Bibliography of Rhetoric and Public Address for
  the Year; DE22

Bibliography of Systematic Theology for
  Theological Students; CA13
Bibliography of Targum Literature; AC24-25
Bibliography of the Continental Reformation; BD3
Bibliography of the Dead Sea Scrolls; AD42
Bibliography of the Reform, ... United Kingdom
  & Ireland; BD43
Bibliography of the Theology of Missions in the
  20th Century; DC13
Bibliography of Third World Missions with Emphasis
  on Asia; DC15
Bibliography of World Mission and Evangelism; DC6
Bibliography [on Christianity and
  Literature]; H67
Bibliography on Church-State Relationships in
  American Education; DA24
Bibliotheca Missionum; DC2
Bibliotheca Theologica; H54
Biblisch-historisches Handwörterbuch; AE8
Bigane, Jack; BD62
Bijbels woordenboek; AE24
Biographical Directory of Negro Ministers; F32
Biography Index; F4
Black Church in the United States; BF41
Black, Dorothy; M3
Black, J. S.; AE12
Bliss, Edwin; DC23
Blondel, Jean-Luc; CB3
Board of Microtext; J53
Bock, Gerhard; F3
Bodensieck, Julius; C32
Bollier, John; A11
Bond, M. F.; BE32
Bong, Rin Ro; DC64-65
Book Review Digest; P1
Book Review Index; P2
Book Reviews of the Month; P11
Booklist; AC3
Books in Print; J31
Books in Series; U32
Books on Demand; J42
Books: Subjects; J21-25
Borchardt, C. F. A.; H65
Born, A. van den; AE24
Boston Theological Institute; A21, U11
Botterweck, G. Johannes; AF11
Bowden, Henry Warner; F33
Bowling Green State University;
  CC13-15, CC31-32
Boyce, Gary C.; BC3
Brandreth, Henry; BE12
Branson, Mark; AA34

Brauer, Jerald; BA23
Brethren Bibliography; BE26
Brethren Life and Thought; BE26
Brinkhoff, Lucas; DE2
British Books in Print; L11
British Humanities Index; S42
British Library; L4
British Library General Catalogue of Printed Books to 1975; L4
British Museum. Department of Printed Books; L1-3, L6-7
British National Bibliography; L12
Brock, Sebastian; AC26
Brockhaus Enzyklopädie; B11
Bromiley, Geoffrey; AE3
Brown, Colin; AF22
Brunotte, Heinz; C16
Buchberger, Michael; C26
Bulletin de théologie ancienne et médiévale; BB13
Bulletin signalétique; S32
Bulletin signalétique 527; T16
Burchard, Christoph; AD44
Bureau of the Census; B41, D16
Burr, Nelson; BF12-13
Buss, Martin; AC7
Buzzard, Lynn Robert; DA21
Byers, David; DA16

CIJE; DD3
Cabrol, Fernand; BB22
Caenegem, R. C. van; BC1
Cahill, P. J.; AF3
Calvin-Bibliographie, 1901-1959; BD52
Calvin Bibliography; BD54
Calvin Bibliography: 1960-1970; BD53
Calvin Theological Journal; BD53-54
Calvini Opera; BD51
Cambridge Ancient History; BB52
Cambridge History of the Bible; AG32
Cambridge Medieval History; BC11
Cambridge Modern History; BE1
Caplan, Harry; DE26
Capps, Donald; DB42
Carson, Don; AA35
Case, Shirley Jackson; BA12
Catalog of the C. Peter Wagner Collection; DC72
Catalog of the Library of the French Biblical and Archeological School; AB5
Catalog of the Middle Eastern Collection; AC22
Catalog of the Oriental Institute Library; AC21
Catalogue de la Bibliothèque de l'École Biblique et Arch. Francaise; AB5

Catalogue général des livres imprimés: Auteurs;
   L41
Catalogue of Books in Dr. William's Library,
   London; BD46
Catalogue of the McAlpin Collection of British
   History and Theology; BD44-45
Catholic Almanac; D21
Catholic Biblical Encyclopedia; AE21
Catholic Dictionary of Theology; CA33
Catholic Encyclopedia; C21
Catholic Library Association; T13-14
Catholic Periodical and Literature Index; T14
Catholic Periodical Index; T13
Catholic University of America; AC1
Catholiques le plus eminents de France et de
   l'étranger; C25
Cave, Alfred; H51
Center for Reformation Research; BD12-13, BD32-33,
   BD62, BD83-84, BD91
Centre de Documentation du C.N.R.S.; T16
Centre de recherche et de documentation des
   institutions chrétiennes; DA4
Chadwick, Owen; BA11
Chapman, Robert; V11
Charlesworth, James; AD23
Chauveinc, Marc; M1
Cheethan, Samuel; BB24
Chevalier, Cyr Ulysse; BC7
Cheyne, T. K.; AE12
Chicago Area Theological Library Association;
   U12-13
Chicago. University. Library; AC22
Chicago. University. Oriental Institute; AC21-22
Childs, Brevard; AA11
Christian Legal Society; DA21
Christian Librarians' Fellowship; T34
Christian Periodical Index; T34
Christian Unity, a Bibliography; BE12
Christian Words; AF23
Christianity and Apartheid; CB32
Christianity and Literature; H67
Christianity in a Revolutionary Age; BE5
Christianity in Latin America; DC72
Christianity in Southeast Asia; DC61
Christianity in Tropical Africa; DC81
Christianity Today; E12
Church-Related and Accredited Colleges and
   Universities in the U.S.; E11
Church-State Relations; DA22
Churches and Church Membership in the United
   States; D17
Clark, Keith; DE12

Classification of the Library of Union Theological
   Seminary; H13
Classified Bibliography of Literature on the Acts
   of the Apostles; AD8
Classified Bibliography of the Finds in the Desert
   of Judah; AD43
Classified Bibliography of the Septuagint; AC26
Classified Catalog of the Ecumenical Movement;
   BE14
Clavis patrum apostolicorum; BB43
Clavis patrum graecorum; BB32
Clavis patrum latinorum; BB31
Clifford E. Barbour Library; AD5, BD72
Collections toward a Bibliography of
   Congregationalism; BE23
Collison, Robert; G1
Columbia University. Psychological Library; DB15
Commenting and Commentaries; AA33
Commission internationale d'histoire
   ecclésiastique comparée; BD11, BD43
Commission on World Mission and Evangelism; DA12
Committee for Theological Library Development; H16
Companion to the Bible; AF1
Comprehensive Bibliography of Modern African
   Religious Movements; DC82
Comprehensive Dissertation Index; M11-13
Concise Dictionary of Christian Ethics; CB12
Concise Dictionary of the Christian World Mission;
   DC21
Concise Sacramentum Mundi; CA32
Congregationalism of the Last 300 Years; BE23
Constable, Giles; BC21
Contemporary Research on the Sixteenth Century
   Reformation; BD1
Cooperative Religion Catalog; H16
CORECAT; H16
Corpus Dictionary of Western Churches; BA24
Corpus Reformatorum; BD51
Corswant, Willy; AE41
Cottrell, Jack; CA11, CB1
Council on Graduate Studies in Religion; M42-43
Council on the Study of Religion; E15-16, M44
Counseling: a Bibliography; DB23
Coxil, H. Wakelin; D1
Creeds of Christendom; CA41
Critical Bibliography of Ecumenical Literature;
   BE13
Critical Bibliography of Liturgical Literature;
   DE2
Critical Bibliography of Missiology; DC4
Critical Bibliography of Recent Discussions of
   Religious Ethics; CB4

Critical Bibliography of Religion in America; BF12
Critical Guide to Catholic Reference Books; A13
Critical History of the Doctrine of a Future Life; CA51
Crooks, George; H53
Cross, F. L.; BA21
Crosse, Gordon; BE32
Crossman, Frederic; DE17
Crow, Paul; BE12
Crusade, The; BC22
Crysdale, Stewart; H62
Cully, Kendig; DD21
Cumulated Subject Index to Psychological Abstracts; DB12-14
Cumulative Author Index for Poole's Index ..., 1802-1906; S13
Cumulative Book Index; J61
Cumulative Subject & Author Index to vv. I-XV of Masters Abstracts; M22
Current Book Review Citations; P3
Current Index to Journals in Education; DD3
Curtis, William; CA42
Cyclopedia Bibliographica; H52
Cyclopedia of Biblical, Theological, & Ecclesiastical Literature; C14

Dallas Theological Seminary; AA12, T21-22
Danker, Frederick; AA2
Darling, James; H52
Darlow, T. H.; AB12
Davies, Godfrey; BD42
Davies, J. G.; DE1
Davis, H. F.; CA33
Dayton, Edward; DC28
De George, Richard; CC1
De Klerk, Peter; H55, BD53-54
De Koster, Lester; BD57
Dead Sea Scrolls; AD41
Decade of Bible Bibliography; AC5
Deighton, Lee; DD5
Dekkers, Eligius; BB31
Delling, G.; AD22
Deutsche Bibliographie; L32
Deutsche Nationalbibliographie; L32
Deutschen Evangelischen Kirchentages; CB15
Deutsches Bücherverzeichnis; L32
Dexter, Henry; BE23
Dictionary Catalog of the Klau Library; H14
Dictionary Catalogue of the Library of the Pontifical Institute of Medieval Studies; BC5-6
Dictionary of American Biography; F24-25
Dictionary of American Religious Biography; F33

Dictionary of Biblical Archaeology; AE52
Dictionary of Biblical Theology; AF3
Dictionary of Christ and the Gospels; AE61
Dictionary of Christian Antiquities; BB24
Dictionary of Christian Biography and Literature; BB26
Dictionary of Christian Biography, Literature, Sects and Doctrine; BB25
Dictionary of Christian Ethics; CB13
Dictionary of Christian Theology; CA22
Dictionary of English Church History; BE32
Dictionary of Hymnology; DE14
Dictionary of Life in Bible Times; AE41
Dictionary of Liturgy and Worship; DE1
Dictionary of National Biography; F53-55
Dictionary of Philosophy and Psychology; CC23
Dictionary of the Apostolic Church; AE62
Dictionary of the Bible; AE11, AE22-23
Dictionary of the History of Ideas; CC22
Dictionary of the New Testament; AE62-63
Dictionary of Universal Biography; F1
Dictionnaire d'archéologie biblique; AE41
Dictionnaire d'archéologie chrétienne et de liturgie; BB22, C25
Dictionnaire d'histoire et de géographie ecclésiastiques; BA25, C25
Dictionnaire de droit canonique; C25
Dictionnaire de la Bible; C25, AE9-10
Dictionnaire de théologie catholique; C25
Dictionnaire du Nouveau Testament; AE63
Diehl, Katharine Smith; DE16
Directory of American Philosophers; CC31
Directory of American Scholars; F41
Directory of Archives and Manuscript Repositories; R3
Directory of Christian Work Opportunities; DC53
Directory of Departments & Programs of Religion in North America; E15
Directory of Ecumenical Institutes, Centers, and Organizations; BE16
Directory of Publishing Opportunities in Journals and Periodicals; V52
Directory of Religious Bodies in the United States; D12
Directory of Religious Organizations in the United States; D18
Directory of Systematic Theologians in North America; CA2
Directory of Theologians in Asia; DC65
Directory of Theological Schools in Asia; DC64
Disciples of Christ Historical Society; BE24
Dissertation Abstracts International; M15

Dissertation Abstracts International Section C ;
  M33
Dissertation Title Index; M43
Dissertations in Philosophy Accepted at American
  Universities; CC12
Dittes, James; DB46
Doctor William's Library, London; BD46
Doctoral Dissertation Abstracts in Religious
  Education; DD17
Doctoral Dissertations in the Field of Religion;
  M42
Dolan, J.; BA31
Dolger, Franz; BB23
Dollen, Charles; BE31
Doors '81; E13
Douglas, James; AE26, BA22
Dreesen, G.; H27
Drouin, Edmond; DA24
Durnbaugh, Donald; BE26

Early Nonconformity, 1566-1800; BD46
Early Sixteenth Century Roman Catholic
  Theologians; BD32
Eastern Asia; DC26
Ebbitt, Wilma; V22
École Biblique et Archéologique Francaise; AB5,
  AD5
Ecumenical Movement in Bibliographical Outline;
  BE12
Ecumenism Around the World; BE16
Education Index; DD2
Educational Resources Information Clearinghouse;
  DD4
Edwards, Paul; CC21
Ehlert, Arnold; CA53
Ehrlich, Eugene; V4
Elements of Style; V23
Elenchus Bibliographicus; T15
Elenchus Bibliographicus Biblicus; AB1
Eleven Years of Bible Bibliography; AC4
Elliott, Charles; DB1
Ellis, John; BF42
Ellison, John William; AG3
Elton, G. R.; BD23
Elwood, Douglas; DC63
Eminent Contributors to Psychology; DB21
Enciclopedia Italiana di scienze, lettere ed arti;
  B14-15
Enciclopedia universal ilustrada europeo-
  americana; B16
Encounter with Books; H29
Encyclopaedia Biblica; AE12

Encyclopaedia Britannica; B1
Encyclopaedia Judaica; C41
Encyclopaedia of the Presbyterian Church in the
  U.S.A.; C37
Encyclopedia Americana; B3
Encyclopedia of American Religions; D11
Encyclopedia of Archaeological Excavations in the
  Holy Land; AE53
Encyclopedia of Associations; B42
Encyclopedia of Biblical Prophecy; AE71
Encyclopedia of Biblical Theology; AF2
Encyclopedia of Bioethics; CB23
Encyclopedia of Christianity; C13
Encyclopedia of Education; DD5
Encyclopedia of Human Behavior; DB33
Encyclopedia of Mission; DC5
Encyclopedia of Missions; DC23
Encyclopedia of Modern Christian Missions; DC22
Encyclopedia of Morals; CB14
Encyclopedia of Philosophy; CC21
Encyclopedia of Preaching; DE28
Encyclopedia of Psychology; DB32
Encyclopedia of Religion and Ethics; C2
Encyclopedia of Religious Quotations; DE44
Encyclopedia of Southern Baptists; C31
Encyclopedia of the Lutheran Church; C32
Encyclopedia of the Middle Ages, Renaissance and
  Reformation; BD21
Encyclopedia of the Social Sciences; B21
Encyclopedia of Theology; CA32
Encyclopedia of World Methodism; C36
Encyclopedic Dictionary of the Bible; AE24
Encyclopédie des sciences ecclésiastiques; C25
English Bible in America; AB14
English-Speaking Hymnal Guide; DE15
Ephemerides Theologicae Lovanienses; T15
Erbacher, Hermann; H63, N15
ERIC; DD4
Erichson, D. Alfredus; BD51
Espasa; B16
Essay and General Literature Index; N2
Essays on Theological Librarianship; H55
Essential Books for a Pastor's Library; H45
Essential Books for Christian Ministry; H46
Eternity Magazine; E13
Ethics [a Bibliography]; CB1
Etudes theologiques et religieuses; CB3
Europa Year Book; B32
European Abstracts; M33
Evangelical Theologians of Wurttemberg in the 16th
  Century; BD33
Evangelisches Kirchenlexikon; C16

Evangelisches Soziallexikon; CB15
Evans, C. F.; AG32
Evans, Charles; J64
Exégèse practique des petits prophètes postexiliens; AC8
Exhaustive Concordance of the Bible; AG1
Expository Dictionary of the Old Testament; AF14
Eysenck, H. J.; DB32

Facelina, Raymond; DC83
Familiar Quotations; DE41
Fant, Clyde; DE28
Ferguson, F. S.; L22
Ferm, Vergilius; CB14
Fey, Harold; BE11
Fields, Don; BE33
Filson, F. V.; AG17
Finegan, Jack; AG31
Finsler, Georg; BD71
Fitzmyer, Joseph; AA3, AD41
Fleming Library; P11
Forming a Theology of Urban-Industrial Mission; DA13
Forthcoming Books; J33
Foundations of Christian Education in an Era of Change; DD13
France. Centre National de la Recherche Scientifique; S32
France protestante et les Eglises de langue francaise; D4
France, R. T.; AA22
Freeman, Harrop; DB23
Freeman, Ruth St. John; DB23
Freidel, Frank; BF1
Freitag, Anton; DC52
French Books in Print; L43
Friars of the Atonement; BE16
Friedrich, G.; AF21
Fritsch, Charles; AC26
Fuller Theological Seminary; AD42, DC15, DC72

Gabler, Ulrich; BD73
Gaffron, H.-G.; AA23
Galling, Kurt; C1
Ganshof, F. L.; BC1
Garber, Glen; CB4
Garrett Evangelical Theological Seminary; BB4, BB11
Gaustad, Edwin; BF31
Geerard, Mauritius; BB32
Gehman, Henry Snyder; AE27
Geils, Peter; L33

Geisendorfer, James; D12, D18
General Catalogue of Printed Books; L1-4
Gesamtverzeichnis des deutschsprachigen
  Schrifttums (GV); L32-33
Gianna, Andrea; DA25
Gill, Athol; CA55
Gillett, Charles; BD44
Glanzman, George; AA3
Glossolalia; CA56
Glueck, Nelson; AB21
Goddard, Burton; DC22
Goldenson, Robert; DB33
Goldingay, John; AA34
Goodspeed, E. J.; BB43
Goodwin, John; DC21
Gordon Divinity School; DC22
Gorzny, Willi; L32-33
Gottcent, John; AB24
Gottsegen, Abbey; DB2
Gottsegen, Gloria; DB2
Graduate Studies in Religion; E16
Graduate Theological Union; H17
Graduate Theses: an Index of Graduate Work in
  Speech; DE23
Graef, Hilda; BB1
Grande encyclopédie; B13
Granger, Edith; DE41
Granger's Index to Poetry; DE41
Grant, F. C.; AE22
Gray, Richard; G2
Greek and Latin Literatures; BB33
Greenslade, S. L.; AG32
Gritsch, Eric; BD3
Grollenberg, Lucas Hendricus; AG13
Grosse Brockhaus, Der; B11
Grossfeld, Bernard; AC24-25
Grove, George; DE11
Grubb, Kenneth; D1
Gründler, J.; D2
Guerry, Herbert; CC11
Guide on the Availability of Theses; M1
Guide to American Catholic History; BF42
Guide to Archives and Manuscripts in the United
  States; R2
Guide to Catholic Literature; H22
Guide to Educational and Employment Opportunities
  for Christian Students; E13
Guide to Higher Education; E12
Guide to Historical Literature; BA2
Guide to Indexed Periodicals in Religion; T2
Guide to Lists of Master's Theses; M3
Guide to Microforms in Print; J51

Guide to Popular Government Publications; R11
Guide to Reference Books; A1-2
Guide to Reference Material; A3
Guide to Religious and Semi-Religious Periodicals; T32
Guide to Religious Literature; H30
Guide to Religious Periodicals; T32
Guide to Reprints; J41
Guide to Social Science and Religion in Periodical Literature; T32
Guide to the Documentation of Psychology; DB1
Guide to the Sources of Medieval History; BC1
Guide to the Study of Medieval History; BC2-3
Guide to the Study of the Holiness Movement; BE27
Guide to Theses and Dissertations; M2
Gustafson, R. K.; CB5

Haberman, Frederick; DE21
Hagen, Kenneth; BD62
Hagenbach, Karl Rudolf; H53
Hale, Frederick; BF11
Hall, Thor; CA1-2
Halvorson, Peter; BF32
Hamburger, Roberta; A14
Hamer, Philip; R2
Hammer, Wilhelm; BD92
Handbook for Scholars; V51
Handbook of Biblical Chronology; AG31
Handbook of Christian Theology; CA23
Handbook of Church History; BA31
Handbook of Denominations in the United States; D14
Handbook of Theological Terms; CA24
Handbuch der Kirchengeschichte; BA31
Handy, Robert; BF22
Harbrace College Handbook; V21
Harmon, Nolan; C36
Harper's Bible Dictionary; AE25
Harper's Encyclopedia of Bible Life; AE42
Harper's Topical Concordance; AG4
Harris, R. Laird; AF13
Harrison, Everett; CA21
Hartman, Louis; AE24
Harvard Encyclopedia of American Ethnic Groups; DC43
Harvard Guide to American History; BF1
Harvey, Van; CA24
Hastings, James; AE11, AE22, AE61-62, C2
Hauck, Albert; C15
Hebrew Union College Annual; AB21
Hebrew Union College-Jewish Institute of Religion; H14, AB21

Hedlund, Mary; BB51
Hedlund, Roger; DC27
Hege, Christian; C34
Hegener, Karen; E1
Heintz, Jean-Georges; H28
Henrichs, Norbert; AB22
Henry, Carl; CB11
Herbert, A. S.; AB13
Herzog-Hauck Realencyklopädie; C11
Herzog, Johann Jakob; C15
Hexham, Irving; CB32
Hilfsbuch zum Lutherstudium; BD61
Hilgert, Earl; H55
Hillerbrand, Hans; BD82-84
Hills, Margaret; AB14
Hines, Theodore; T2
Historian's Handbook; BA1
Historical Abstracts, 1775-1945; BE4
Historical Association; BA11
Historical Atlas of Religion in America; BF31
Historical Catalogue of Printed Editions of the
  English Bible, 1525-1961; AB13
Historical Catalogue of the Printed Editions of
  Holy Scripture; AB12
History of Christianity; BA32
History of Creeds and Confessions of Faith; CA42
History of Ideas; CC3
History of the Christian Church; BA33
History of the Church; BA11, BA31
History of the Churches in the U.S. & Canada; BF22
History of the Ecumenical Movement; BE11
History of the Expansion of Christianity; DC51
Hodes, Franz; F3
Hodges, J.; V21
Höfer, Josef; C26
Horst, Irvin; BD81
Hospers, J. H.; AC23
Howard University Bibliography of African &
  Afro-American Religious Studies; H64
Hubbard, Robert; AA34
Huldrych Zwingli im 20. Jahrhundert; BD73
Humanistic Psychology; DB2
Humanities, The; A5
Humanities Index; S41
Hurd, John; AD1
Hurst, John; H53-54
Hussite Movement and the Reformation in Bohemia,
  Moravia and Slovakia; BD91
Hyamson, Albert; F1
Hymn and Scripture Selection Guide; DE3
Hymn Society of America; DE12
Hymns and Tunes: an Index; DE16

267

ICUIS Working Bibliography on World Hunger; CB33
Illustrated Bible Dictionary; AE5
Illustrated Guide to Abbreviations; V41
Index of Articles on the N.T. & the Early
   Church ... in Festschriften; AD3-4
Index of Reviews of New Testament Books Between
   1900-1950; P12
Index Patristicus sive Clavis Patrum
   Apostolicorum Operum; BB43
Index to Festschriften in Jewish Studies; N14
Index to Jewish Periodicals; T33
Index to Literature on Barth, Bonhoeffer and
   Bultmann; CA54
Index to Periodical Literature on Christ and the
   Gospels; AD6
Index to Periodical Literature on the Apostle
   Paul; AD9
Index to Religious Periodical Literature; T11
Index to Theses Accepted for Higher Degrees in the
   Universities of Great Britain; M32
Indexed Periodicals; S1
Indices Theologici; T23
Infodex; AC2
Information Please Almanac; B31
Information Retrieval in the Field of Bioethics;
   CB21
Inslag van die Calvinisme in Suid-Afrika; H66
Institute for Scientific Information; S43, S52
Institute for the Study of American Religion; D12
Institute of Mennonite Studies; BD82
Institute on the Church in Urban-Industrial
   Society; CB33, DA12-14
Instructions for Contributors; V33
Intercristo; DC53
International Bibliography of Historical Sciences;
   BA3
International Bibliography of Research in Marriage
   and the Family; DB22
International Committee of Historical Sciences;
   BA3, BD11, BD43
International Directory of Philosophy and
   Philosophers; CC32
International Ecumenical Bibliography; BE15
International Encyclopedia of Psychiatry,
   Psychology, Psychoanalysis & Neurology; DB31
International Encyclopedia of the Social Sciences;
   B22-23
International Glossary of Abbreviations for
   Theology and Related Subjects; V42
International Index; S16
International Microforms In Print; J51
International Missionary Bibliography; DC6

International Missionary Council; H23
International Review of Biblical Studies; AB2
International Review of Mission; DC6
International Standard Bible Encyclopedia; AE3-4
International Who's Who; F13
Internationale Bibliographie der Zeitschriften-
   literatur; S33
Internationale ökumenische Bibliographie; BE15
Internationale patristische Bibliographie; BB12
Internationale Personalbibliographie; F2-3
Internationale Zeitschriftenschau für Bibel-
   wissenschaft und Grenzgebiete; AB2
Internationales Abkürzungsverzeichnis für
   Theologie und Grenzgebiete; V42
Interpretation; AA4
Interpreter's Dictionary of the Bible; AE1-2
Introduction to Christian Education; DD12
Introduction to Theology; H51
Introduction to United States Public Documents;
   R12
Introductory Bibliography for the Study of
   Scripture; AA3
Inventory of Marriage and Family Literature; DB22
Irregular Serials & Annuals; U23

Jackson, Samuel Macauley; DC5
Jacques Cattell Press; F41
James, Gilbert; DA15
Jedin, Hubert; BA31, B41
Jellicoe, Sidney; AC26
Jenni, Ernst; AF12
Jesus Christ Our Lord; CA52
Jewish Encyclopedia; C42
Johnson, J. Edmund; H61
Joint Council on Research in Pastoral Care and
   Counseling; DB44-45
Jones, Charles; BE27
Jongeling, B.; AD43
Jordak, Francis Elliott; CC2
Journal of Biblical Literature; V33
Journal of Religious Ethics; CB4
Joy, Charles Rhind; AG4
Judson Concordance to Hymns; DE17
Julian, John; DE14

Karpinski, Leszak; H3
Karrenberg, F.; CB15
Kasch, Wilhelm; DD16
Katholieke universiteit te Leuven; H27
Keeler, Mary; BD42
Kelly, Balmer; AA4
Kempff, Dionysius; BD58

Kennedy, James; A12
Kepple, Robert; T1
Key Words in Church Music; DE13
King, Henry; DE26
Kissinger, Warren; AD10-11
Kittel, G.; AF21
Klassen, A. J.; BE25
Klau Library; H14
Klauser, Theodor; BB23
Knower, Franklin; DE27
Kraeling, Emil G. H.; AG14
Kraft, Henricus; BB43
Krause, Gerhard; C17
Krentz, Edgar; H55
Kwiran, Manfred; CA54

Lampe, C. W. H.; AG32, BB41
Langevin, Paul-Emile; AB3-4
LaNoue, George; DA23
LaSor, William; AD42
Latourette, Kenneth; BA32, BA41, BE5, DC51
Law and Theology; DA21
Leclercq, Henri; BB22
Lee, Sidney; F53-54
LeMaistre, Catherina; CB31
Leon-Dufour, Xavier; AE63, AF3
Lescrauwaet, Josephus; BE13
Lewanski, Richard; E22
Lexikon der christlichen Kirche und Sekten; D2
Lexikon für Theologie und Kirche; C26-27, CA32
Li, Tze-Chung; A6
Liao, David; DC26
Liberation and Salvation; DC72
Library of Congress; J1-2, J11-15, J21-26, J52, R1, U1, U3-4
Library of Congress Shelflist: Religion, BL-BX; H15
Library Research Guide to Religion and Theology; A12
Lietzmann, Hans; BB23
List of Bibliographies of Theological and Biblical Literature; G22
Literature of Christian Ethics, 1932-1956; CB5
Literature of Medieval History, 1930-1975; BC3
Literature of the Doctrine of a Future Life; CA51
Literature of the World in Translation; BB33
Literature of Theology; A11, H54
Littell, Franklin; BA42
Little, Brooks; BE22
Little, Lawrence; DD15
Living Themes in the Thought of John Calvin; BD57
Livingstone, E. A.; BA21

Livres de l'année-Biblio; L42
Livres disponibles; L43
Loetscher, Lefferts; C12
Louvain, Universite Catholique de; BA13
Lovejoy, Clarence; E2
Lovejoy's College Guide; E2
Loyola University of Chicago; A22
Lueker, Erwin; C33
Lutheran Cyclopedia; C33
Lutheran World Federation; C32
Lutherbibliographie; BD63
Lutherjahrbuch; BD63

McAlpin Collection of British History & Theology; BD44-45
McCabe, James; A13
M'Clintock, John; C14
McCurry, Don; DC25
McDormand, Thomas; DE17
McGrath Publishing; D18
Macgregor, Malcolm; BD47
McKenzie, John; AE23
McLean, George; CC43
Macmillan Altas History of Christianity; BA42
Macmillan Bible Atlas; AG11
MacQuarrie, John; CB13
Malatesta, Edward; AD7
Malcom, Howard; H55
Mann, Nicholas; BD21
Mansell; J1-2
Manual for Writers of Term Papers, Theses, and Dissertations; V32
Manual of Style; V31
Marconi, Joseph; S1
Marrou, Henri; BB22
Marrow, Stanley; AA1
Martin, Ira Jay; CA56
Martin, Jochen; BA41
Masters Abstracts; M21-22
Matthews, Donald; U14, U16
Mattill, A. J.; AD8
Mattill, Mary; AD8
May, Herbert Gordon; AG16
Mayer, Frederick; D13
Mead, Frank; D14, DE44
Medieval Monasticism; BC21
Meer, Frederik van der; BB51
Meissner, William; DB43
Melanchthonforschung im Wandel der Jahrhunderte; BD92
Melton, J. Gordon; D11-12
Member's Handbook; V33

Menendez, Albert; DA22
Menges, Robert; DB46
Mennonite Bibliography; BE25
Mennonite Encyclopedia; C35
Mennonitisches Lexikon; C34
Merchant, Harish; H29
Methodist Periodical Index; T42
Methodist Union Catalog; BE22
Methodist Union Catalog of History, Biography, Disciplines, and Hymnals; BE22
Metzger, Bruce; AD3-4, AD6, AD9, AD12
Meyers enzyklopädisches Lexikon; B12
Meyjes, Guillaume; BD21
Microfilm Abstracts; M15
Microform Holdings from All Periods; BD12
Microform Publishers Trade List Annual; J54
Microform Review; J51, J54
Middle East; DC25
Migne, P.-J.; BB32
Miller, Donald; AA4
Miller, J. Lane; AE25, AE42
Miller, Madeleine; AE25, AE42
Mills, Watson; P12
Minister's Library; H41-42
Mission Beyond Survival; DA14
Mission Handbook; DC24
Missionary Research Library; DC1, DC13, DC61
Missions Advanced Research & Communication Center; DA2, DC14, DC24
Mitros, Joseph; H2
Mode, Peter; BF14
Modern History Abstracts, 1775-1914; BE4
Mohrmann, Christine; BB51
Mol, Hans; D3
Montminy, Jean; H62
Moore, Helen-Jean; DD15
Morehead, Joe; R12
Morris, Raymond; H23
Mosher Library; T21-22
Mosher Periodical Index; T22
Moule, H. F.; AB12
Moyer, Elgin; BA26
Muldoon, Maureen; CB34
Muller, Gerhard; C17
Multipurpose Tools for Bible Study; AA2

Nag Hammadi Bibliography, 1948-1969; AD24
National Catholic Almanac; D21
National Council of Churches; BE12, DA23, D17
National Faculty Directory; F42
National Foundation for Christian Education; C13
National Historical Publications Commission; R2

National Historical Publications and Records
 Commission; R3
National Register of Microform Masters; J52
National Union Catalog; J11-15
National Union Catalog of Manuscript Collections;
 R1
National Union Catalog, Pre-1956 Imprints; J1-2
Native American Christian Community; DC41
Nave, Orville; AG5
Nave's Topical Bible; AG5
Neff, Christian; C34
Negenman, Jan; AG15
Negev, Avraham; AE51
Neil, Stephen; BE11
Neill, Stephen; DC21
Nelson, Marlin; DC15
Nelson's Complete Concordance of the Revised
 Standard Version Bible; AG3
Nelson's Expository Dictionary of the Old
 Testament; AF14
Nevin, Alfred; C37
New Atlas of the Bible; AG15
New Bible Dictionary; AE26
New Books in Print; J33
New Cambridge Modern History; BE2-3
New Cambridge Modern History, v.2; BD23
New Catholic Encyclopedia; C22-24
New Columbia Encyclopedia; B4
New Encyclopaedia Britannica; B2
New Grove Dictionary of Music and Musicians; DE11
New Guide to Popular Government Publications; R11
New International Dictionary of New Testament
 Theology; AF22
New International Dictionary of the Christian
 Church; BA22
New Schaff-Herzog Encyclopedia of Religious
 Knowledge; C11
New Serial Titles; U2-U4
New Testament Abstracts; AD2
New Testament Commentary Survey; AA35
New Westminster Dictionary of the Bible; AE27
New York Times Index; F14, S19
New York Times Obituary Index, 1858-1968; F14
Newman, William; BF32
Newsletter of the Association for the Development
 of Religious Information Systems; A22
Newsome, Walter; R11
Nickels, Peter; AD21
Niesel, Wilhelm; BD52
1978 Directory of Theological Schools in Asia;
 DC64
1979 Directory of Theologians in Asia; DC65

Nineteenth Century Readers' Guide to Periodical Literature, 1890-1899; S14
North American Protestant Ministries Overseas; DC24
North, Robert; AC8
Noshpitz, Joseph; DB4
Novum Testamentum; AD24

OT/ANE Permucite Index; AC2
Oberschelp, Reinhard; L32
O'Brien, Betty; N11
O'Brien, Elmer; N11
O'Brien, Thomas; BA24
Ofori, Patrick; DC81
Ökumenische Bibliographie; DD16
Old Testament Abstracts; AC1
Old Testament Books for Pastor and Teacher; AA11
Old Testament Commentary Survey; AA34
Old Testament Dissertations; AC7
Ollard, Sidney; BE32
Oriental Institute; AC21-22
Orr, James; AE4
Oxbridge Directory of Religious Periodicals; U21
Oxford American Dictionary; V4
Oxford Bible Atlas; AG16
Oxford Dictionary of the Christian Church; BA21
Oxford English Dictionary; V4

Paetow, Louis; BC2-3
Pantzer, Katharine; L22
Parables of Jesus; AD10
Paris. Bibliotheque Nationale; L41
Parkland College, CB6
Parks, George; BB33
Pastoral Care and Counseling Abstracts; DB44
Patristic Greek Lexicon; BB41
Patrologiae; BB32
Patrologie; BB1
Patrology; BB1-3
Pauly, August Friedrich von; BB21
Pauly-Wissowa; BB21
Pauly's Real-Encyclopädie der classischen Altertumswissenschaft; BB21
Payne, J. Barton; AE71
Peatling, John H.; DD22
Peddie, Robert; L5
Periodical and Monographic Index to Literature on the Gospels and Acts; AD5
Periodical Articles on Religion; T31
Perrin, P. G.; V22

Personal-Bibliographien aus Theologie und
   Religionswissenschaft; H63
Peterson's Annual Guide to Graduate Study; E1
Pettee, Julia; H13
Pfeiffer, Charles; AE6, AE52
Philosopher's Guide; CC1
Philosopher's Index; CC13
Philosopher's Index: Retrospective Index to
   non-U.S. Publications; CC15
Philosopher's Index: Retrospective Index to U.S.
   Publications; CC14
Philosophical Documentation Center; CC13-15,
   CC31-32
Philosophy of Religion; CC42
Piepkorn, Arthur; D13, D15
Piercy, William; BB26
Pinnock, Clark; CA12, CC41
Pinson, William; DE28
Pipkin, H. Wayne; BD72
Pirot, L.; AE10
Pittsburgh Theological Seminary; AD5, BD72
Pollard, Alfred; L21-22
Pontifical Institute of Medieval Studies; BC5-6
Pontificia Universita' Urbaniana; DC3
Poole's Index to Periodical Literature; S11-13
Popst, Hans; L33
Potchefstroomse University for Christian Higher
   Education; H66, BD1
Poulton, Helen; BA1
Pre-56; J1-2, AB11
Preliminary Bibliography for the Study of Biblical
   Prophecy; AB23
Pre-Nicene Syrian Christianity; BB4
Presbyterian Historical Society; BF43
Princeton Religion Research Center; D19
Princeton Theological Seminary; AA5, CA13, DA1
Profiles in Belief; D15
Protestantism in Latin America; DC71
Pseudepigrapha and Modern Research; AD23
Psychoanalysis and Religion; DB47
Psychological Abstracts; DB11-14
Psychological Abstracts: Cumulative Author Index;
   DB16-17
Psychological Studies of Clergymen: Abstracts of
   Research; DB46
Psychology of Religion; DB42
Public Affairs Information Service; S18
Publishers' Trade List Annual; J34
Pulpit Eloquence: a List of Doctrinal and
   Historical Studies in English; DE26

Quasten, Johannes; BB2
Quinn, Bernard; DA16

Rahner, Karl; C26, CA31-32
Rambo, Lewis; DB42
Rand McNally Bible Atlas; AG14
Ransohoff, Paul; DB42
Rea, John; AE6
Read, Conyers; BD41
Reader's Digest Almanac; B31
Readers' Guide to Periodical Literature; S15
Reader's Guide to the Great Religions; H1
Readings for Town and Country Church Workers; DA16
Real-Encyclopädie der classischen Altertumswissenscahft; BB21
Realencyklopädie für protestantische Theologie und Kirche; C15
Reallexikon für Antike und Christentum; BB23
Recent Homiletical Thought; DE25
Recherches éthiques aux États-Unis; CB3
Recommended Reference Books and Commentaries for a Minister's Library; AA32
Redgrave, G. R.; L21-22
Reference Catalogue of Current Literature; L11
Reformation, The; BD23
Reformed Journal; CB32
Regazzi, John; T2
Reich, Warren; CB23
Reid, Joyce; AG13
Reike, Bo; AE8
Religion au Canada; H62
Religion in America, 1979-80; D19
Religion in American Life; BF12-13
Religion in Canada; H62
Religion in Geschichte und Gegenwart; C1
Religion Index One: Periodicals; T12
Religion Index Two: Festschriften, 1960-1969; N11
Religion Index Two: Multi-Author Works; N12-13
Religions; H2
Religious Bodies, 1936; D16
Religious Bodies of America; D13
Religious Books and Serials in Print; J36
Religious Education; DD11, DD17, DD22
Religious History of the American People; BF21
Religious Leaders of America; F35
Religious Liberty; DA25
Religious Life of Man; H3
Religious Reading; H71
Religious Studies Review; M44, DB41
Religious and Theological Abstracts; T35
Renaissance/Reformation Bibliography; BD4
Renewals; A21, BF41

Répertoire bibliographique des institutions
 chrétiennes; DA4
Répertoire bibliographiqus des institutions
 chrétiennes. Supplement; DA5
Répertoire des sources historiques du Moyen Age;
 BC7
Repertorium Biblicum Medii Aevi; AA31
Research in Education; DD4
Research Libraries and Collections in the United
 Kingdom; E23
Researches in Personality, Character and Religious
 Education; DD15
Resources for Christian Leaders; DA2
Resources in Education; DD4
Retrospective Index to Theses of Great Britain and
 Ireland, 1716-1950; M31
Review of Religion; M42
Revue d'histoire ecclésiastique; BA13
Revue de Qumran; AD44
Reynolds, Michael; M2
Rhetoric and Public Address; DE21
RIC; DA4
RIC Supplement; DA5
RIC Supplement 30; DC83
RIC Supplement 47-49; DA25
Richardson, Alan; AF4, CA22
Richardson, Ernest; T31
Riley, Mary; CC12
Ringgren, Helmer; AF11
Roach, John; BE3
Robert, Stephen; E23
Rogers, A. Robert; A5
Roget's International Thesaurus; V11
Romig, Walter; H22
Rost, Leonhard; AE8
Rounds, Dorothy; AB7
Rouse, Richard; BC4
Rouse, Ruth; BE11
Routley, Erik; DE15
Rowe, Kenneth; BE22
Rowley, H. H.; AC4, AE22, AG13, AG15, BB51
Ruoss, George; E21
Rwegera, Damien; DC83

Sacramentum Mundi; CA31-32
Sacramentum Verbi; AF2
Sadie, Stanley; DE11
Saint John's Gospel, 1920-1965; AD7
Saint Louis University; H72
Sample, Robert; BB4
Sandeen, Ernest; BF11
Sayre, John; A14, H43, AA32

Schaff-Herzog Encyclopedia; C11
Schaff, Philip; BA33, CA41
Schalk, Carl; DE13
Scholer, David; AA21, AD24
Scholler, Rainer; L33
School Question; DA24
Schottenloher, Karl; BD31
Schreckenberg, Heinz; AD25-26
Schultz, Lawrence; BE26
Schwarz, J. C.; F34-35
Schwertner, Siegfried; V42
Schwinge, Gerhard; A15
Scott, David; AE42
Seagreaves, Eleanor; CB31
Search for Environmental Ethics; CB31
Selected Bibliography in Western Languages; DC62
Selected Bibliography in Western Languages, Classified and Annotated; DC63
Selected Bibliography on Moral Education; CB6
Selective Bibliography for Christian Apologetics; CC41
Selective Bibliography for the Study of Christian Theology; CA12
Selective Bibliography for the Study of Hymns, 1980; DE12
Selinger, Suzanne; BD4
Seminary Review; CA11, CB1
Senaud, Auguste; BE12
Serial Bibliographies for Medieval Studies; BC4
Serial Bibliographies in the Humanities and the Social Sciences; G2
Sermon on the Mount; AD11
Sheehy, Eugene; A1-2
Shelf List of the Union Theological Seminary ... in Classification Order; H12
Short-Title Catalogue of Books Printed in England; L21-24
Shunami, Shlomo; G23
Sieben, Hermann Joseph; BB44
Sills, David; B22
Sims, Michael; DC16
Sinclair, John; DC71
Singer, Isadore; C42
Sixteenth Century Bibliography; BD13
Smith, Wilbur; AB23, G22
Smith, William; BB24-25, DE41
Social Science Reference Sources; A6
Social Sciences and Humanities Index; S17
Social Sciences Citation Index; S52
Social Sciences Index; S51
Social Scientific Studies of Religion; H61
Society for Old Testament Study; AC3-6

Society of Biblical Literature; V33, AD3-4
Sociological Abstracts; DA11
Sonne, Niels; M41
Source Book and Bibliographical Guide for American Church History; BF14
Sources and Literature of Scottish Church History; BD47
South African Theological Bibliography; H65
South Asia; DC27
Southeastern Pennsylvania Theological Library Association; U14
Southern Baptist Convention, Historical Commission; T41
Southern Baptist Periodical Index; T41
Southwestern Baptist Theological Seminary; H46, P11
Speech Communications Association; DE24
Speech Monographs; DE21-23, DE26
Spencer, Claude; BE24
Spencer, Donald; DE3
Sprague, William Buell; BF44
Springer, Nelson; BE25
Spurgeon, Charles; AA33
Starr, Edward; BE21
Statesman's Yearbook; B33
Statistical Abstract of the U.S.; B41
Statistical and Historical Annual of the States of the World; B33
Stegemann, H.; AA23
Stegmüller, Friedrich; AA31
Steinmueller, John; AE21
Stephen, Leslie; F53
Stewardson, J. L.; BB11
Stoekle, Bernhard; CB12
Stokes, G. Allison; DB41
Streit, Robert; DC2
Strong, James; AG1, C14
Strunk, William; V23
Studies in Missions: an Index of Theses on Missions; DC14
Study and Evaluation of Religious Periodical Indexing; T1
Stuiber, Alfred; BB1
Subject Catalog; J26
Subject Collections; E32
Subject Collections in European Libraries; E22
Subject Guide to Books in Print; J32
Subject Guide to Reprints; J41
Subject Index of Books Published Before 1880; L5
Subject Index of the Modern Works Added to the Library; L6-7
Subject Index to Periodicals; S31

Subject Index to Select Periodical Literature; T21
Suggested Bibliography for Ministers; H44
Suid Afrikaanse Teologiese Bibliographie; H65
Sullivan, Kathryn; AE21
Suttle, Bruce B.; CB6
Systematic Theology [a Bibliography]; CA11
Systematic Theology Today; CA1
Systematisches Verzeichnis der wichtigsten Fachliteratur; AA23

Targum and New Testament; AD21
Taylor, John; V41
Taylor, Marvin; DD11-13
TEAM-A Serials; U15
Temple, Ruth; BB33
Tenney, Merrill; AE7, AE28
Themelios; BD2
Theological Bibliography in the Eighteenth Century; H55
Theological Book List; H23-26
Theological Dictionary of the New Testament; AF21
Theological Dictionary of the Old Testament; AF11
Theological Education Association of Mid-America; U15
Theological Education Fund; H23-26
Theological Encyclopedia and Methodology; H53
Theological Index; H55
Theological Students Fellowship; AA34-35, CA12, CA41
Theological Word Book of the Bible; AF4
Theological Wordbook of the Old Testament; AF13
Theologische Literatur des Jahres; H74
Theologische Literaturzeitung; H73-74
Theologische Realenzyklopädie; C17
Theologische Rundschau; H75
Theologischer Jahresbericht; H76
Theologisches Begriffslexikon zum Neuen Testament; AF22
Theologisches Handwörterbuch zum Alter Testament; AF12
Theologisches Taschenlexikon; CA32
Theologisches Wörterbuch zum Alten Testament; AF11
Theologisches Wörterbuch zum Neues Testament; AF21
Theology Digest; H72
Thernstrom, Stephan; DC43
Thiselton, Anthony; AA35
Thomas Müntzer; BD84
Thompson, William; DE25
Tippett, A. R.; DC12
Titles in Series; U31
Tobey, Jeremy; CC3
Todd, Robert; H44

Toohey, William; DE25
Tools for Bible Study; AA4
Tools for Theological Research; A14
Toomey, Alice; G12
Totok, Wilhelm; L32
Town and Country Church; DA15
Trinity Journal; H44
Trinterud, Leonard; BF43
Trotti, John; H21
Tübingen Universitätsbibliothek; T23
Tummers, Deodatus; DC4
Turabian, Kate; V32
Turnbull, Ralph; DA3
Turner, Harold; DC42, DC82
Turner, Nigel; AF23
Tushingham, A. D.; AG12
Twentieth Century Abstracts, 1914- ; BE4
Twentieth Century Atlas of the Christian World; DC52
Twentieth Century Encyclopedia of Religious Knowledge; C12
20 Centuries of Great Preaching; DE28
Two Hundred Fifty Years of Brethren Literature; BE26
Tylenda, Joseph; BD53
Tyndale Fellowship for Biblical Research; AE26

Ulrich's International Periodicals Directory; U22
Ulrich's Quarterly; U24
Unger, Merrill F.; AF14
Union Catalog of the Graduate Theological Union Library; H17
Union List of Periodicals; U11, U14, U16
Union List of Serials; U12-13
Union List of Serials in Libraries of the United States & Canada; U1
Union Theological Seminary, New York.; H11-13, BD44-45, DC1
Union Theological Seminary, Virginia; CB5, H45
United Methodist Church. Commission of Archives and History; C36
United Methodist Periodical Index; T42
United Presbyterian Church in the U.S.A.; DD14
United States. Bureau of the Census; B41, D16
United States Doctoral Dissertations in Third World Studies; DC16
Unity and Religion, a Bibliography; BE12
Universitas Catholica Lovaniensis; T15
Université Catholique de Louvain; BA13
University Microfilms; J42, M11-15, M21-22, M33
University of Chicago; AC21-22
University of Chicago Press; V31

Unreached Peoples; DC28
Urban-Rural Mission Office; DA12
Urbano, Henrique; H62
Urech, Edouard; AE41

Van Leunen, Mary-Claire; V51
Vatican II; BE31
Verbeke, Gerhard; BD21
Verbum Domini; AB1
Verzeichnis lieferbarer Bücher; L31
Viening, Edward; AG6
Vigouroux, Fulcram Grégoire; AE9
Vismans, T. A.; DE2
Vocabulaire biblique; AF1
Vocabulaire de théologie biblique; AF3
Voces; BB44
Vogel, Eleanor; AB21
Vorausdruck für das Einzelfach Neues Testament; AA23
Vorster, W. S.; H65
Vos, Howard; AE6
Vriens, Livinus; DC4

Wace, Henry; BB25-26
Wagner, C. Peter; DC28, DC72
Wainwright, William; CC42
Walford, A. J.; A3
Wall, C. Edward; S13
Walt, B. J. van der; BD1
Walters, LeRoy; CB21-22
Waltke, Bruce; AA12, AF13
Wardin, Albert; BE33
Warshaw, Thayer; AB25
Washington Theological Consortium; U16
Watson, Robert; DB21
Weber, Otto; C16
Webster's Biographical Dictionary; F11
Webster's Collegiate Thesaurus; V12
Webster's New Collegiate Dictionary; V2
Webster's Third New International Dictionary of the English Language; V1
Westermann, Claus; AF12
Western Religion; D3
Westminster Dictionary of Christian Education;DD21
Westminster Dictionary of Church History; BA23
Westminster Dictionary of Worship; DE1
Westminster Historical Atlas to the Bible; AG17
Weston College School of Theology; AD2
What Asian Christians are Thinking; DC63
Wheatcroft, Les; H62
White, E. B.; V23
White, William; AF14

Whitely, William; BE21
Whitten, M.; V21
Who was Who; F52
Who was Who in America; F22-23
Who was Who in Church History; BA26
Who's Who; F51
Who's Who in America; F21
Who's Who in Religion; F31
Who's Who in the Clergy; F34
Who's Who in the World; F12
Wickens, Robert; DA15
Wiener, Philip; CC22
Williams, E. L.; DC83
Williams, Ethel; F32, H64
William's Library, London; BD46
Wing, Donald; L23-24
Winter, Ralph; BA32
Wolman, B. B.; DB31
Wood, A. Skevington; BD2
Woods, R. L.; DE43
Working Bibliography on World Hunger; CB33
World Almanac and Book of Facts; B31
World Bibliography of Bibliographies; G11-12
World Bibliography of Bibliographies, 1964-74; G12
World Christian Handbook, 1968; D1
World Christianity: Eastern Asia; DC26
World Christianity: Middle East; DC25
World Christianity: South Asia; DC27
World Council of Churches; BE14, DA12
World Directory of Theological Libraries; E21
World Methodist Council; C36
World of Learning; B34
World Treasury of Religious Quotations; DE43
World's Committee of Y.M.C.A.; BE12
Wright, George; AE54, AG17
Writer's Guide and Index to English; V22
Wyckoff, DeWitte Campbell; DD14
Wycliffe Bible Encyclopedia; AE6

Yearbook of American & Canadian Churches; D20, E11
Yizhar, Michael; AD45
Young, Robert; AG2

Zeitschrift für evangelische Ethik; CB2
Zeitschriften Inhaltsdienst Theologie; T23
Zeman, Jarold; BD91
Zondervan Pictorial Biblical Dictionary; AE28
Zondervan Pictorial Encyclopedia of the Bible; AE7
Zondervan Topical Bible; AG6
Zweite Vatikanische Konzil; C27
Zwingli-Bibliographie; BD71
Zwingli Bibliography; BD72

Reference —
Use in the Library Only